LOGIC IN A POPULAR FORM

T0373077

THE INDIA LIST

Sumanta Banerjee

LOGIC IN A POPULAR FORM

ESSAYS ON POPULAR RELIGION IN BENGAL

LONDON NEW YORK CALCUTTA

Seagull Books, 2019

Text © Sumanta Banerjee, 2002, 2019
ISBN   978 0 8574 2 6161

First published by Seagull Books in 2002

British Library Cataloguing-in-Publication Data
A catalogue record for this book is available from the British Library

Typeset by Seagull Books, Calcutta, India
Printed and bound by Hyam Enterprises, Calcutta, India

CONTENTS

ACKNOWLEDGEMENTS

The essays included in this volume were written over the past several years, and the ideas were primarily conceived during my association as an Honorary Fellow with the project on Socio-Religious Movements and Cultural Networks in Indian Civilization, which was formulated by the Indian Institute of Advanced Study (IIAS) of Shimla in 1991–92, and lasted till 1995.

The earliest of the six essays is 'The "Pir" and the "Narayana"—A Syncretistic Accommodation in Bengali Ritual and Folklore', which was presented at a seminar at the IIAS during 3–7 May 1993. It is being published here for the first time. Of the other essays, an earlier draft of 'From Aulchand to Sati-Ma: The Institutionalization of the Karta-bhaja sect in Nineteenth-century Bengal', was presented at a seminar on 'Organizational and Institutional Aspects of Religious Movements' at IIAS in October 1994. It was published in *The Calcutta Historical Journal*, VOL. XVI, NO. 2, July–December 1994. A slightly abridged version of it was later included in *Organization and Institutional Aspects of Indian Religious Movements*, edited by Joseph T. O'Connel and published by IIAS in 1999. 'The Changing Role of Kali in the Bengali Popular Psyche' is a revised version of a paper read out at a lecture organized at the Seagull Bookstore in Calcutta by Seagull Foundation for the Arts in February 1998. 'The Ambiguities of Bharat Mata' is an elaboration on a talk delivered at a seminar on State, Community and Women, organized by the Women's Development Centre of Deshbandhu College, New Delhi in March, 1999.

The two other essays—'Bamakshyapa of Tarapeeth: The Dramatist of Popular Angst' and 'Radha and Krishna in a Colonial Metropolis'—are new chapters based on my later researches, which extended beyond the lifespan of the original IIAS project.

I would like to acknowledge the suggestions offered by fellow collaborators engaged in the IIAS project, particularly Professor J. S. Grewal, who guided the project as the Director of the Institute. I would also wish to express my gratitude to Ms Anjum Katyal of Seagull Books, without whose perseverance the present collection could not have been brought together.

Dehradun, 2002

INTRODUCTION

I

Historians of popular religion and culture may be described as the ragpickers of history. They build up their resources from the leftovers of historical research. They scrape together from the dustbin of history all the crumbs of information which are discarded as useless by the scholars of the 'great tradition', and the little asides and observations made (en passant) by historians after chronicling the birth and growth of the well-known, established religious orders.

But by piecing together these crumbs, historians of popular religion try to reconstruct the mental world of the unheard populace and give voice to their usually unknown beliefs and customs. They open up interesting possibilities for the writing of history in a way which can unfold to modern readers the various dimensions of popular logic embedded in the socio-religious life of the lower orders. Through their own religious vocabulary and rituals, these people try to make sense of the world, cope with its hazards, negotiate with the arrival of modern science in their society, and finally, attempt to give a meaning to their own existence.

The essays in the present collection are an attempt to rediscover some of the aspects of this multi-faceted image of popular religion in the context of nineteenth-century Bengal. They also try to re-examine the relevance of some of the beliefs and rituals that have flowed down from that past and continue to survive in Bengali society today.

These essays are an extension of my earlier study of nineteenth-century Bengali popular culture in *The Parlour and the Streets* (Seagull Books, 1989). Investigations during that study revealed to me the intricate relationship between popular culture and popular religion. I have therefore tried in these essays to expand on some of the ideas relating to the latter, which were suggested, but left undeveloped, in my earlier study.

In the present introduction, however, I seek to go beyond the scope of the particular topics covered by the essays in this volume, and deal with questions related to theories of popular religion as well as the historian's responsibility in India today. I also hope to engage in a productive dialogue with historians, social scientists, social activists, as well as many others, who may have to interact with the beliefs and customs of popular religion in India, in the course of working in their respective areas of functioning. Such a dialogue is essential, since I am fully aware of the risk involved in seeking to make contact with a mentality, the motivations and manifestations of which, in religious forms, may appear to contradict the norms of scientific logic.

II

Maybe because of the humble origins of the historiography of popular religion, it is being belatedly and grudgingly recognized today as a subject of serious historical research. This is one of the many little ironies of history. While it is the oldest form of religion in the world, popular religion remains the youngest in the list of academic disciplines. It is only recently that some modern historians, mainly from Europe, have begun to discover the importance of popular religion in past societies and attempt to unravel the 'mentalities' of the populace which shaped it.[1]

Popular religion had long loomed large as a shadowy presence in the investigations and findings of folklorists and ethnologists. But it had remained incidental to their main areas of research. It needs to be recognized in its own right as a separate field of study that requires different tools of investigation of a multidisciplinary nature.

As the oldest form of logic, popular religion expresses the first stammering efforts of mankind to rationalize existence—human, animal and natural. Its reasoning powers prodded the human mind to find out causes concerning birth and death, the movements of the heavenly bodies, the regular changes in seasons, the growth and decay of vegetation, rain and drought, thunder and lightning, eclipses and earthquakes, etc. These, and a score of inexplicable phenomena, haunted the troubled imagination of the primitive mind. In its desperate urge to find reasons, it speculated on the basis of whatever evidence it could gather, and invented myths: trying to connect one phenomenon with another, tracing the effect in one happening to what it thought was the cause in another, and imagining the existence of some spirit or superhuman power or god behind all the mystifying events. Through all this ran the anthropomorphic tendency to make the world 'significantly humanlike' by imagining that animals and objects can have the same feelings and qualities as humans, and hence a superhuman power, or God or several gods could appear in human or any of these forms. Such beliefs functioned as intellectual explanations of events, or of the general order of things.[2] It was the popular way of organizing their experiences and rationalizing them. Explaining religion as a 'general theory of the world', Karl Marx described it as its 'logic in a popular form'.[3]

Thus, what we define as popular religion is a product of a collective rationality which developed primarily from and within the rural community's consciousness, often independent of the ecclesiastical codified scriptures of the learned clergy. The tribal gods and religious rituals, animistic beliefs and practices predate the birth of organized religions. Similarly, Indian rural communities (as well as urban, in certain circumstances) gave birth to local godlings who were far removed from the deities worshipped in the Vedas or the Upanishads. Thus, we come across Bana-bibi and Dakshin Ray in the Sunderbans of Bengal, who are still worshipped by the local people for protection from the tigers which invade their villages. All over Bengal, Shitala, a goddess not to be found in any of the doctrinal Hindu religious scriptures, continues to be worshipped by devotees seeking protection from small-pox. It would be worthwhile to find out whether the official claim of eradication of small-pox all over the world has eroded the popularity of Shitala among the villagers in Bengal.

Popular logic had created new deities in response to problems and crises which they had never faced before, even in a purportedly scientifically ordered world like Bengal under British colonial rule. When cholera broke out for the first time in Bengal in 1817, the rural community invented and added Ola-bibi, the goddess of cholera, to their divinities.[4]

The presence of diseases and death led respectively to a corpus of popular religious therapeutics (e.g. faith cure, magic, witchcraft, etc) and popular religious obsequies (as different from the funeral ceremonies ordained by the established religious orders) which are found among certain tribal and Dalit or lower-caste communities. The various legends about the creation of the world, the birth of the human being, the procreation of the species, that are current even today among the different tribal communities—whether among the Santhals and Mundas in eastern India, or the Nagas and Mizos in the northeast—testify to the continuity of an alternative popular religious tradition that is primarily oral, and runs parallel to the written religious explanations of the birth of the universe and humanity as propounded in the scriptures that are venerated by their respective followers—Christians, Muslims and Hindus among many other religious communities.

The oral character of popular religion has shaped it in a way that is different from the written religious texts. Explaining the differences, Jack Goody points out that oral religion is more flexible and accommodating than written religion, where words tend to 'fix' the deities and the rituals. In oral religion, a myth is more malleable, since the popular systems of beliefs are open-ended, adapting and adopting new beliefs in the course of their journey through verbal renderings from one generation to another, from one country to another. But in literate religions, the dogma and services are rigid. The rituals are repeated in a verbatim fashion under a centralized direction with no deviations allowed. Besides, unlike the universalistic concerns and moral injunctions of literate religions, popular beliefs and practices, by the very nature of their birth and development, are particularist and local culture-specific. Their speech and action are embedded in specific contexts—during seasons of sowing and harvesting which differ from one country to another, or when misfortune strikes certain communities in the form of sickness or death, drought or floods, events whose irregularity compels the eliciting of favours from the local divinities they have created.[5]

But the differences should not make us imagine a strictly binary distinction between the two trends—the flexibility of the oral culture of popular religion and the rigidity of the ethical injunctions of the written texts of the religious establishments. In a bid to explain the highly complex relationship between the two in medieval Europe, modern theoreticians of popular religion appear to be divided. Some have tended to dismiss popular religion and culture as vulgarized versions of the scriptures written by the clergy.[6] Others like Jacques Le Goff, feel that folkloric elements in popular religion were suppressed by the church, or destroyed, or partially adapted to the demands of official ideology.[7] Mikhail Bakhtin describes popular religion and its cultural manifestations as a counter-system that constantly opposes and demystifies the established order and the established religion.[8]

While acknowledging this conflict between popular religion and the church in medieval Europe, Aron Gurevich expresses a slightly different view when he states:

> The opposition of popular to ecclesiastical culture should
> not be understood simplistically, because it was not just

an opposition . . . The dialogue of two principles of medieval culture can be understood only if we do not consider them divorced or antithetical. It should be conceived of not as a debate between two metaphorically opposed entities, not as a 'dialogue of the deaf', but as the presence of one culture in the thought and world of the other, and vice versa.[9]

In the Indian context, historical findings suggest that popular beliefs and customs that still survive predate the arrival of Aryan culture. The theologians of the later literate religious orders usurped and metamorphosed them in their religious scriptures. The history of Brahmanical adoption and adaptation of primitive and tribal rituals and deities is well documented by historians like D. D. Kosambi. In Bengal, Abanindranath Tagore, the renowned painter who also analysed Bengali popular rituals that were still current in the early 1940s, after meticulously examining their roots and transformation, came up with the theory that the Hindu theologians first tried to impose the Vedic gods and their grand ceremonial style of worshipping on the indigenous population, 'by crushing the freedom and spontaneity of their efforts and thoughts'. Later, these theologians accepted some of their deities and rituals, but transformed them in a way as to 'pass them off as scriptural' in order to 'preach the greatness of Hindu divinities'.[10] Abanindranath's theoretical proposition, formulated in the early 1940s in the context of Bengali popular religion, anticipates in a large measure the theory propounded by Jacques Le Goff in the 1980s, when he talked about similar suppression of folkloric elements in popular religion by the dominating classes in medieval Europe, and their later adaptation to suit the official ideology.

Although popular religion and institutionalized theology in India had interacted over centuries, borrowing from each other and exchanging ideas and practices, this does not rule out the power of the Brahmanical hierarchy, at certain stages in the history of this interaction, to suppress the religious beliefs and practices of the lower orders, or marginalize them within a religious order. The transformation of the Vaishnavite movement in Bengal, initiated by the religious reformer Chaitanya in the sixteenth century, is a revealing illustration. Its upper-caste and upper-class interpreters (the six disciples of Chaitanya, known as the six Goswamis) could institutionalize what Chaitanya initially conceived as an egalitarian and flexible system, into a hierarchically ordained replica of the caste-based Brahmanical order.[11]

Historians of popular religion therefore will have to shuttle back and forth between the past and the present, the oral and the literate traditions, between the remnants of the primitive spontaneous and unorganized religious rituals that continue to survive in popular religious customs and festivals on the one hand, and the scriptures of the established religious orders that dominate the socio-religious milieu of the Indian upper-class educated gentry, on the other.

This leads us to the next important dimension—the time frame of popular religious beliefs and customs. Are they static, remaining in an unchanged form, retaining passively vestigial traces from the past? Among continental historians, Emmanuel Le Roy Ladurie appears to favour this view, when in the context of medieval and early modern France, he argues that history essentially stood still as far as the great mass of people were concerned. Despite new developments that were taking place at the higher level which affected a conspicuous minority, the beliefs and behaviour of the majority remained static for a long period—implying a certain inertia in popular psychology that resisted changes.[12] Or, did changes take place in popular religious attitudes and practices in a long process of evolution in the *longue durée* (long duration), as suggested by Michel Vovelle?[13]

In the Indian context again, we find that popular divinities had never remained fixed and immutable. Images were consciously contrived, and new images were added by the popular psyche, to serve immediate interests (as in the case of the goddesses of diseases mentioned earlier). In some cases, popular religious sects and practices had over the ages become institutionalized (as the essay on the Karta-bhaja sect in this volume will indicate). At times, we come across a hybrid offspring like Kali. Her demoness-like destructive passion recalls the traces of her birth—possibly from a mating between a primitive tribal vision, and a later Brahmanical theological concept of a mother goddess. Through her long evolution in a history of *longue durée*, she served as a symbol of different types of power to meet the changing needs of the people, varying from age to age or community to community (as described in the essay on Kali in this volume)—as a tribal mother goddess in a hoary past, a deity worshipped by dacoits in eighteenth-century Bengal, a political symbol of revolutionary nationalism at the turn of the twentieth century.

One can also take the case of the Radha-Krishna motif—an intrinsic part of both the literate and the oral religious traditions in Bengal. The former is represented by the Chaitanya-led Vaishnavite theology, known as Gaudiya Vaishnavism, and the latter by a multi-faceted system of popular religious beliefs and practices of different syncretic cults. In popular culture in particular, this religious intent of the Radha-Krishna text had been quite often overtaken by the secular potentialities of its subtext, which has its birth in an old romantic folk legend prevalent among the Abhira cowherd community of north India. In the colonial metropolis of Calcutta, this old subtext of the Radha-Krishna legend was used by popular poets, singers and dancers to subvert the prevailing rules and norms imposed by the religious and social establishments—a subject examined in the essay on Radha and Krishna in this volume.

III

It would be interesting in this connection to analyse briefly the complex interaction between popular religion (as a part of the 'little tradition', as different, though not always opposed to, the 'great tradition'), and the colonial establishment in Bengal. The perceptions of the first generation of colonial rulers were marked by a peculiar mixture of revulsion and attraction, hostility and conformity, towards the deities worshipped by the local people. Trained in the

Christian doctrine, the European visitors and settlers were shocked by the proliferation of images of multiple popular deities that they saw in Bengal. Among them, Kali was, of course, the main object of their curiosity. While many, like the inveterate nineteenth-century English traveller Fanny Parks, found the figure of Kali 'disgusting', we come across an interesting instance of her predecessors in Bengal paying homage to the same goddess. John C. Marshman tells us, in his *The Life and Times of Carey, Marshman and Ward* (1859) about a deputation of English officials and soldiers in the mid-eighteenth century, who went in a procession to Kalighat to make a thanksgiving to the goddess in the name of the East India Company for its success in Bengal![14] Such encounters between Hindu religion and the early generation of English settlers often led to rather bizarre instances of acculturation. A senior English army officer, Major General Charles Stuart (1758–1828) made a collection of Hindu idols, and, like pious Hindus, walked down from his residence in Wood Street in Calcutta to the Ganga for his daily bath. He was known among his contemporaries as Hindu Stuart, and his tomb, which still stands in a Christian cemetery on Park Street in Calcutta, was modelled on a temple with figures of Hindu deities on a carved gateway.[15]

But, while allowing the worshipping of popular deities, the colonial administration did begin to intervene in certain religious practices from the nineteenth century onwards—like sati among the upper-caste Bengali Hindus, or human sacrifices at the altar of Kali, or the ritual of self-flagellation at the Chadak festival.

At the same time, relationships were being constructed at the higher level in colonial Bengal between the respective 'great traditions' of the Orient and the Occident from the end of the eighteenth century onwards. Under the patronage of Warren Hastings, translations of Sanskrit classics and Brahmanical and Islamic laws were being undertaken by a generation of British Orientalists. The Asiatic Society of Bengal in general, and William Jones (who founded it in 1784) in particular, played an important role in the introduction of the Indian 'great tradition' to scholars and literati of the European 'great tradition' (like Goethe, among others). The latter tradition also soon became accessible to the new generation of English-educated Indians by the turn of the nineteenth century. This interaction was made possible by the mediation of the colonial power.

No such interaction between the 'little traditions' of the West and the East was possible, since they enjoyed neither the privilege of having their respective translators and interpreters introduce themselves to each other, nor the patronage of a mediating power. Further, in the nineteenth century, these 'little traditions'—both in England and in India—were facing increasing pressure from the state authorities as well as the upper classes in their respective countries, leading to their marginalization. For instance, while in Bengal the colonial administration was coming down on popular street entertainments like 'sawngs' or pantomimes, in England during the same time the street art of mumming (acting in dumb shows), and village church bands and choirs, among other popular entertainments, were facing pressure from the state and its agencies of discipline, regulation and repression.[16]

The establishment of the British colonial system, however, exposed the Indian 'little tradition' to a new religion—Christianity. In keeping with the tradition of acculturation in their religious beliefs and habits, some of the old Bengali syncretic sects often adopted and adapted the new practices introduced by the Christian missionaries. Thus, the Karta-bhaja sect followed a set of ten rules and fixed every Friday for a confession session by its members, reminiscent of the Biblical Ten Commandments and the Catholic practice of confession respectively (see essay in this volume). Similarly, another sect of popular religion in nineteenth-century Bengal, the Ram-Ballabhis, used to sing a song praising at the same time Kali, the Christian God and Khoda of the Muslims.[17]

IV

These syncretic religious sects occupy a special position in the history of Bengali popular religion, creating a subculture of their own. One nineteenth-century Bengali scholar listed some 50-odd syncretic sects which were flourishing all over India during his lifetime and which traced their descent from the seventeenth-eighteenth century. Among them, at least 40 were found in Bengal.[18] They included (besides the above-mentioned Karta-bhajas and Ram-Ballabhis), the Lalanshahis who were followers of the famous mystic poet Lalan Fakir, the Shahebdhanis, the Darbeshis, the Bala-Harhis, the Auls and Bauls, among others. Most of these popular sects were offshoots of the post-Chaitanya Vaishnavite movement, and some developed under the influence of Sufist ideas.

It is important to note that their popularity continues to survive even today in Bengali rural culture—in both West Bengal of India and Bangladesh on the other side of the border. While on a trip to a village in Nadia in West Bengal, bordering Bangladesh, sometime in the 1990s, a distinguished West Bengali scholar and collector of folk songs heard the story of a Baul singer, Sadananda Khyapa, who gave a moving account of his experience in Bangladesh. Sadananda recounted how he had crossed over to Bangladesh without legal travel documents. Being a Baul, he wanted to visit Kushthia (in Bangladesh) which is the birthplace of Lalan Fakir, who is venerated by Bauls all over the Bengali subcontinent. Sadananda was arrested by the Bangladesh police soon after he crossed the border, and was taken to the nearby police station. The police inspector there was a Muslim called Nasiruddin, who sprang a pleasant surprise on a petrified Sadananda with a strange request. Nasiruddin asked him to sing a 'kirtan'—a Bengali devotional song in praise of the loves of the traditionally worshipped Hindu divine couple, Radha and Krishna. Sadananda sang for hours, while a totally absorbed Nasiruddin listened with his eyes closed. At the end, the police inspector opened his eyes, and burst out with the words: 'Jay Gour!' ('All Praise to Gour'—the traditional form of greeting among Bengali Vaishnavites). He then turned to Sadananda, and said: 'Can you imagine how I have missed a kirtan all these years ever since you Hindus left for Hindustan?'[19]

It is necessary to understand the development and abiding popularity of these syncretic sects in a dual context—first, the socio-religious composition of Bengali society at the time of their birth, and secondly, the cultural tradition that continues down to the present times in rural society, where people require songs and music not only for entertainment, but also for their deep spiritual needs.

To go back to the socio-religious past which gave birth to these sects and their songs, we should note that at the top of the Bengali society at that time there were the twin religious establishments— one ruled by the Brahmanical order according to strictly laid down hierarchical caste-bound norms for the Hindus, and the other by the 'ashrafs' (Muslim aristocrats and clergy who claimed descent from the earlier Arab, Turkish, Afghan and Mughal settlers) for the Muslims. Both sought to institutionalize their own mechanisms of socio-religious control over their respective followers, with the aim of purging them of the many pre-Brahmanical and pre-Islamic beliefs and customs that they shared, to hegemonize them instead under their respective religious doctrines.

Below this horizontally stratified minority of the dominating Hindu and Muslim classes at the top, there was another and a larger world of lay members of society. Among the Hindus, starting from the bottom, they consisted of the traditional occupational castes like Harhis (scavengers), Chamars (tanners), and Doms (who cremated dead bodies), who were relegated as untouchables in the Hindu religious hierarchical order. Then there were the farmers, agricultural labourers, artisans, and small traders who came from the middle and lower-caste Hindu society. Among the Muslims also, although Islamic theology is against any discrimination among its followers, in practice in Bengal, the labouring 'atraf', 'ajlaf' (ranging from cultivators to tailors, cobblers and washermen) and 'arjal' (sweepers, scavengers and others engaged in occupations considered lowest in the hierarchy in the list of professions in contemporary Bengali Muslim society) communities were looked down upon by the ashrafs. Members of all these various rural lower orders could never be totally hegemonized by the orthodox religious establishments under their respective norms of doctrinal purity. They continued to lead an eclectic lifestyle—Muslims participating in Hindu religious festivities, and vice versa; or both sharing local religious practices and rituals of an animistic nature, which harked back to a tradition of collective memories (e.g. worshipping of godlings or 'pirs'). It was these communities of the lower orders in Bengali society which formed the base of the popular syncretic sects that developed in the past. Despite the 1947 Partition that split them apart, and the later socio-economic changes that have taken place since then in the countryside of West Bengal and Bangladesh, these rural communities continue to sustain the culture of popular religion.

These syncretic sects still share certain common characteristics from the past. First, most of them were founded (between the seventeenth and nineteenth centuries) by humble people of obscure origins belonging to the depressed and poorer castes among the Bengali Hindu and Muslim population, like Balaram Harhi (founder of the Balarami sect), Aulchand (of the Karta-bhaja sect), Shahebdhani (by whose name his sect is known), to mention a few.

Secondly, their belief systems and rituals lay stress on the equality of human beings, irrespective of their caste origins, religious denominations and gender differences. They renounce polytheism, idol worship and formal observance of caste regulations. Women enjoy a more expansive space in their system of beliefs and rituals, compared to the position allotted to them in the orthodox Hindu, Islamic, or Christian religious systems. To add a word of caution however—at the ground level, this space also is quite often intruded upon by the patriarchal tendencies that dominate these sects, almost all of them still being structured around subservience to their male founders. We shall come to this a little later.

But when we reach the third facet of these syncretic sects, we discover that beyond the externalities of their practices there is a deeper philosophical dimension to their belief systems. Unlike the particularist and local culture-specific trends in the other spheres of popular religion (e.g. worship of local deities, rituals surrounding the cosmic circle, rites of passage, etc.), they delve into universalist spiritual concerns. But they make a daring departure from the orthodox religious practice of respecting the Supreme Being as something extraneous, and superior to the individual's body and soul, which can be worshipped from a distance only, in the form of images of its various manifestations (e.g. Shiva, Vishnu, Brahma, etc.). Instead, these mystic poets of the syncretic sects humanize the Supreme Being by formulating the concept of it as an Intimate Beloved (Moner Manush), or the Man of the Heart, as described in the Baul songs, whose abode, they believe, is the human body itself, and whose seat is the human heart within it. Human knowledge, according to them, thus lies in knowing one's own self, wrestling with the hurdles embedded in that self (described in these songs as *shara-ripus*, often identified as the six sins of lust, anger, greed, addiction to drinks, infatuation and envy), and by overcoming them, reaching that Supreme Being.

Thus, the human body acquires an important position in the songs (as well as the rituals) of these popular religious mystics— often as a microcosm of the universe and human existence. It has given birth to a distinct literary genre—the songs of *dehatattwa* (i.e. around the idea of the human body as a metaphor).[20]

The desire, among these syncretic sects, to humanize the concept of the Supreme Being in the form of an Intimate Beloved, can indeed be traced to the earlier culture of the Sufi and Bhakti movements that spread in different parts of India in the fifteenth-sixteenth century. But this trend of humanizing the divine in the songs of the Bengali syncretist sects also harks back to an earlier tradition of domestication of divinities in popular Bengali folk narratives like the Mangal-kavyas, where the god Shiva and his consort Parvati were moulded in the image of a typical poor Bengali village couple quarrelling over mundane things, or the songs about the divine couple Radha and Krishna who appeared in the earthly role of a pair of romantic lovers in the familiar pastoral setting of the Bengali countryside, torn by common human passions like love and jealousy. This folk tradition of shaping the gods and goddesses in human form—even to the extent of attributing to them all the human frailties—had already paved the way for the popular acceptance of divinities in intimate terms in Bengal. The founders of the syncretic cults and their singers who appeared on the scene in the seventeenth–eighteenth century lifted this tradition to a higher level by conceptualizing the divine itself—as different from the individual divinities worshipped by the people—in intimate terms as a soulmate. Known as 'maromis', or mystic poets, some of the poet-composers of these syncretic sects (like the Lalanshahis, Karta-bhajas and Bauls), through a marvellous combination of experience, imagination and observation, created songs in the popular idiom that achieve an intensity which rivals that reached by the poetry of the 'great tradition'. These songs establish a rough register of the innate concerns that have continued to agitate human minds through centuries—the riddle of the relationship between body and mind, the stresses and strains that pull the soul apart between the desire to believe in an Absolute Power and the failure to comprehend it, the tensions between the certain knowledge of the final end of the human body and the unending appetite for elongating it. These poet-composers of popular religion found in poetry the only way to achieve a higher kind of knowledge necessary to move beyond the quotidian existence bound by the limitations of contemporary knowledge. Listening to their songs, one remembers the words of the famous modern poet-philosopher of the Afro-French (Negritude) movement, Aime Cesaire: 'Poetic knowledge is born in the great silence of scientific knowledge.'[21]

Cesaire's provocative proposition rings a bell, and takes us back to the haunting epigrammatic verse composed by Lalan Fakir (1772–1890) some two hundred years ago: *'Jakhon Nihshabdo Shabdere Khabey, Takhon Bhaber Khela Bhenge Jabey'* ('When silence devours sound, the sport of existence will end').[22] He captures in these two stark lines the apocalyptic vision of the destiny of human existence, by counterposing the two polarities of the world of senses—sound and silence—the former representing life, and the latter the emptiness into which it is sucked at the end. Lalan's verse is an expression of a rational conclusion, formulated in poetic terms, of sensuous experiences. It can be described as intuition that is synonymous with the 'lightning recapitulation of rational processes', a term used by a modern European historian writing about similar instances in the history of popular religion in medieval Europe.[23]

Most of these songs of the folk poets of the religious syncretic sects—which they still continue to compose, adding new imagery borrowed from contemporary reality—are in an enigmatic language of codes, made up of words loaded with symbolic and suggestive connotations, described as *sandhyabhasha* (often translated as 'twilight language', i.e. half expressed and half-concealed, or interpreted as a derivation from *abhisandhi*, which when translated loosely, means a secret plot). This is in the long tradition of the use of enigmatic metaphors to disguise the real meaning of the philosophic message, or to express it in the form of riddles, as found in the old Bengali Buddhist Charya songs, Tantrik literature, and in later times, the poems of Kabir, among others. Explaining the use of this particular style in the religious literature of such sects and mystic preachers, modern scholars have linked it with their desire to maintain the secrecy of their rituals and create a language of their own which was accessible only to the initiated.[24]

But in the case of the Bauls and similar other popular religious sects of eighteenth–nineteenth century Bengal, the old literary tradition of resorting to *sandhyabhasha*, or an enigmatic idiom, could have been forced upon them by certain pressures that they faced in their contemporary surroundings. Their syncretic creed based on an eclectic adoption and adaptation of beliefs and customs from different religious sources, was frowned upon by the orthodox theocracy which felt that the purity of religious doctrine was being diluted and distorted by the lower orders. Besides, these syncretic sects empowered the lower-caste people with a faith that helped them to assert their freedom as individuals, since they taught them that humanity could not be divided along caste or religious lines. Such self-assertion by their lower-caste followers often posed a challenge to the upper-caste Bengali landlords in the eighteenth–nineteenth century. We hear of an incident in a village in Nadia, where the Brahman landlord took offence at the temerity of a lower-caste member of the Balarami sect who did not bow his head to show him respect. Despite a thrashing by the landlord's men, he kept on saying that he would never bow his head to anyone except his guru Balaram Harhi, the founder of the sect.[25]

Threatened by the spread of such beliefs and actions, the orthodox religious establishment and the upper-class leaders of society launched a systematic campaign against the Bauls and members of other syncretic sects. In nineteenth-century Bengal, we hear of leading members of the Hindu bhadralok society, ranging from Sivanath Shastri to Sri Ramakrishna, denouncing the Karta-bhaja sect.[26] At the same time, influential Muslim leaders like Munshi Meherullah and Golam Kibria, as well as Muslim-edited journals like *Islam Pracharak*, were launching a vicious offensive against the Bauls.[27] This could have forced many such sects to go underground, and reinforced the old tradition of enigmatic code language in their songs.

Despite this history of repression, the syncretic sects and their wandering minstrels still survive in the Bengali countryside. It is the confluence of a variety of streams in their belief systems and cultural output—described earlier—which continue to nourish their popularity. As evident from the previously narrated experience of the West Bengali Baul who crossed over to Bangladesh, even today the cultural and spiritual needs of the villagers are met by the songs of such folk religious poets. They do not worship idols, or have temples or any institutionalized infrastructure, or a professionally trained priesthood, with the aim of organizing their followers. But they weave human concerns in an allegorical tapestry of spiritual concerns that reminds the common people of the powerful emotional capacities that they possess, like romantic love and the willingness to sacrifice everything for that love (as narrated by them in the Radha-Krishna kirtans), and the possibilities of rallying these basic human urges and powers in a spiritual direction. They remind them of the futility of their present pursuit of a fragile consumerist goal, and the need for identification with a higher ideal during their lifetime.

V

The popularity of these wandering minstrels of the Bengali syncretic sects, like the Bauls, Fakirs, Darbeshis, can be traced to their
creative ability to communicate metaphysical messages through
songs that reach out to the common people.

But when we come to the other vastly spread different popular
religious creeds, we find a variety of belief systems and practices
which are still operating in both traditional, and, surprisingly,
certain segments of modern Bengali society. They include general
customs like the worshipping of the goddess of small-pox Shitala,
or of a saint (like Satyapir)—the rituals surrounding whom are
analysed in one essay in this volume—and faith in magical cures
(through offerings to images or memorials of saints, or wearing
amulets, etc., a subject touched upon in the essay on the Karta-
bhaja sect).

We also come across instances of institutionalization of some
of these traditional popular religious beliefs and customs, and
iconization of the folk preachers who introduced them—mainly
through sustained efforts by their followers to build up a halo
around the spots where they operated. Two representative examples of how such spots developed into pilgrimages are Ghoshpara
in Nadia (associated with the founder of the Karta-bhaja sect) and
Tarapeeth in Birbhum, which was an isolated cremation ground
when the late-nineteeenth century Tantrik anchorite Bamakshyapa
chose it for his religious meditation (discussed in an essay in this
volume). It is interesting to observe how in both the cases mercantile and commercial interests influenced in a large measure their
development as religious pilgrimages.

These various facets of popular religion in Bengal pose a problem for those inside the camp of the more 'advanced' religions
which reject the little gods and pagan practices, and believe in an
Ultimate One of some sort, for example, Buddhism, Islam, Christianity, the Hindu concept of the Absolute—Brahma—and Jewish
monotheism. Their followers quite often continue to practise rites
that predate the birth of these new religions, or are prohibited by

their respective clergymen. For instance, Christian converts among the tribal communities continue to pay homage to images of their old gods. Indian Muslims in certain places worship local saints like pirs in blatant violation of the codes of orthodox Islam.

These beliefs and customs represent a microsystem of power in the society of the lower orders, which is also in a constant dialectical relationship with the macrosystem of power that had been shaped by the alliance of the religious establishment and the ruling classes at the top. The microsystem rules the populace in their daily existence—through its local mother goddesses like Bana-bibi or Ola-bibi, or the shamans and witch doctors. The macrosystem wields power over them in the wider context—when the Brahman priest is invited to preside over a wedding ceremony, when the mosque calls the Muslim followers to prayer, when the Hindus pay their obligatory visits to pilgrimage centres spread all over India, or when the Muslims undertake Haj to Mecca.

The engagement between popular religion and modern scientific rationality had also been fraught with problems. There had been a tendency among some representatives of the latter to dismiss popular religion as a relic from the early childhood of mankind, and as an anachronism in societies where it still survived. Max Weber, for instance, drew a sharp line between magical practices of the past and the emergence of a professionally trained priesthood which, according to him, made religion 'rational' through the combination of metaphysical thought and ethics. In this conceptual framework of his, he appears to deny the peasantry any rational thinking when he describes them as 'so strongly tied to nature, so dependent on organic processes and natural events, and economically so little oriented to rational systematisation'.[28]

Even when we look back at anthropologists who had tried to explain popular religious beliefs and customs in the framework of the terms of reference of scientific rationality, we find that their efforts were often stymied by intellectual limitations imposed by time and space. Thus one of the pioneers of cultural anthropology in the early decades of the twentieth century, while acknowledging that the myths invented by the people had their 'source in reason' and originated in 'that instinctive curiosity concerning the causes of things', described them as 'mistaken explanations of phenomenon, whether of human life or of external nature . . . being founded on ignorance and misapprehension.'[29]

While this indeed provides an analysis of the myths that dominate popular religion, the logic on which their critique is based is flawed to a certain extent. The reasons proferred for their dismissal—'mistaken explanations' and 'ignorance and misapprehension'—are not enough to muster conviction even among followers of modern scientific rationality. The growing realization that scientific statements can never be certain (which does not necessarily lead to the rejection of the rational pursuit of science) might make many accuse modern science of similar 'mistaken explanations' and 'ignorance and misapprehension'.

VI

The relationship between popular religion and modern science therefore needs to be redefined. In this connection, the observations made by one modern commentator on popular religion, while comparing primitive magic with modern therapies, are worth quoting: 'Magic, for those who practise it, is a system of compensations, guarantees and protections, a vital form of self-preservation. We may resort to drugs, or to the psychiatrist's couch, when we feel our sanity is endangered; the 'primitive' will consult his witch doctor who may prescribe the temporary observance of some taboo.'[30] We may add—without rejecting in the least the tangible effects of advances made in medical science—that despite the achievements, the diagnosis and treatment of a modern psychiatrist or a physician can still be as flawed as those of a primitive witch doctor.

In other words, neither religion nor science can claim certainty in knowledge, if we assume that knowledge is complete and it alone would provide something that is definitely true and permanent for the entire universe. The storehouse of knowledge has changed from time to time depending on the inventions of scientists and the ability of reasoning by contemporary rationalists. Following fresh discoveries as well as the recognition of the need for new methodologies to examine evidences of the past, scientists of every generation put to test the conclusions arrived at by their predecessors—who had also claimed a rational basis for their opinions in their times.

Such changes in our knowledge, however, do not invalidate the basic principles of scientific enquiry. They rather make its followers critically self-conscious of their own flaws and help them to look for methods of transcending them, since such an enquiry is defined by the obligation to question and to test.

But there is another aspect to the claim to certainty in knowledge. Whether in religion or science, it has been used as an instrument of power to enforce and retain control in every society. An alliance between the religious establishment and the ruling classes based on an agreement on the contemporary concept of certainty in knowledge, had laid down laws and shaped rules that sought to bind society in a homogeneous unit under a hegemonic control, as under a Brahmanical or an Islamic hierarchical order, as mentioned earlier. Similarly, the scientific revolution also, with all its potential to free society of religious tyranny, has resulted at times in instituting scientific authoritarianism, by attributing to itself certainty of knowledge. This often delegitimizes alternative ways of understanding reality, and helps the ruling powers to impose an authoritarian system of values and a uniform model of development on society to serve their own interest, in the name of science.

The unilinear deterministic claim that modern science alone can solve all the problems of humanity—what may be described as scientism—needs to be questioned. It is quite evident that scientific knowledge, its inventions and operations, are mediated by a variety of factors ranging from the priorities of those who patronize scientific investigations in a particular direction, to the individual inclinations and limitations of scientists pursuing their respective goals. As Robert Oppenheimer observed: 'a great part of the present scene arises not from what we have learned, but by its application in technology. This, in turn, rests on an organization of the economy and on our political arrangements. Neither of these derives from, nor is in any tight way related to, the sciences, because, although the growth of knowledge is largely responsive to human needs, it is not fully so.'[31]

Most of the theoreticians and practitioners of modern science have realized through centuries of experiments and experiences that the whole of physical reality cannot yet be explained fully in terms of one comprehensive and unilinear formalism. This of course does not mean that we should give up the search for explaining that reality through scientific enquiry. But in order to enrich and expand the scope of such an investigation, it may be necessary to take a fresh look at the various popular perceptions that explain physical reality in a different framework of references, and to try to understand why the beliefs and customs that represent such perceptions still continue to survive. These need to be looked at through a prism that is different from a historical approach that explains piety and rituality from a deterministic and unilinear point of view and often assumes a dismissive tone. At the same time, the new prism does not necessarily have to be a rear-view mirror that magnifies and valorizes every past popular religious belief and practice. Many which still persist in India should indeed be rejected as negative and retrograde trends (e.g. witchcraft involving human sacrifices, as well as witch-hunting leading to lynching of women, sati or burning of widows, female circumcision among certain communities, female infanticide, untouchability, etc.). They violate the universally acknowledged modern codes of humanitarian values and norms, besides rejecting one of the fundamental duties enjoined upon the citizens of India by their Constitution—'to develop the scientific temper, humanism and the spirit of inquiry and reform' [Part IVA(h)].

Yet, in Indian popular religion, such inhuman propensities also coexist with opposite trends that continue to sustain certain values and practices which are in conformity with the concepts of 'humanism' and 'the spirit of reform' as understood according to today's universal humanitarian standards. These trends, as we have discussed earlier, are represented in a large measure by the Bauls and similar syncretic sects.

How do historians in India negotiate with these different trends in popular religion—often conflicting with each other—which continue to impinge on our society even today?

VII

Any search for an answer to this question is invariably bound up with another equally tricky question: what are the responsibilities of historians? No one can deny that their primary responsibility is to their discipline, the rules that govern it which require them to master their basic tools of investigation, analysis and exposition irrespective of the political views to which they might adhere.

At the same time, however, we must remember that historians are not operating in a vacuum, or on a level playing field of a symmetrically ordered universal academic fraternity who share common social concerns and priorities in research. We may point out in this connection the different situations in which historians of popular religion are undertaking research in India and Europe (the latter being the location of the main centres of modern research in popular religion).

The historians in the West today are engaged in chronicling and analysing medieval popular religious beliefs and practices in their countries, many of which are no longer extant and do not affect their social environment and everyday experience in a major way. While these historians are diachronically comparing successive periods of popular religion of a past that allows them a certain distance, in the Indian social context today historians have to synchronically negotiate with two cultures—of the past and the present—that coexist in our country. This reality quite often denies our historians of popular religion the privilege of detachment that is enjoyed by their counterparts in the West.

This is inevitable in the Indian context, since the past, and particularly the medieval era of Indian history, are not yet a closed chapter. Historically, there has been no total rupture between the medieval and the modern. The former flows into the latter. Collective hopes and aspirations, societal fears and prejudices, religious beliefs and practices that have been handed down from the past continue to rule the life of communities in India in a way that has almost disappeared from societies in the modern West. They are not exotic, remote objects of academic research, but leap out from history and break in upon the consciousness of the present generation of Indians. It is this specific historical context which distinguishes the space of research of the historians of popular religion in India from their counterparts in the West. The issues that engage the attention of the Indian historians in this area, at times, overlap with current societal and political concerns in India.

The dilemma facing the historians of Indian popular religion might be seen as originating in the very construction of history as a discipline. From a strict adharance to the rules of that discipline, historians may not like to mix up their area of study—the past—with the present. Contemporary reality, they may argue, is too close for historians to be objective in their assessment.

This raises certain questions. Are historians certain that their narration and analysis of the past can ever resurrect it in its pristine form, despite their loyalty to the rigid rules of their discipline? How many among them can honestly claim to have met the austere standards set by Marc Bloch who declared: 'whoever lacks the strength, while seated at his desk, to rid his mind of the virus of the present, may readily permit its poison to infiltrate even a commentary on the Iliad or the Ramayana'?[32] Historians may consciously refuse to 'readily permit' the present to infect their research about the past. But can their subconscious remain totally uncontaminated by the pressures of the present that may indirectly shape their views about the past? As Oppenheimer suggested in the case of scientific research, in historical research also both extraneous and subjective factors mediate in the historian's search for knowledge.

In the present conditions in India, historians who aim at meeting Marc Bloch's standards may have to become schizophrenics of sorts—split into halves by the constant tension between two pulls. As disciplined historians they are required to totally separate their academic involvement in their specific domains of research from their concerns over surrounding socio-political issues that may impinge on their daily living as well as intellectual existence.

But some of these current issues, which can be described as the 'virus of the present', to quote Marc Bloch, may have developed from the residues of the past which these historians are researching. If historians are recognized as agencies of intellectual enlightenment, is it not their responsibility then to touch upon the present implications of the findings from their researched past, even if these may be peripheral to their main subject?

In other words, historians living and working in India today can seldom afford to remain ensconced within boundaries strictly determined by the traditional rules of their discipline, which are increasingly being threatened by the sheer pressures of the surrounding reality. They are compelled to realize that the object of their study is no longer a past wrapped in a prophylactic incapable of contaminating the present, or which itself is immune to contamination by the present. The writing and interpretation of medieval Indian history provide an interesting illustration. They are taking place today under the shadow of wide-ranging socio-political concerns. The entire controversy over the Babri Masjid and its demolition, among academic circles in India today, suggests how a historical past is revived, reinterpreted and recycled in different ways in the present. Historians of academic repute are no less participants in this process than politicians.

Should historians of popular religion in India then stop at just explaining the internal logic in past religious beliefs and behaviour patterns, an endeavour which in itself is an engrossing adventure? It involves entering into a past and a total immersion into the ocean of popular religion to get under its waters and into its depths, a methodology born from what is described by some as the 'Baptist theory' of history.[33] Or, should historians of popular religion dive into the waters, but surface, and explain and analyse the bearing of the persistence of such popular religious beliefs and customs on the collective psychology and behaviour of Indian society today?

Among those subscribing to the latter approach, there seems to be a frequent tendency to emphasize only those aspects of popular religion that they find useful to defend their present understanding of secularism. They discover in the Bhakti and Sufi movements in particular a source of inspiration today to remind Indian society of an alternative tradition of religious and cultural pluralism and harmony, as distinct from the current dominant trends of religious exclusivity and mutual antagonism. Such reminders have often been harnessed recently to attempts to fight violent manifestations of religious intolerance and sustain the secular fabric of our fragile polity.[34]

Although their efforts are praiseworthy, a few words of caution may be relevant in this connection. First, it is necessary to remember that the Bhakti and Sufi traditions which are being recalled today took their birth at a particular historical juncture to address contemporary socio-religious needs which were totally different from the concerns being faced by modern Indian society. Without in the least undermining the scholarship or the well-meaning efforts of those secular-minded individuals and organizations who are drawing inspiration from these sources, I doubt whether by selectively using these traditions to pick out from them certain songs and messages that suit today's secular agenda (e.g. those that speak of the universality of humankind and reject differences between Hindus and Muslims, or the upper and lower castes), we can fight the menace of modern communalism. If we choose to uphold only one cultural facet (such as the songs and poems about Hindu–Muslim unity) and decontextualize it from the wider religious and philosophical perspective of the Bhakti and Sufi movements, as historians of popular religion we may be doing injustice to the particular type of world outlook that these traditions represented. Failed political radicals in the West also have often turned to the humanitarian aspects of past religions in the tremulous hope of reviving egalitarian sentiments. Describing such trends as 'religious fellow-travelling', one perceptive observer from the West has pointed out that theirs is a 'piety without content, a religiosity without either faith or observance'.[35] At the political level too, the tendency to bank on the Bhakti and Sufi messages as a last resort to fight communalism betrays a certain intellectual inadequacy for meeting the new historical challenge thrown up by the rise of what is known as 'religious fundamentalism'. Those in India who are seriously committed to the task of putting an end to religious conflicts and establishing a society based on values that would respect both the pluralistic norms of religious harmony as well as secular principles, can indeed draw inspiration from whatever sources are available to them—indigenous and external, traditional and modern. But they will have to create their own new tools—both ideological and operative—to fight effectively their modern enemies, just as the Bhakti and Sufi reformers some five centuries ago invented a parallel ideology and strategy to challenge the prevalent religious orthodoxy.

There is another trend among certain historians and social scientists who are intervening in the contemporary debate in India on traditional religious beliefs and practices. They would prefer to explain them exclusively within the framework of the terms of reference of these religious systems themselves, and defend them accordingly. This approach to tradition appears to be a part of a wider ideological attempt to challenge the premise of Western modern science and rationality, and posit the two traditions of Indian popular religious beliefs and Western Enlightenment in a binary way. They denounce modern science as representative of the crass commercial adventurism of Western colonialism, and trace its destructive potentialities to the Enlightenment. They thereby tend to throw the baby of rational discourse out with the bath water of the Enlightenment. In an ideological backlash against the scientism of post-Enlightenment rationality, they appear to project the past society of India as an idyllic alternative to the present—the former reconstructed often in the shape of a Gandhian rural utopia. In these efforts, they even appear to go to the extent of defending traditional prejudices and practices (like valorization of sati) that go against all humanitarian norms, on the plea that such beliefs and behaviour represent the higher ideals of self-sacrifice handed down from a pristine past.[36]

While questioning much of the post-Enlightenment rationality that shaped colonial policies in India, we cannot at the same time reject the fundamental principle of critical reasoning that originally inspired the philosophers of the Enlightenment, and cannot but remember that it was this tradition of the Enlightenment which offered the colonized intellectuals the tools to challenge colonial rule, all their limitations notwithstanding.

The criticism of scientism by anti-Enlightenment intellectuals is a rather dangerous tendency. By launching an attack on science itself, it plays into the hands of the modern proponents of religious obscurantism.

It is necessary therefore to sound a word of caution against the trend of valorizing all popular religious beliefs and practices as the ideal alternative to the present drift towards religious violence and crass consumerism. As pointed out earlier, popular religion in India is not a seamless whole of humanitarian values and altruistic behaviour. Age-old prejudices continue to dictate certain practices in popular religion. Even within the folds of the same popular religious sect, one can find that the community spirit and solicitiousness which cut across religious, caste and gender differences quite often go hand in hand with the most atrocious practices which are carried out by its followers, again dictated by the same popular logic that makes them believe that these are penances that act as therapies (for example, dragging disabled people to a tank regarded as sacred, and ducking them in the hope of their recovery, at the Ghoshpara fair in Bengal).

The other aspect of popular religion which needs to be reviewed from today's standards of gender rights is the position of women in its various belief systems and practices. Although, at an abstract level, women are quite often worshipped as a mother goddess in many of the popular religious cults, in their rituals the

space that women enjoy is created within the patriarchal framework of values and structures. Among the Karta-bhajas, for
instance, while Saraswati, the wife of their preacher Ramsharan
Pal, is still worshipped as Sati-Ma, in the *dandikhata* ritual at the
Himsagar tank in Ghoshpara, the women pilgrims are not spared
the physical coercion of dragging their bodies to the temple of Sati-
Ma, if they happen to be barren (considered to be an inadequacy
among women according to the patriarchal social norms which
tend to ignore similar male inadequacies like impotence and steril-
ity). Similarly, in Tantrik rituals—followed by certain popular religious cults—although the female is considered to be essential (as
shakti, or the source of power) as a partner of the male in the *sadhana* or devotional exercises, in the sexual practices that are
required by these rituals, the woman is usually found to be in the
passive role of the recipient, according to both the interpreters of
Tantrik theology and eyewitness accounts of Tantrik practices, such
as Bhairabi-chakra.[37]

VIII

How then do the ragpickers of history assemble their inventory
into a meaningful pattern that would allow the readers to see and
understand the past as well as the present of popular religion?

As one leading historian of popular religion observed some
time ago: 'an irrational and (at least for some) atemporal phenomenon—and one thus historically irrelevant—could be studied in a
(rational), but not (rationalistic) key.' He then suggested that it was
possible to 'reconstruct a culture radically different from our own
... in spite of the intervening filter.'[38]

In the Indian context, historians of popular religion have a dual
task—'reconstructing' the culture of the popular religion of the
past, and redimensioning our understanding of those currents of
popular religion which are still prevalent in our society.

We therefore have to readjust the 'intervening filter' which we
are using in the present. It is necessary to understand the validity
of two separate cultural truths—one of the past, the other of the

present—and recognize at the same time that in the Indian situation the past lives in the present. We have to open up our awareness to the existential problems faced by a people living in a past threatened and besieged by natural calamities, famines and diseases, and the outlet which they sought for their collective fears and hopes in beliefs and rituals. It was a form of rationalization for them. Reason dictates methods and machinations for survival, and also invents theories to justify them.

When we come to the present, we find that some of the old religious beliefs and rituals—often dictated by the same popular logic of the past—persist in our society, albeit transformed in certain ways. We also discover the emergence of new religious icons and customs, mainly in urban society (e.g. the goddess Santoshi Ma; godmen like Sai Baba, Mahesh Yogi, Rajneesh among others, and the practices of their followers). How do we open up our awareness to these developments? How do we explain their persistence despite modern scientific forays into both traditional and modern societies?

They need to be examined in the light of the various requirements and desires of the different strata of our people. A compelling need among some makes them believe in visions and miracles, and makes possible the emergence of these phenomena in their perception. While trying to explain them, we should take into account the expectations of popular religiosity based on its own ways of ratiocination. The popular mind may find the explanations offered by modern science, or the solace preferred by the theology of the established religions, inadequate. Visions or miracles (attributed to shamans in traditional societies, or anchorites like Bamakshyapa in Bengal during the late nineteenth–early twentieth century), or dreams and hallucinations—often self-induced by the use of drugs by both the anchorites and their followers—were, and still are in certain situations in modern India, often the poor man's necessary modes of coping with an inhospitable reality. One of the leading continental historians of popular religion in modern Europe, Piero Camporesi, described the socioreligious psyche of the poor in medieval Italy in terms which bear resemblance to that of modern India: 'The flight of the ragged and starving masses . . . into artificial paradises, worlds turned upside down and impossible dreams of compensation originates from the unbearability of the real world, the low level of sustenance, dietary deficiency and (for contrast) excesses; these inspired an unbalanced, incoherent and spasmodic interpretation of reality.'[39]

The survival of such dreams among the populace, as well as the proliferation of new divinities and godmen/godwomen in the modern urban milieu, can be traced to both the tradition of collective fears and hopes that flow from the past, and new anxieties and aspirations, which, ironically enough, are being fuelled by the inventions of modern science. On the one hand, the rapid scientific development of the destructive power of armaments and the widespread ecological destruction wrought by technology have created a whole host of new fears and uncertainties among a section of the population who are directly affected by them. On the other hand, the increasing influence of 'hi-tech' industries, communication media and the consumerist values they preach have led to the birth of new ambitions and norms of behaviour among another section. While these avenues opened up by modern science offer them immense opportunities to gain wealth and recognition, they have to join a rat race to gain them. The fierce cutthroat competition creates new types of tensions and apprehensions among members of this parvenu social class, or those aspiring to join them. If the beleaguered unlettered laymen in rural society need to create deities or godlings to satisfy their urge for protection from calamities, and solace from some higher authority, the insecure educated gentry in the Indian urban society need a guru or a godman to solve problems at their level.

Certain trends in traditional popular religion and those in the newly emerging modern religious sects (e.g. led by godmen like Rajneesh) appear to converge. Both are operating outside the institutionalized framework of the traditional established religious systems. Both open their doors to all, irrespective of the religious denomination to which they may belong.

But the similarity stops there. We have to make a distinction between the two types of socio-religious needs and the responses of the two different societies which give birth to them. The fears and hopes of the members inhabiting these two environments are produced under different conditions. A comparison of the popular deity Satyapir worshipped in Bengal, and the famous godman Rajneesh who had an international following, would explain the point. The minds that lay themselves open to Satyapir are shaped by attitudes and values which are not only traditional, but shared by a multitude encompassing both the rich and the poor, rather than an exclusive elite. The story narrated during the rituals reflects a craving for social justice in community terms. The followers of Rajneesh on the other hand, come from widely different sociocultural backgrounds, both indigenous and foreign, but are brought together temporarily at one level in their search for a balm for their personal tensions and anxieties. They are a part of a cosmopolitan elite which seems to be torn between the material allurements that globalization may offer them as a privileged group and the fears and sense of uncertainty that it threatens them with. They seem to be more concerned about their individual salvation, in rituals that are packaged in the form of group therapies. This is a far cry from the collective memories and concerns that are represented by congregations of people who share a long and common tradition of socio-religious and cultural customs, that one can observe at a recital of Satyapir's hagiography, or at the Ghoshpara fair, or at the festival of Bauls at Kenduli. It is these latter varieties of human experiences that continue to sustain the pluralism that one finds in the various types of popular religion in India, warts and all.

The very fact that, unlike in the West, the microsystem of power of popular religion still functions in India, provides the historian with a rare opportunity of directly observing its practices and understanding the popular psyche in a manner that opens up possibilities of writing history in a new way.

I

THE CHANGING ROLE OF KALI
IN THE BENGALI POPULAR PSYCHE

Our daily life creates our symbol of God. No two
ever cover quite the same conception.

Sister Nivedita[1]

Different conceptions of God—or a superhuman power—at various levels of Bengali society had created numerous symbols over
the ages. In popular religion, these symbols had taken shape in a
multiplicity of local deities that are still worshipped in the countryside. Significantly enough, most of them are mother goddesses.
Kali can trace her origins to this hoary tradition of mother-worship
in Bengali popular religion.

But popular divinities inhabit a fluid space. Although when
they are born, they are meant to meet immediate needs, they never
remain fixed within their original boundaries. They are pushed by
their devotees to move over to the wider area of general concerns.
Thus these deities glide from one situation to another with a flexibility that defies historical and social boundaries. By digging into

the history of popular religion, one can excavate a treasure trove of myths of how old gods took on new appearances at a certain stage, consciously contrived deities emerged from the imagination of the populace to undergo yet another transformation at some later age. New mythologies and symbols are created every time to make them serve contemporary needs.

It is in the context of these multiple facets of popular religion in Bengal that the position of the goddess Kali is being located, and her evolution in the history of the Bengali psyche being traced. The aim is to understand the logic of the myth of Kali, as well as the internal logic of the religious conceptions that changed from time to time. This will enable us to recover the way in which the Bengali popular mental universe was articulated in relation to religion. There is no intention here to get involved in the debates over the subtleties of the highly complex theological interpretations of Kali made by adherents belonging to different schools of thought—interpretations which in their own right deserve a scholarly exam-ination beyond the scope of the present study. What is being attempted here is an examination of the relationship between cer-tain socio-religious practices and rituals in Bengal, and their ideo-logical counterparts in myths and postulates as created by the Bengali collective consciousness, which varied from one period to another. The ancestry of Kali is being traced to her origins in nat-ural phenomenon, collective needs, rituals of popular religion, etc. and her development is monitored through various phases till the turn of the twentieth century, when the Bengali middle-class men-tal universe was prepared for an instinctive alliance between reli-gion and politics.

I am following a hypothesis that is distinct from the theoretical assumption that a divinity or religious icon originally conceived by the lower orders remains stagnant and immune to external influ-ences. On the contrary, I find that the history of the concept and role of the Kali image in Bengal demonstrates the tremendously innovative capacities of the devotees of a primitive goddess to refashion the image of Kali by endowing it with new powers according to their contemporary social and political needs. These devotees initially came from the rural lower orders, and later from the urban Bengali middle classes. This again demonstrates the interfacing of two forms of religious consciousness—the popular and the elite, the rural and the urban—which Aron Gurevich describes as a 'dialogue conflict.'[2]

Primitive Sources

To start with, the original concept of Kali can be traced back to the development of the mother goddess in primitive society—which is found all over the world. The concept of the mother goddess again can be traced to the primitive collective consciousness about the procreative powers of the woman. In an agrarian society, the idea of the mother goddess as the deity of procreation was reinforced by the practice of agriculture, which found that the earth was procreative, yielding food. The fertility cults followed in agrarian societies indicate the development of the mother goddess into a deity presiding over agricultural operations. The term Annada (one who gives rice) or Annapurna (one who never denies food) used in Bengali for the mother goddess Durga is a significant pointer to this stage of transformation in her gradual evolution. Interestingly enough, the role of the mother goddess was not restricted to her powers as a source of procreation (specifically in the form of Shasthi, the goddess worshipped for the birth and protection of children), and fertility only, but expanded into other roles also—as the benevolent protector of the community against diseases or predatory animals as well as in the various fearsome incarnations of the deity of destruction—Brahmani, Sidhheshwari, Rankini (identified with, or springing from, Kali) among others.[3]

There are two significant features which deserve attention. First, the bulk of the corpus of such divinities worshipped by the rural Bengalis were, and still are, female. Secondly, they are represented usually by crude images, or even stones stamped sometimes with sindur (vermilion), and worshipped at a spot called the *thaan* (distortion in colloquial Bengali of the word *sthana*, or a place) usually situated at the end of a village. Most of these goddesses are propitiated with the sacrifice of animals or birds. The fact that the Brahman-dominated Hindu religious establishment looks down upon such practices (Manu in fact, denounced worshippers of such deities as *patit* or degraded) indicates that these village mother goddesses are a legacy of pre-Aryan rural collective religious beliefs and practices.[4]

The question is: what is the relationship between the benign and beneficent mother goddess Annapurna and the ferocious divinity of destruction, Kali? In ancient mythology, the mother goddess as the source of procreation and the mother goddess as destroyer were not separate and opposite icons, but incarnations of the same spirit that encompassed birth and death. She was perceived as an omnipotent but rather unruly goddess who brought forth and fostered all creatures, and yet simultaneously devoured them. Heinrich Zimmer picturesquely describes the dual role of the goddess in popular perception: 'Relentlessly, she swallows back like a monster the beings that she produces . . . This recognition of the negative aspect of the maternal principle descends from the antiquity of the neolithic. It is one of those perennial images that persisted in the popular religions of the non-Aryan branches of the Indian folk'.[5] It should be remembered that most of the advances in Neolithic civilization, such as food production, pottery making and domestication and milking of cattle, were started by women. It was not without reason that what was regarded as the super-human was shaped by its devotees in the form of a female deity in the ancient days, and even in the later Brahmanical theology came to be defined as the Adya-Shakti (or primeval female power). To her, the primitive mind attributed fecundity and growth as well as decay and death, both in nature and human existence.

Archaeological records as well as popular legends suggest that mother goddesses vested with protective and curative powers and depicted in the form of fearsome effigies were widely worshipped by the aboriginal population in eastern India (including Bengal) long before the arrival of Aryan culture in that part of the country. Later Buddhist influences led to the incorporation of these aboriginal goddesses into the Mahayana-Vajrayana pantheon.

One Vajrayana Buddhist goddess was known as Parna-Shabari. The suffix *shabari* harks back to the oft-repeated references in ancient scriptures to the custom of worshipping mother goddesses by the aboriginal Shabars (hunters, forest-dwellers) in eastern India. She is represented as a young woman clothed in tiger-skin and tree-bark, with solid rings hanging from her ears, trampling upon all diseases. In the hymn meant to propitiate her, she is described as a *dakini* (witch) and *pishachi* (female fiend).[6]

Among other village goddesses depicted in similar fearsome form, the image of Rankini, said to be a local version of Chamunda, the destructive mother goddess found in the ancient Puranas, seems to have been an object of popular worship in Bengal for ages. Her name appears in the medieval Bengali poetic folk ballads called Mangal-kavyas, which resuscitated the primitive deities of eastern India, claimed them to be local incarnations of the gods and goddesses of the ruling Aryan culture, and narrated their exploits and magical powers. Till some years ago, a ruined temple of this goddess was still extant in Indra village in Medinipur in West Bengal. According to one observer, the worship of Rankini actually started from the tribal-dominated Singbhum area (now a part of Bihar) bordering Bengal, and spread to neighbouring villages in Medinipur, Bardhaman, and other districts. Made of stone, her image was installed and worshipped in the midst of dense forests.[7] Worshipping of the goddess was apparently accompanied by human sacrifice, a practice which continued till the beginning of the nineteenth century, as evident from a report in a contemporary Bengali newspaper about a similar incident in a temple of Rankini in a village in Bardhaman.[8]

Incidentally, the word *rankini* in Bengali means a poor woman. Was this again a transformation of the mother goddess into a deity representing poverty? Was she made into a symbol of hunger, who had to be propitiated with human sacrifice? Was her worship more common during periods of drought and impending famine? One could hazard these guesses in the light of certain observations made by a nineteenth-century British official who toured rural Bengal, and who noted that human sacrifices were resorted to in the villages 'in order to avert the famine', and that among aboriginal tribes in the south-west of Birbhum, such sacrifices were made 'with a view to procuring the early arrival of the rains.'[9]

But let us come back to what Zimmer describes as the 'negative aspect of the maternal principle.' The terrifying figure of the mother goddess was born in the primitive mind from the cosmic terror that the human being felt in the presence of Nature. Behind the triumphant thought of renewal of life through fecundity, there lurked the fear of natural disasters and the threat of disease and death. To the primitive mind it was a nightmarish universe peopled with both real predatory animals and unpredictable natural forces like earthquakes and floods, as well as imaginary creatures, phantasmagoric monsters, sinister witches, who were held responsible for all the ills that the human being suffered. It was a universe in which humankind felt pursued with a diabolical perseverance by these evil spirits. The primitive mind sought to externalize and objectify this innermost sense of fear and terror by constructing a grotesque image, the figure of the black goddess, depicting her with all the terrifying attributes that man feared: a wreath of severed heads dangling from her neck to her knees, dripping blood, bared fangs. These basic ingredients that went into the shaping of her image remained constant. But more and more macabre features and bloodcurdling stories came to be added to the image over the ages.

The Grotesque in Popular Religion

The terrifying shape of the destructive goddess horrifies us by both its monstrosity and its gruesomeness. The conception of these twin facets of the goddess is rooted in a long tradition of the grotesque in popular imagination. The misshapen anatomy had long been a part of popular folklore, which indulged in free play with the human body, often adding to it animal limbs leading to good-humoured anatomical fantasies or celestial drolleries, like the image in Indian mythology of Ganesha with an elephant head. At the same time the gory malignance attributed to some of these grotesque creatures of popular imagination had always held fascination for the popular poets and their listeners, as found in the fairy tale and mythological descriptions of demons and ghosts, rakshasas and asuras. Their conception emphasizes the idea of eating and devouring. We therefore find in their descriptions repeated stress on visual attributes like lolling tongues, teeth tearing apart human flesh, half-devoured bodies hanging from their mouths, blood streaming from their lips.

Kali belongs to the latter domain of Bengali popular imagination. As evident from her visual image, as well as the description of that image in scriptural texts, a particular concept of the human body was crucial to her construction. It is interesting to note that unlike other grotesque creatures or gods like Ganesha, Kali's body is not a mixture of human and animal parts. She possesses a human body but with features that recall the painful disintegration and final end of that body, dancing in the cremation grounds, surrounding herself with putrefying limbs and skulls, spouting blood, and trampling upon the body of a man who is alternatively described as *shava* (a dead body) or a fallen Shiva. She thus forewarns of the ominous destiny of the human body—the body that, to quote Mikhail Bakhtin, 'fecundates and is fecundated, gives birth and is born, devours and is devoured, drinks, defecates, is sick and dying.'[10] It is this stark and merciless inevitability evoked by Kali that makes her all the more frightening. She is not some distant half-human half-animal creature, but a very recognizable female form, indulging in an orgy of bloodthirsty destruction.

It is also significant that this gruesome and grotesque mother goddess is painted black, the colour of night. To the primitive human being, the darkness of night was haunted by the unknown, the mysterious and the fearful. In fact, in the Rigveda, there are propitiatory verses addressed to a Ratri Devi (goddess of night), requesting her to protect human beings from tigers and thieves. According to some later commentators like Swami Abhedananda, the renowned disciple of Ramakrishna, it was this goddess who was later turned into Kali in Hindu scriptures.[11]

Besides the colour of her skin, the other features of the black goddess also suggest symbolical associations. The bloodstained tongue that hangs out, for instance, has been interpreted as the symbol of fire. The *Mundakopanishad* describes fire as having seven tongues, the first of which is called Kali. The all devouring power of fire filled the primitive people with awe. With its licking tongues it consumed the sacrificial offerings. Its dancing flames devoured the corpses of the dead. From this experience, it is easy to imagine the image of the dark goddess with protruding tongue dancing on the cremation ground. The familiar sight of the black smoke coiling up over the burnt white ashes could have inspired some imaginative poetic mind in later days to conceive the image of the dark Kali trampling on the white body of Shiva.

A different interpretation of the protruding tongue is however offered in a Bengali legend. The image of Kali as worshipped in Bengali religious functions, was reported to have been visualized by a sixteenth-century Tantrik scholar Krishnananda Agambagish on the model of a Bengali village housewife of whom he had a sudden glimpse. The story goes that one night he sat wracking his brains, but failed to find the best way to represent the goddess. As usually happens in such legends, Kali herself appeared to him in a dream and asked him to fashion her image after the first figure he saw on waking up the next morning. Coming out from his room in the morning, the first thing he saw was a dark-complexioned milkmaid. She had her right foot placed forward, and with her left hand she was collecting cowdung from the earth. Then with her right hand she was plastering the walls of the house with a handful of the cowdung (which when dried could be used as fuel cakes). Because of her labour, she was perspiring, and with the back of her right hand she was trying to wipe the sweat off her forehead. As a result, the sindur on her forehead had got smeared and reddened her eyebrows; her *ghomta* (veil) had fallen off, leaving her hair all tousled. When she abruptly found herself face to face with Krishnananda, she became conscious of her dishevelled appearance, and in the typical Bengali female manner of expressing bashfulness, she put out her tongue and lightly bit it.[12]

This supposedly became the model of the Kali icon which is worshipped all over Bengal.

But significantly enough, Krishnananda selectively adopted
only a few postures and features of the milkmaid (her dark skin,
the raised right foot—to be placed on the chest of the prostrate
Shiva—her dishevelled hair, and the protruding tongue). The rest
of the Kali image is a far cry from the shy village maid. Modelled
on the various representations found in the Puranas, but primarily
derived from the Tantrik tradition, the Kali that is worshipped in
Bengal is a fierce-looking icon, which again emphasizes the
grotesque in popular tradition. While in the *Markandeya-purana*,
Kali, although terrifying in her appearance, covers her hideous
nakedness with a tiger-skin, in other versions, particularly in
Bengal, she has shed all her clothes and dances naked. Although
her body is buxom with rounded breasts and heavy hips, her face
looks fiendish, her teeth are large fangs and blood drips from her
tongue. This image is based on a description found in the Tantrik
hymns read out in her praise. Although composed in Sanskrit,
these supplicatory hymns contain mantras, or incantations which
are just a combination of certain sounds that hark back to tribal
chants. This has given rise to the speculation that the Tantrik
beliefs and rituals surrounding mother-worship are actually
derived from aboriginal religious customs.[13]

The Erotic and the Macabre

An intriguing feature of Tantrik hymns is that while describing the
features of the goddess, they usually bring together both the erotic
and the macabre. Thus Dakshina Kali—the most popular representation of the goddess in Bengal—is hailed as *bigalitachikure*
(hair hanging loose, evoking the image of a woman in passionate
ecstasy) as well as *srikkadwandwasradharadwadharabadane* (blood
streaming from the two ends of her mouth). She has a pair of
large and prominent breasts (*peenastana*), but her neck is garlanded with a wreath of human skulls (*mundasragatishayalasatkan-
thi*) touching the nipples. Described as totally naked (*digambari*),

she is celebrated for a girdle made out of severed hands of dead bodies that decorate her heavy hips (*gatasunang bahuprakara kritakanchiparilasannitambang*). The next verse locks the concepts of death and love in a tight embrace:

> *Shibabhirghorabhih shabanibahmundasthinikaraih*
> *Parang sankeernayang prakatita chitayang harabadhung*
> *Prabishtang santushtamuparisuratenatijubating . . .*[14]

(Oh, wife of Hara! Terrifying jackals are all around. The entire place abounds with the skulls and bones of dead bodies. In the middle, a funeral pyre is burning. In this cremation ground, you, Young Lady, feel happy engaging in coitus with Shiva, with you on top of him.)

The proximity between sexuality and death had fascinated the human mind from time immemorial. The awareness that the body is the site of both, had inspired the human imagination to construct motifs that bring the two together in some form or other. Occult Tantrik practices like necromancy, or copulation in cremation grounds, and the mantras accompanying them, apart from being exercises in overcoming fear and revulsion among the devotees, are also a brutal and direct way of reminding the human mind that even the utmost moment of bliss (in physical union) is doomed to extinction. But there seems to be more to it. There is a sense of finality that marks both the climax in sexual union and the physical extinction of the body, temporarily in the former case, permanently in the latter. If sexual union reaches its climax in orgasm, the human body reaches its end with the release of the last breath in death. George Bataille argues that human beings play at death in erotic abandonment, and describes orgasm as *la petite morte*.[15]

Shades of History

But apart from being associated with the primitive attitude towards night, the colour black in which Kali is painted could suggest certain historical developments, as indicated in some of the stories in the Puranas. It would be interesting to examine these stories and hazard speculations. In the *Shiva-purana* and the *Padma-purana*, for instance, we come across a delightful episode about a quarrel between Shiva and Parvati. Shiva apparently taunted Parvati for her dark skin, comparing their relationship to a black serpent entwined around a pale sandalwood tree: '*Bhujangibasita shubhre sangslishta chandane tarou.*' An angry Parvati worshipped Brahma and received his blessing, enabling her to shed her dark skin and acquire a fair complexion which entitled her to the honorific Gauri (literally meaning fair-complexioned). The dark skin she shed was turned into another goddess called Ekanangsha, who was identified with the earlier mentioned goddess of night, Ratri.[16]

Can we venture to discover deeper symbolical meanings in the story? The black Durga was probably a goddess of the aboriginal dark-skinned people whom the Aryans conquered. In an attempt to adopt her and make her a consort of their fair-skinned god, they made her shed her skin. But to allow the aborigines to worship their old goddess, in their myth they transferred Durga's original skin to another goddess.

In a different myth relating to the birth of Kali, we could perhaps discover traces of another historical phase—when matriarchy faced patriarchal intrusions. In the *Markandeya-purana* and *Durga-saptati* we are told about two demon brothers, Shumbha and Nishumbha, who were enchanted by the beauty of the goddess Durga, and sent their messenger to her, carrying a proposal. Durga however told the messenger that she had promised to marry only that man who could defeat her in a battle. The two brothers then sent their army under their commander Chanda and his brother Munda to capture the recalcitrant goddess. An angry Durga knitted her brows, and there emanated from her frown a black goddess called Kali. She is described as 'Karalabadana . . . Bichitra-khatwangadhara Naramala-bibhushana/ Dwipicharmaparidhana Shushkamangsati-bhairaba/ Atibistarabadana Jihbalalanabhish-ana/Nima-gnaraktanayana Nadapuritadingmukha.[17] (She has a frightful face . . . she carries a strange-looking skeletal weapon in her hands and a necklace of human heads hangs around her neck;

she is clad in tiger skin and her skin is all withered; she has a huge mouth with her tongue lolling out horribly; her bloodshot eyes are sunken deep and she is filling the universe with the roars of a lion.)

In the gory battle that ensues, the new goddess devours all the soldiers and chariots of the demons, kills Chanda and Munda, and finally offers their heads to Durga as trophies of her victory. The latter then baptizes Kali with a new name—Chamunda—in memory of her killing of the two brothers.

All through the narrative, we notice the unmistakable stress on the prowess of the female. Durga rebuffs the male demands and challenges the two demon brothers to fight her. When their messenger fails to persuade her, Shumbha and Nishumbha send the powerful commander of the demon army, Dhumralochan, to apprehend her. But just one roar from Durga reduces him to ashes! The next time around Chanda and Munda are sent to carry out the task, but the goddess does not even deign to touch them, creating another goddess (rather than a god) to annihilate them.

Is the entire story, a paean to women's courage and power, an allegory for matriarchal power fighting threats from male domination? Was it invented during a particular period when various factors, like the introduction of new tools of production and the important role of men in their use, were leading to their increasing incursions into the hitherto female-dominated world of social norms and practices? How is it that the story not only continued to survive even after the defeat of the matriarchal system but also got incorporated in the later Puranas?

It is here that we should acknowledge our debt to the power of the oral tradition in India. Unlike written and printed literature, which is fixed and therefore more vulnerable to censorship and suppression by the ruling powers, the oral tradition can survive as a subterranean stream that can always cheat the authorities by changing its course, taking different forms. It retained its continuity and prevailed over the religious diktats of successive indigenous socioeconomic systems and external conquering powers, whether Aryan, Greek, Turk, Mughal or European. While retaining its myths and legends, the Indian oral tradition was not, however, a closed system. It was open-ended enough to recognize the new beliefs and mythologies that were introduced with each turn in the historical development of Indian society. It accepted them and transformed them in accordance with both the outlines of the past myths and the needs of contemporary society. That is how we get a Kali who preserves all the traces of an aboriginal past, and also acquires the new features of a Buddhist, and later a Brahmanical, deity.

Indian religious myths and legends as handed down to us should not be taken as ossified representations of fixed beliefs and practices of a certain period—they need to be recognized as a corpus shaped over generations by both the populace and the clergy, which carry layers of historical strata that added newer and newer stories from their respective periods to the original myth. It is up to the modern historians of popular religion to analyse these myths and classify their various components according to their historical origins, as far as it is possible to disentangle them.

Following this course, when we examine recorded history, we find that these mother goddesses of the matriarchal era were adopted by a succession of established religious orders in Bengal, which indicated the continuing hold of these icons on popular faith and belief even after the end of matriarchy. In later Buddhism for instance, during its transition to Vajrayana, these mother goddesses were already being incorporated into the Buddhist pantheon, as evident from the earlier mentioned Parna-Shabari. It appears that still later during this period, the multiplicity of the numerous local mother goddesses was sought to be streamlined into one uniform shape under the prevailing Shakta cult (based on the concept of the archetypal female power, manifest in Shakti, as a consort of the male deity who can be roused only by her touch), which had become popular in Bengal by the seventh and eighth centuries.[18] Thus the Bengali Buddhists, during the Pala kingdom, conceived the mother goddess Tara in two forms: one as a gentle, and the other as a fierce-looking deity called Ugra-Tara. In

the latter form, she looks like a descendant of the terrifying primitive goddesses worshipped by tribals like the Shabars.[19]

The next stage of accommodation and incorporation began
under the Hindu Brahman kings in Bengal around the eleventh
century. The local aboriginal goddesses, already reincarnated in
the form of Tara by the Buddhists, were usurped by the Brahmanical order and incorporated into its pantheon as Sati. One can
recapitulate the familiar mythological story about Sati in order to
re-examine how the religious beliefs of the non-Vedic and pre-
Vedic people were grafted onto the stem of Vedic religion. Daksha,
the father of Sati, organized a yagna, to which he refused to invite
his son-in-law Shiva. When Sati wanted to attend the ceremony,
Shiva obstructed her. In protest, Sati assumed the forms of ten
goddesses (*dasha-mahavidya*) to confuse and terrify Shiva: Kali,
Tara, Rajrajeshwari, Bhubaneshwari, Bhairabi, Chhinnamasta,
Dhoomabati, Bagalamukhi, Matangi and Mahalakshmi. A frightened Shiva then relented, and allowed Sati to go to the Daksha-
yagna. But when she arrived there, her father Daksha began to
abuse Shiva. On hearing this, in anguish, Sati ended her life on
the spot. A distraught Shiva came and lifted his wife's body on his
shoulders and began a dance of destruction. In order to prevent
him from destroying the universe, Vishnu with his famous
chakra—the lethal battle-wheel—cut Sati's body into pieces, and
they flew in all directions, settling down in different parts of the
country, which came to be known as *peethas*, or sacred spots in
memory of Sati.

There are several interesting aspects to this story into which
one can read a host of meanings recalling popular folklore, historical stages in the evolution of society and religion, and interlacing
of beliefs and practices of one religion with those of another. First,
there is this myth of Sati's incarnation as *dasha-mahavidya*.
Here, the mother goddess who in primitive religion was single
(even when she had a consort, the latter's name rarely figured in
folklore; we are not told, for instance, of the male consorts of
Shitala, Ola-bibi, Bana-bibi, and other goddesses who still survive
in rural society) is now identified as the wife of a male god, Shiva.

Did this indicate a transition from a matriarchal to a patriarchal society? But even after this transition, she continued to be revered as a powerful goddess, as an intractable legacy from a tradition which needed to be fully controlled and transformed according to the requirements of the ruling ideology. Was it the necessity to concede to this popular traditional faith in the omnipotence of the mother goddess that made the myth-makers and theologians of the later era invent the concept of the *dasha-mahavidya* so as to accommodate the various tribal goddesses within the form of a single deity? Almost all the ten incarnations hark back to the images of the primitive tribal mother goddesses—grotesque in form, awe-inspiring, macabre.

The Sati myth also lends itself to another historical interpretation. One of the pioneer historians of Calcutta suggested that one could read in it the 'story of the dismemberment of a kingdom'. According to his speculation, Daksha, the ruler of the kingdom, drunk with power, brought about anarchy:

> Destruction threatens everywhere; anarchy reigns supreme. At this stage the preserver appears and parcels out into various sections the kingdom which now lies a helpless corpse. He . . . plants the seeds of new life in spots that lie far apart, so that each spot may become a centre of independent growth. Thus interpreted, the legend may be taken to refer to the emigration of the Aryans from Daksha's country and their colonization of different parts of India.[20]

An interesting instance of how this mythological tale underwent an imaginative interpretation at the level of popular religion in Bengal, with significant socio-historical bearings, has been provided by an Aghori (a type of Tantrik practitioner) of Bakreshwar, a pilgrimage centre in Birbhum. According to him:

> Shiva . . . was the hero, the god of the non-Aryans. In the opinion of the Aryans, the followers of Shiva were degraded, fallen . . . Shiva used to live in Kailash . . . (and) did not live in (other parts of) the Himalayas, since the

Himalayas were the heaven of the Aryans, under their control. But he married a girl from these Himalayas. She, the
daughter of an Aryan ruler, having heard of his (Shiva's)
virtues, intensely propitiated him to be able to garland him
(as her husband) . . . When Uma (another name of Sati,
Parvati, Durga—the daughter of the Aryan ruler Daksha)
married Shiva, all the Aryan gods were mad with anger.
How could Shiva dare to marry the daughter of an Aryan
ruler! They looked for an opportunity to teach him a les-
son, or test his prowess. It was because of this that the
Daksha-yagna ceremony was organized. But when (at this
ceremony) the Aryans got to know about Shiva's divine
supernatural powers, they lost their pride; they had to bow
down to Shiva. Shiva then became Maheshwara (the highest among all the gods).[21]

The other interesting aspect of the myth of Sati relates to the
peethas, or the sacred spots where her different limbs were
supposed to have fallen. Hindus believe that there are 51
recognized *peethas* spread over different parts of India and neighbouring areas, under which these limbs are buried. Curiously
enough, unlike those situated in the north and the west which are
to be found in rather isolated spots, separated from each other by
vast distances (e.g. Hinglaj in Baluchistan in the northwest of
today's Pakistan, Jwalamukhi in the Punjab), the *peethas* in the east
and northeast seem to be concentrated in a cluster, a closely knit
zone. At least 13 *peethas* are situated in the Bengali-speaking areas
of today's West Bengal and Bangladesh, eight in the eastern and
northeastern regions (including the famous Kamakshya temple in
Assam), at least two in Nepal and one in Tibet (the famous Manas-
Sarovar). Archaeological excavations in some of these sites have
revealed the remains of mother-deities, indicating that these spots
had been sites of worship in the pre-Aryan days. Most of
the goddesses worshipped in these ancient sites were depicted
in the grotesque form of destructive and devouring images. It
suggests that the later religious orders, in recognition of the
strongly entrenched pre-Aryan religious and sociocultural beliefs

and practices surrounding the mother goddess that continued to mark the lifestyle of the aboriginal population in Bengal and the northeast, chose these spots to woo these people and invented new myths to adopt them into their respective religious frameworks.

The next significant thing that strikes us is the source of the concept of *peethas* as sites of relics of Sati's body. The concept appears to have been borrowed by the Brahman theologians from the Buddhist religious practice of collecting the remains of Buddha's body and worshipping them. After Buddha died, his hair, nails, tooth, bones, etc. were taken away by his devotees and placed in different spots all over the country upon which stupas were erected. These became Buddhist pilgrimage spots. This Buddhist tradition was evidently assimilated by the Brahman theologians, giving rise to the concept of the *peethas*.

The incorporation of the time-honoured, venerable spots of pilgrimage that were common to both the tribal and later Buddhist devotees, into the later list of the 51 *peethas* suggests an interesting process of religious negotiation between the Brahman and the non-Brahman traditions of the past. Since popular religious beliefs and practices revolved around these spots, the Brahman theologians sought to co-opt them, divest them of their tribal origins and Buddhist influences, and reinterpret them within the framework of their own Puranas and myths.

In Bengal in particular, the main site where the negotiation between Brahman theology and pre-Brahman religious practices took place was the field of Tantrism. In the period following the Turkish invasion in the thirteenth century, the Brahmans gravitated towards the Tantrik tradition of Bengal, in a large measure adopted its views and rituals, and modified them according to their needs. Explaining their motivation, one later day Bengali historian traced it to their loss of ruling power, and the consequential erosion in their control over society after their defeat at the hands of the foreign invaders. While in the heyday of their rule they could afford to ignore and look down upon the traditional beliefs and practices of the Bengali lower orders, once dispossessed of ruling power they sought to re-establish their authority over society by wooing these same lower orders and accepting some of their religious views and customs. Noting the changes brought about in Tantrism by Brahman influence, he observed:

> The brahmans of Bengal gradually adopted Tantrik customs, became successful practitioners of the cult and began to rule over society. It is because of their efforts that Buddhist Tantra began to be decked in a brahmanical mode. Krishnananda (Agambagish), Brahmananda, Tripurananda and others, through their composition of various Tantrik texts, re-introduced in Tantra the influence of the caste-division-based social hierarchy (*varnashramadharma*) . . . In order to bring the Bengalis under Brahmanical rule, the brahmans of the past had to make a lot of compromise with Tantrik and Buddhist religion . . .[22]

Kali in Calcutta

When we move from the medieval to the modern era in Bengal, we come across yet another interesting example of how obscure religious spots can be adopted and transformed into important pilgrimage centres in accordance with changes in society and economy. It is again centred on the primitive mother goddess—the famous shrine of the goddess Kali in Kalighat, situated in south Calcutta.

Curiously enough, the name of Kalighat does not occur in any of the old Puranas or Sanskrit scriptures that list the *peethas*. Even when we find its mention in popular Bengali folk narratives composed between the end of the fifteenth and the sixteenth century (e.g. Bipradas Pipalai's *Manasamangal* written in 1495 and Mukundaram Chakravarty's *Chandi-kavya*, written sometime between 1580 and 1585), its authenticity is quite often challenged by modern historians of Calcutta.[23]

It is only in sixteenth-century texts like Krishnananda Agambagish's *Brihattantrasar* and *Tantrachuramoni*, that Kalighat is mentioned as a pilgrimage centre. A latter-day Purana, the *Bhavishya-purana*, giving a list of pilgrimage spots, mentions: '*Govindapura prante cha Kali Suradhani tata.*' ('And Kali appears on the banks of the river Suradhani'—Hooghly). Why did the Kali of Kalighat assume importance in the sixteenth century? The village Govindapur came up in the mid-sixteenth century when the Sheth and Basakh traders migrated here from their earlier trading centre at Saptagram. The silting up of the river Saraswati on which Saptagram was situated necessitated the shifting of their trading centre to a more convenient place, which happened to be Govinda-pur on the banks of the Hooghly, which in those days opened up the entry route for the European traders to Bengal. Besides, this village—Govindapur—was situated close to Sutanati, which was inhabited by *tantees* (weavers) whose textiles, known for their fine craftsmanship, could be imported.

Once these Sheth and Basakh traders settled down in Govin-dapur and turned it into a trading centre, it began to attract atten-tion from other parts of the country. Before their arrival, there was already an image of Kali in the old village, but legends and literary records suggest that it was a *gujhya-Kali*, or a hidden Kali (if trans-lated literally) meaning a goddess worshipped in secrecy. It was installed in the middle of jungle. The original inhabitants of this area, aboriginal fishermen (Pods, Jalias, Bagdis) and hunters and woodcutters like shikaris, byadhs, among others, offered worship to the dreaded goddess according to old aboriginal rites, which also included human sacrifice.[24] According to legends, this makeshift temple of Kali was destroyed in an earthquake sometime in the fif-teenth century, and the image was then said to have been trans-ferred to a spot in Bhawanipur in south Calcutta, the area where today's Kalighat is. (This was, in those days, a part of the Govinda-pur area.) Incidentally, Bhawani is another name for the mother goddess.

At the end of the sixteenth century, Raja Basanta Ray was said to have built a small temple at the site, replacing the earlier thatched mud hut which sheltered the Kali image. From this period, we get to know the names of the priests of the Kali temple. Bhubaneshwar Chakravarty was the first in a long succession of priests who continued to look after the temple for centuries.[25]

But it was from the early eighteenth century that the Kali of Govindapur began to acquire importance among the gentry. The Sabarna Chaudhury zamindars, who by then had acquired the proprietorship of the area, and had settled down in Barisha nearby, were instrumental in developing the site, and improving the temple. From an obscure deity of the lower castes, the goddess Kali emerged as a highly respectable object of worship of the upper castes and classes. Her worship was now performed in public instead of in secret as in the past. The shrine also began to attract pilgrims from around Calcutta. From then on, claims were made about Kalighat being one of the *peethas*. Legends were floated which said that the toe of the right foot of Sati fell there, a belief which still inspires pilgrims to visit Kalighat, although it does not figure in the original list of 51 *peethas*.

The next phase in the transformation of the temple at Kalighat began from the end of the eighteenth century. Thereby hangs an interesting tale. Kaliprasad Dutta was the son of a wealthy Kayastha family of Hatkhola in north Calcutta. He had a Muslim mistress, known as Anar Bai. When his mother died, the orthodox Brahmans of Calcutta ostracized him because of his liaison with a Muslim, and refused to attend the funeral ceremony. Since the funeral rites without the attendance of Brahman priests were considered incomplete according to Hindu law, a distraught Kaliprasad approached a leader of the Hindu community of Calcutta, Ramdulal Dey, a millionaire trader. Ramdulal sought the advice of Santosh Ray, the then patriarch of the Sabarna Chaudhury family, the original proprietors of Calcutta. Santosh Ray suggested that Kaliprasad offer a large amount of money to the Brahman priests and invite them to a feast. A grateful Kaliprasad offered Rs 25,000, which the Brahmans donated to Santosh Ray, who started building the Kali temple at its present site. It took seven to eight years to build, and was completed in 1809, after Santosh Ray's death.

From then on, all through the nineteenth century, rich citizens of Calcutta added to the temple complex, building annexes and offering gold. Jaynarayan Ghoshal of Bhukailas (Khidirpur) presented four silver arms, two gold eyes and gold and silver ornaments to the goddess. Gopeemohan Thakur spent Rs 10,000 on the worship of the goddess in 1811. Interestingly, Europeans living in Calcutta in those days also presented offerings to Kali in Kalighat, soliciting favours. As mentioned earlier, John Marshman tells us about a deputation from the Government which 'went in procession to Kalighat and made a thanks-offering to this goddess of the Hindus, in the name of the (East India) Company, for the success which the English have lately obtained in this country. Five thousand rupees were offered. Several thousand natives witnessed the English presenting their offerings to this idol.'[26] Another British observer, the Reverend James Ward, chaplain of St John's Church in Calcutta in the early years of the nineteenth century, in his *Views of the History & c., of the Hindus*, writes: 'I have received accounts several times of Europeans, or their native mistresses, going to this temple and expending thousands of rupees in offerings ... Very lately a gentleman in the Hon'ble Company's service, who had gained a cause at law, presented thank-offerings to Kali which cost two or three thousand rupees'.[27]

Stories of massive expenditure on sacrifices of buffaloes and goats at Kalighat hit the headlines of contemporary newspapers. Rev. James Ward tells us that the monthly expenses for the worship of the deity under all heads amounted to 'sicca rupees 6,000, or Rs 72,000 a year.' The worshipping of the goddess was not confined to the Kalighat temple only. Rich families of Calcutta organized Kali pujas in their mansions on a lavish scale. Practices like the drinking of alcohol and the consumption of the meat of sacrificed animals, which used to be a part of primitive rituals associated with the worshipping of the mother goddess, and which were later incorporated by Buddhist and Shakta practitioners into their Tantrik rituals, were transformed into gala sessions of drinking and fine dining in the rich Shakta households of nineteenth-century Calcutta.

Such events formed the staple of popular jokes among the common people of the city. Some of these jokes illuminate the fascination for the bizarre in urban popular culture, a trend shaped by the tradition of myth making in India. As in the myths about ancient mother goddesses and Kali, weird things happen in these popular anecdotes also. But instead of being gruesome, these droll narratives of the urban wags turn out to be hilarious caricatures of the devotional practices of the worshippers of the same goddess of destruction and death, Kali, who at another level inspired awe and respect amongst these very wags. Let us examine one such story that made the rounds in those days. It was about the family of Kalishankar Ghosh of Shobhabazar of north Calcutta. Both the masters and the servants of this fabulously rich household were dyed-in-the-wool Shaktas for whom alcohol was the lifeline to Kali, and therefore they drowned themselves in it from morning till night! One evening, when Kalishankar was relaxing after his *sandhya ahnik* (evening prayers), his servant came to massage his feet. He found his master lying in bed with one foot stretched out. The other foot was obviously tucked beneath his thigh. But the servant, like his master, totally sozzled, could not trace the hidden foot. So, after he finished massaging the outstretched foot, he started looking for the missing foot all over the house. He approached Kalishankar's wife, who, being a devout Shakta, was also dead drunk. When asked about her husband's other foot, she ordered the servant to look for it at the *ahnik* spot (where the daily prayers were offered) in the house. Failing to find the foot there, the servant went back to his master with tears in his eyes, and begged his pardon for losing his foot. Kalishankar, in an alcoholic stupor of generosity, smiled at his servant and assured him not to worry, his foot must have been taken away, along with the *naibedya* (the food offered to the deity and later distributed among the devotees) by the Brahman priest who conducted the evening prayers. The servant then rushed to the house of the Brahman priest—who must have also been quite high at that hour of the evening—who assured the servant that if he had brought away the master's foot by mistake, he would take it back as soon as he found it in his house![28]

Clearly, Kali had travelled a long way from the jungles of Govindapur of the fifteenth century. Urbanization transformed a godling into a rich goddess. But in spite of the expensive ornamentation and the rich paraphernalia of her worship, the image of Kali basically remained the same—the hands holding the scimitar, a wreath of severed heads around her neck, a lolling tongue and a prostrate Shiva under her feet. Here was an excellent example of the transformation and elevation of a tribal goddess into an extravagantly decorated image, all the while retaining its original conceptual ingredients—the ferocious visage, the terror-inspiring ambience, the macabre imagery that marked the conceptualization of the mother goddess in popular religion. This is a clear illustration of the interlacing of two forms of religious consciousness, the popular one nurtured by the lower orders, and the elite form developed by the establishment, into a complex synthesis—another example of the 'dialogue conflict' described by Aron Gurevich.

Kali of the Bengali Underworld

Along with this historical transformation of Kali in early nineteenth-century Calcutta, socioeconomic forces in contemporary Bengal were reshaping the image of Kali in different directions.

Almost contemporaneous with the development of the Kali temple in Kalighat in the south, there was another shrine dedicated to a goddess called Chitteshwari in the north. Although the name is not found in any of the ancient or later Hindu and Tantrik scriptures, according to local beliefs it was another name for Kali. This temple was set up in what is now Chitpur, some time in the late sixteenth century. Contemporary and later legends suggest that it was worshipped by a dacoit called Chitu. Chitpur could have been named after either the goddess, or the dacoit. Or was the goddess named after the dacoit?[29]

The association of Kali with dacoits was an old one. We come across references to dacoits worshipping her in the Vindhya-parvata near Benaras in north India in *Harivamsha* and other texts. Still later, in the seventeenth-century Bengali biography of

the Vaishnavite reformer Sri Chaitanya, *Chaitanya Bhagavat* by
Vrindavan Das, we hear of the dacoit Kenaram shouting the war
cry 'Victory to Kali!' In certain parts of Bengal, on village outskirts,
one could find Kali temples which were known as the haunts of
dacoits, the deity known as *dakate-Kali*. The tradition of human
sacrifices and bloody rituals associated with Kali attracted dacoits
to this particular deity. She became the goddess of the underworld.
Tantrik practices opened up an easy path for dacoits and other
denizens of the underworld, providing them with a religious sanction for their activities, a sort of psychological reassurance. The
murders they had to commit in the course of their dacoities could
be explained away as *balis*, or sacrifices at the altar of Kali.

There was a rise in the incidence of crimes like dacoities and
murders in Bengal in the late eighteenth–early nineteenth century.
This was a period when the Mughal reign was on the wane, and
the East India Company was consolidating its rule over Bengal.
It was a period of utter disorder—collapse of the traditional village
economy, dislocation of thousands of families from their homes
and occupations, agricultural disasters and famines. A devastating famine wiped out one-third of the population of Bengal in
1769–70. Following the Permanent Settlement of Lord Cornwallis
in 1793, there was an increasing incidence of dacoities. James Mill
in his evidence before the Select Committee appointed to investi-
gate the effects of the Permanent Settlement was reported to have
admitted that it was this that had led to the impoverishment of the
peasantry in the Bengal countryside and had driven many among
them to dacoity. In 1835, the government set up a Dacoity Com-
mission to find ways and means to stop dacoity, to no avail.[30]

This essay does not purport to enter the debate over whether
the history of such dacoities should remain imprisoned in the cat-
egory of common 'crimes' (as described by British officials in
those days), or be re-allocated a space under the newly constructed
major concept of 'social banditry', or under the rubric of 'anti-colonial rebellions' (as some of these types of dacoities have been designated by several modern historians).[31] We are for the present
limiting our investigation and analysis only to the relationship

between dacoities and the worshipping of Kali during a particular period in the history of colonial Bengal.

The dacoits were known to move around in gangs, and offer prayers to Kali before undertaking any venture. Kali was identified with Shakti, and they expected her to endow them with the courage and power necessary to carry out their actions. The most organized and prominent among these gangs were the *thugs*, or *thugees*, who were notorious for enticing unwary travellers and then strangling them. While their primary motive was robbery, murdering the victims became a secondary compulsion, motivated by the need to silence them. Thus robbery and murder became co-terminous in *thugee* practice, the murdered victims legitimized as offerings to Kali. Although such practices had existed among dacoits in the past, the *thugee* cult grew apace in the troubled times of the inter-mission between the decline of the Mughal empire and the con-solidation of the British colonial system. It had a wide network operating all over north and central India, stretching even to Bengal, where we hear the name of a Bengali *thugee* called Ramlochan Sen.[32] It was during the tenure of Lord William Bentinck as the Governor-General of India that the *thugees* were eliminated under operations launched by Captain William Sleeman.

In this connection, it may be worthwhile to mention a new myth that evolved around Kali during this period which suggests how popular imagination could refashion tradition and create new folklore in order to justify necessities. This myth seeks to explain the origin of the *thugs* or *thugees*. According to the ancient myth (in the *Devi Bhagavata*), when Kali fought with the *asura* Raktabeeja and inflicted wounds on him, with every drop of blood from his wounds, new *asuras* emerged. The traditional myth tells us that Kali licked up these drops before they could be reborn as *asuras*, which explains why her tongue perpetually hangs out. (This again stresses the presence of a certain logic in popular myths. In order to explain every phenomenon, a cause is invented.) This story of the old myth was however given a twist in a new myth that came into currency during the eighteenth century. According to this version, Kali could not prevent the proliferation of *asuras* however hard she tried, either by killing them, or by licking up the blood to pre-empt their birth. There had to be a bloodless way of eliminating them, since every drop of blood would give birth to an *asura*. So Kali created two heroes and gave each a noose made out of a scarf, with which they strangled every *asura* as he was born. When they had thus eliminated all the *asuras*, a gratified Kali gifted them this noose with the blessing that it would help their descendants to earn their living. It is these two heroes created by Kali, who were claimed by the *thugees* to be their ancestors, continuing to strangle victims with a latter-day version of this noose.[33]

Kali in a Poet's Vision

A different conception of Kali was being fashioned in another part of the Calcutta society of that period, far away from the Kali that was being redecorated in Kalighat temple and worshipped by nouveau riche patrons in their mansions, or the old goddess of the underworld who was being propitiated by the followers of Chitu the dacoit. In the early eighteenth century—sometime around 1730—an 18-year-old youth arrived in Calcutta from a village in 24-Parganas. His name was Ramprasad Sen. Looking for a job, he finally found one as a clerk in the office of a Bengali dewan, or an estate manager (Gokulchandra Ghoshal of Khidirpur according to one source, Durgacharan Mitra of Sutanati according to another). Being of a poetic bent, Ramprasad spent most of his time in office writing verses in his accounts book. Almost all these verses were dedicated to Kali, and it was a new conception of Kali, an attempt to domesticate the fearful goddess in mystical terms.

In calling upon Kali, Ramprasad reduces himself to the position of the ideal child, his relationship with the mother goddess becoming an allegory for the game of life. The Great Mother, who is both the creator and the destroyer, plays with her children—human beings—like toys. Sometimes she pampers them, sometimes discards them. But unlike inanimate toys, they have feelings, and therefore they respond, like children again, now gay, now petulant, now despairing. Ramprasad expresses all these various shades of human feelings in a social existence which is tossed by waves of success and adversity.

His conception of Kali was in line with the popular Bengali literary tradition of domesticating divinities (like Shiva and Parvati in the Mangal-kavyas, or Radha and Krishna in the 'padabali kir-tans' [lyrical ballads]). Here Ramprasad was trying to lock horns with the dreaded goddess, challenging her, laughing at her, com-plaining about her misdemeanours, and then again supplicating to her as her child. Ramprasad evokes a dual image of Kali as the mother goddess who is both bountiful and destructive. There is also a rather ambivalent erotic approach, with frequent stress on her nudity. To describe the unclad Kali he often uses the colloquial Bengali term *langta* which evokes a sense of the body in the raw, warts and all, but intimate and inviting in its sensual and sexual nakedness, different from the Sanskritized chaste term *nagna* or *nagnika*, which would correspond to the English word 'nude', implying a more elegant but distant and inaccessible female form.[34] The following lines addressed to Kali, for instance, turn the mother goddess almost into a shameless hoyden:

> Kali go keno langta phero
> Chhi Chhi kichhu lajja nei tomar
> Apni langta, pati langta
> Ma go, amra sabe mori laje[35]

> (Kali, why do you romp around naked? Fie on you! Don't you have any shame? . . . You are naked, so is your hus-band . . . Dear Mother, we all die of shame for you . . .)

At another moment Ramprasad pretends to give up worship-ping Kali, playfully complaining about her nakedness, as well as demonstrating the traditional patriarchal prejudice against female assertiveness:

> Aar torey naa dakbo Kali,
> Tui meye hoye oshi dhorey langta hoye ron korili.[36]

> (I'll never call upon you again, Kali. How could you, being a girl, have held a sword and stripped naked to fight a battle?)

It would be interesting to analyse Ramprasad's psychology of mysticism. Coming from the upper-caste Hindu class, he could have suffered from the same ambivalence that marks the Shakta cult, born as it was from the 'illegitimate' union of aboriginal customs and Brahmanical theology. While acknowledging the omnipotent mother goddess, attracted by the traditional concept of the all-powerful Adya-Shakti, was he also torn between his total devotion to Kali and the impulse to completely submit to a goddess, and social prejudices about the position of women in his society, an inherited repulsion for the assertive and self-willed woman?

Take another verse where Ramprasad's personal suffering and privation intrude upon his devotion to the mother goddess:

Karunamoyee ke baley torey dayamoyee,
Karo dugdhete batasha,
Amar emni dasha, shakey anna mele koi?[37]

(Who would call you compassionate and merciful? You serve sweet milk to some people, while here I cannot even find rice to go with my spinach!)

A more intimate and aggressive approach is found in the following verse:

Ebar Kali tomaye khhabo
Ebar tumi khhao, ki ami khhai Ma,
Dutor ekta korey jabo
Dakini Jogini duto, tarkari banaye khhabo.
Tomar mundo-mala kerey niye.
Ambale sambhar charabo.[38]

(I'll devour you now, Kali. I'll decide once and for all whether you eat me, or I eat you. I'll make a vegetable curry of your two companions Dakini and Jogini. I'll snatch away your garland of skulls and make a spicy sauce out of it).

In Ramprasad's songs, which still remain an integral part of life in Bengal, Kali is described in the common language of the people. Sister Nivedita paid the best tribute to Ramprasad when she said, 'The shrewd mother-wit of a peasant joins with the insight of a great poet, not only to express the finest of fine emotions—the joy of being inferior, but to hint in the same words, at the secret of existence.[39]

Kali in Politics

A new phase in Kali's transformation begins at the end of the nineteenth century. By the last quarter of this century, the Bengali bhadralok society had become politically organized. In this early phase of a newborn spirit of patriotism they turned back to ancient Hindu myths and the history of Hindu kings and their exploits to derive inspiration and self-confidence in their politics of negotiation with the English rulers. The stage in Bengal was set for an alliance between religion and politics.

The image of Kali played a crucial role in this alliance. In 1882, Bankim Chandra Chattopadhyay's *Anandamath* came out. The concept of Mother India fighting the colonial demons was borrowed from the age-old concept of the mother goddess crushing the asura. Bankim, through the words of the sannyasi Satyananda, presents three phases of Mother India's development—the Mother as she was in the past, the Mother as she is now in the present, and the Mother as she will be in the future. The Mother in her present phase is depicted as Kali, enveloped in darkness, painted black, deprived of everything, and hence naked.

This historical image of Kali was familiar to every Bengali household, because of the dominance of the Shakta tradition in Bengal. According to British official records, in mid-nineteenth-century Bengal, at least three-fourths of the Bengali population belonged to a Shakta cult.[40] In continuation of this tradition, destruction, sacrifice and death, familiar motifs associated with Kali, came to dominate Bengali thinking as the country woke up to the twentieth century. The political turmoil began with the division of Bengal in 1905. The symbolism of Kali was now extended by bands of armed revolutionaries to sanction the political assassination of British officials and their Indian agents. They solicited the blessings of Kali, and followed the ritual of touching the sword, sometimes letting out blood as a symbol of sacrifice, recalling thus the rites of the old dacoits, although on a different level.

A significant development associated with the reinterpretation and relocation of Kali in a dominant position in the radical politics of late nineteenth century–early twentieth century Bengal was the gradual retreat of Vaishnavism and the Bhakti cults in the face of the revival of the Shakta tradition. This had far-reaching socio-political consequences.

It is necessary to recall in this connection that in the post-Chaitanya period in Bengal, during the seventeenth and eighteenth centuries, various popular religious cults emerged as offshoots from the Gaudiya Vaishnavite mainstream. They were mostly founded by members belonging to the depressed castes among the Bengali Hindu and Muslim poor. Their rituals and lifestyle reasserted the message of equality between castes, religious communities and men and women. What is significant is that these popular Vaishnavite sects were founded upon an amalgamation of Bhakti and Sufi ideas, and thus cut across Hindu–Muslim barriers.

With the reassertion of the Shakta tradition in the socio-politcal scene of Bengal, represented by the Goddess Kali with her message of violence and destruction, the gentle and non-violent tradition of Vaishnavism with its stress on harmony and peaceful coexistence beat a retreat. The militant image of Kali was more relevant and necessary to the rising Bengali Hindu nationalist movement than the amiable image of the god Krishna which the Vaishnavites had fashioned. It was the warrior-god Krishna of the *Bhagavad Gita*, rather than the lover-god Krishna of the padabali kirtans that appealed to the revolutionaries. As a result, while the Muslims in rural Bengal could find a space in the traditional syncretic framework of the eclectic rituals of the various Bhakti and Sufi sects, they found themselves rather alienated from the exclusivity of the reinterpreted cult of the mother goddess with its stress on Hinduism, and quite often, bias against Muslims (as found in the contemporary nationalist discourse). There were, of course, exceptions among Muslims. The famous revolutionary poet Kazi Nazrul Islam composed a large number of songs in praise of Shyama or the goddess Kali. Among other such Muslim poets were Mirza Hussain Ali and Mohammed Sultan.

The decline in the popularity of Vaishnavism in the face of the Bengali Hindu middle-class-led militant anti-colonial campaign in the late nineteenth century recalls the fate suffered by the Sufist cults among Muslims, which had to retreat under the pressure of the offensive mounted against them by the Wahhabi and Feraizi leaders of the anti-British movements in the 1830s and 1840s. A rigorous concept of austere purification marked both the Hindu and Muslim-led campaigns. Leaders of both the communities, although separated by more than a half century, felt that only such purification could prepare their respective followers for self-sacrifice and instil in their minds the confidence to overcome their enemies. This purification, according to them, was only possible by returning to (or by reinterpreting, or even reinventing) their respective religious myths, beliefs and rituals which were essential ingredients of the collective inheritance of their people. The Wahhabis and the Feraizis of the early nineteenth century reinvented a purist Islam (from a selective interpretation of the texts to suit their needs) that required purging Muslims of adulterations like syncretistic customs, faith in pirs, etc., preparing them to fight extraneous domination (British colonial power). The late nineteenth-century Bengali Hindu politicians similarly resurrected a mother goddess, re-emphasized her aggressive qualities, reinterpreted her role in the anti-colonial movement, and demanded from their followers total surrender to her. Virulence of faith was the cornerstone of both the political campaigns. Neither could allow any eclecticism, syncreticism, permissiveness, tolerance, dissent or non-conformity in their movements.

Conclusion

The various stages in the development of Kali from the misty past of aboriginal folklore to the firm terrain of modern history, suggest a number of shifts in the boundaries of the representation of the image in response to circumstances. Although the original image maintained the basic ferocious contours and its worship retained some of the bloody rituals, its role changed over the centuries. The extraordinary stability of the mother-cult, reinforced in the very heart of the modern era in urban Calcutta in the early nineteenth–early twentieth century (which coincided with neo-Hindu revivalism) indicates that rituals that were originally intended to influence nature or overcome the fear of death or disease do not necessarily die out when rational means of controlling nature or overcoming such fear are developed. Rational argumentation and the deployment of empirical evidence coexist with inherited beliefs, which resurface and get reinterpreted according to new situations and demands.

It is this legacy of the collective unconscious that sustains the hold of the mother goddess on the Bengali popular psyche even today, sometimes at the subterranean level, sometimes overtly. Among modern Bengali creative artists, it was the film-maker Ritwik Ghatak who alone tried to capture this spirit in a theoretical framework to demonstrate the continuity and pervasiveness of the archetype of the Great Mother's dual image in Bengali society, in both its benign and ferocious forms. In his films, it becomes a symbol of both her nourishing functions and her destructive force. In *Meghe Dhaka Tara*, made in 1960, the image of the heroine Neeta recalls that of the goddess Annapurna as the nourishing force and provider (in her impoverished family) who pines for a sight of the mountains (the abode of Shiva) all through her life, and sees it 'only when the hour of the final Union (with the Absolute) approaches, and the God of Destruction (Shiva) in the shape of Mahakal (Time Eternal) takes her into his final embrace of ultimate extinction.'[41]

The reappearance of the mother goddess as a destructive icon strikes us with sudden terror—like the little girl Sita in that

THE CHANGING ROLE OF KALI 65

haunting sequence of Ritwik's immortal film *Subarnarekha* who, during her gleeful solitary loitering, is startled by the apparition of the goddess Kali appearing out of the blue. For a moment, she is terribly frightened. But soon after she realizes that the frightening image of Kali that she saw was not real. It was only a professional village folk-artiste known as a 'bahurupi', who decks himself up sometimes as an animal, sometimes as a colourful deity, to entertain the rural people. Explaining the sequence, Ritwik says that the bahurupi never wanted to scare the little girl: 'she just came across him.' Ritwik's next observation goes beyond this innocent world of childhood fright when he adds ominously: 'I somehow feel that the entire human civilization has just 'come across' the path of the archetypal image of this terrible mother.'[42]

In the long history of the development of the image of the mother goddess, the reinterpretation of Kali at a certain stage also led to a patriarchal construct of the icon, as is evident from her remodelling by the rich patrons of eighteenth- and nineteenth-century Calcutta, and later during the militant national movement, when the male leadership revived the myth and refashioned the image of the deity to suit their political interests. When female power in society, which originally gave birth to the mother goddess, lost its position, the image that women themselves created as a representation of their own power began to be usurped by male rulers and religious interpreters through the successive ages.

It is this history of tensions between the original concept of Kali as a mother goddess which was shaped by women in power on the one hand, and the later versions moulded by generations of her male devotees on the other, that awaits a serious analysis by scholars—through interdisciplinary exchanges among historians, anthropologists, and others involved in exploring our past. It is a fascinating history of sights and sounds that is yet to be composed by a choreographer-historian sensitive to the primitive drum beats and the steps of the tribal dances that traditionally continue to celebrate the mother goddess in obscure villages, as well as to the violent rhythms of a later political celebration of the image of a Kali which was made to inspire vengeance against a foreign oppressor—or which today has been reduced to a mere excuse by the local gangsters of Calcutta to extort money from the citizens to subsidize their revelries!

II

THE 'PIR' AND THE 'NARAYANA'—
A SYNCRETISTIC ACCOMMODATION
IN BENGALI RITUAL AND FOLKLORE

This essay is a preliminary attempt to enter a complex socio-religious and cultural area of popular beliefs and practices which can be traced to a past which still eludes our efforts to structure it according to our present concepts, which continue to influence a large part of current folk culture in different areas of the country.

For the present purpose, I am choosing a particular syncre- tis-tic tradition in Bengal, the beginnings of which can be found in the socioeconomic changes that were taking place in the fifteenth–sixteenth century. But the phenomenon of its continuation in the villages of Bengal still awaits a proper investigation that needs to be based on what Jacques Le Goff describes as 'historical ethnology.'[1]

The syncretistic tradition which is being selected revolves round a deity, variously known as Satyanarayana and Satyapir in different parts of Bengal. The earliest extant manuscripts quoted by collectors and critics[2] can be traced to the seventeenth and eighteenth centuries, but internal evidence from them suggests that the cult of Satyanarayana and Satyapir could have flourished in the late fifteenth–early sixteenth century during the reign of Sultan Alauddin Hussain Shah in Bengal. This Sultan and his successors preceded Akbar in encouraging the growth of an eclectic culture based on traditional indigenous religious beliefs and rituals as well as the lately arrived Islamic ideas and legends (primarily of a Sufist character, since Bengal was exposed to Islam first through Sufi preachers from the closing years of the twelfth century).[3] It was during this period that translations of Sanskrit epics into Bengali and the recording of floating popular legends and folklore in the form of manuscripts by Bengali poets were patronized by the court of the Sultans of Bengal. As one Bengali literary historian pointed out almost a century ago, 'We believe that it is the conquest of Bengal by the Muslims that has led to the good fortune of the Bengali language. The Muslims, whether they came from Iran, or Turkey or any other place, they turned completely into Bengalis once they settled down here. They began living surrounded by their Hindu subjects and neighbours.' He then described the social environment—which continued to be a living reality in rural Bengal even in his times: 'The bells of the Hindu temples rang beside mosques. Muharram, Eid Sabe(ba)rat rubbed shoulders with Durga puja, Raas festival and Holi.'[4]

It is in this social environment that one should try to locate the birth of the Satyanarayana and Satyapir cults. The norms of the ritual laid down in the available texts to worship the deity, as well as the oral narrative that is essential to follow the ritual, reflect a curious amalgam of customs and beliefs that are conventionally divided into traditional blocks of separate Hindu and Muslim faiths and practices. It is not as if such divisions did not exist, since, as already mentioned, the orthodox religious elite—both among the Hindus and Muslims—sought to consolidate their control over their respective communities by insisting on a puristic adherence to rituals and religious customs that aimed at keeping the two communities apart. But thanks to the permissive Sufist character of the early Islamic proselytizers in Bengal (who succeeded in winning over a large number of the Hindu lower-caste people who turned

to Islam to escape the humiliation imposed by Brahmanical dis-
criminatory practices), and the tolerant attitude of the sixteenth-
century Muslim rulers of the Shah dynasty who played an important part in patronizing Bengali language and literature, the
initial sense of hostility against the Muslim invaders among the
Bengali community (during the wars of succession in the thirteenth century which disrupted life in general) gave way to a sense
of security and desire for adaptability among the masses. A sort of
intermingling of Islam on the one hand and animist, Buddhist
and Hindu beliefs on the other took place in the exchange of
themes and motifs in sixteenth–seventeenth-century Bengali literature. We find Muslims composing poems on the Radha-Krishna
theme of Vaishnavism (like Akbar Shah Ali, Nasir Mahmud, Fakir
Habib, Sheikh Jalal)[5] as well as Hindu poets imbibing motifs from
Islamic thought (like Kshemananda of the seventeenth century
acknowledging the Koran in his 'Manashar Bhashan' as one of the
many sacred objects along with popular Hindu amulets). Another
seventeenth-century Hindu poet Krishnaram Das composed a ballad in praise of Kalu Gazi, a Muslim pir worshipped by all for protection from tigers in the Sunderbans area of south Bengal. A
blending of two (possible) historical figures—a Hindu guru Matsyendra and a Muslim warrior of the seventeenth century, Masnad
Ali—led to the formation of Pir Machandali in Medinipur in West
Bengal, in whose praise a Bengali Hindu poet Sitaram Das composed a ballad.[6]

The emergence of the syncretistic Satyapir or Satyanarayana
during this period was therefore not an isolated development. It
was part of an evolving sociocultural tradition. The extant texts
describing the exploits of the popular saint provide us with an
excellent opportunity to establish contact with the common folk of
medieval Bengal who have disappeared into the past, but who were
trying to make sense of, and cope with, the surrounding reality
with the help of a cultural and religious resource base. This base
consisted of inherited traditions as well as attempts at reworking
these traditions in the light of the new socio-religious developments following the Muslim conquest. In the process, these people

and their poets—both Hindus and Muslims—created a variegated repertoire of folk ballads, 'panchalis' (popular songs, usually devotional, interspersed with rhymes for fast recitation) and rituals about Satyapir and Satyanarayana over almost 300 years (from the sixteenth to the nineteenth century). The various versions of the exploits of the syncretistic saint—available from different parts of Bengal, and at different periods—reflect a variety of stimuli that the authors could have received from the different socioeconomic environs prevailing in their respective areas and periods. The story line, however, remains common—running like a thread through all the versions that span both time and space in Bengal, which indicates the continuity of an inherited cultural and religious tradition at the popular level that coexisted with (and perhaps preceded) the norms established by the Brahman priests and the Islamic clergy.

The Methodology

It is quite possible that most of the meanings of exploits of the saint and the adventures of his devotees found in the different versions of the Satyapir folklore are today lost to us. They were embedded in the context of a living reality which was rarely recorded in modern historical terms, and which can never be recaptured.

We do not know, for instance, the exact occasions during which the tales were recited and the rituals accompanying them observed, the background of the narrators, or the composition of the audience. We can merely hazard guesses by relating the emergence of the folklore to the historical period on the basis of internal evidence available from extant texts, which again—let us hasten to add—could have gone through a process of transformation and contamination, from oral narrative through handwritten manuscript to printed book. Therefore, investigation into any medieval cultural phenomenon—whether in Bengal or any other part of India—requires a 'judicious use of documentation and a well-grounded imagination.'[7]

Using this methodology, we may venture to suggest that the emergence of the Satyanarayana or Satyapir folklore and ritual[8] represented a stage in the historical evolution of a popular belief system that embraced a host of similar syncretistic cults and deities of a dualistic religious character. In the rural milieu of medieval Bengal, both Hinduism and Islam were tempered with animist survivals, creating a realm of 'double faith', or even 'multiple faith'.

In order to explore the 'mentalite' of the medieval Bengali populace through an examination of the Satyapir and Satyanarayana texts, we propose to take up representative samples from selected parts of Bengal, composed by both Hindu and Muslim authors. We attempt to show not merely what people thought, but also how they thought, how they construed the world, invested it with meaning, and infused it with emotion. We shall be working back and forth between the text and the context.

The Composition and the Plot of the Tale

By the term 'composition', we mean the sequence of functions which runs as a basic thread through all the main versions of the folk tale of Satyapir-cum-narayana. This composition lies at the bottom of the many 'plots' of the various versions. 'Composition is a constant factor; the plot a variable one.'[9]

The composition of the main story is based on the following sequence: (i) a poor Brahman who lives by begging is visited by a Muslim fakir who declares himself an incarnation of Narayana, or Vishnu, and advises the Brahman to offer him 'shirni' (an offering of sweets mixed with other ingredients which is served to Muslim saints); (ii) the Brahman follows his advice and becomes rich; (iii) his prosperity attracts the attention of a merchant, who, learning about Satyapir from the Brahman, promises to propitiate the saint with regular offerings of shirni if the pir gives him a daughter; (iv) the merchant's wife gives birth to a daughter, who after some time is married off to an eligible young man; (v) the merchant forgets to keep his promise to offer shirni to Satyapir, and sets off on a voyage with his son-in-law towards a kingdom located somewhere

near today's Sri Lanka; (*vi*) Satyapir gets annoyed at this dereliction
of duty and punishes the merchant by planting stolen goods from
the local king's treasury in the merchant's ship at the port of the
kingdom; (*vii*) the king arrests the merchant and his son-in-law on
charges of theft and throws them in a dungeon; (*vii*) back in the
merchant's home, his wife and daughter propitiate Satyapir, beg
his forgiveness and plead for the return of the merchant and the
son-in-law; (*ix*) Satyapir relents and appears before the king in a
dream, asking him to release the merchant and the son-in-law; (*x*)
the two are released and set sail for home: (*xi*) as they approach
home, the merchant's daughter who was offering shirni to
Satyapir, in her hurry to greet her father and husband, drops the
offering on the floor; (*xii*) annoyed by her carelessness, an angry
Satyapir sinks the merchant's ship and both the merchant and his
son-in-law are drowned; (*xiii*) realizing her mistake, the daughter
hurries back to her room and picks up the shirni and eats it; (*xiv*)
now that the pir is made happy, the ship surfaces, the merchant
and his son-in-law are restored to life, and they reach home with
all the treasures that they had acquired during the voyage—to live
happily ever after!

As should be evident from the familiar sequence of events, the
formation of the Satyapir folklore echoes the age-old fairy tales—
the begetting of children through the grace of some god; voyages
to foreign lands; adventures and mishaps suffered by the main
characters; rewards for good acts and punishment for misdeeds,
even if inadvertent; and finally, the triumphant return home. But
the old fairy tales were being re-interpreted in accordance with the
new forms of consciousness of the people of medieval Bengal. As
a result, the old and the new entered into hybrid formations, like
'Satyapir-cum-narayana.'

The compositional core of the tale highlights three motifs that
get repeated. The role of the deity—marked by two sets of duality:
now as a pir, the next moment as Narayana; as a benign deity to
those who faithfully pay him obeisance; and as a destructive one
towards those who ignore him, or are careless in carrying out the

required rites. The second and the third motifs—the voyage and the ritual of making shirni, offering it to the pir, and eating it—are intertwined. The misfortunes and adversities faced on the sea and in a foreign land constitute the episode of the voyage, which becomes the axis of the tale. The shirni becomes the magic agent that helps the characters to overcome all difficulties, whether man-made (like imprisonment) or natural (like the shipwreck).

The Deity

In the different medieval versions of the folk tale (variously titled 'Satyapirer panchali', 'Satyanarayaner bratakatha', 'Satyanarayaner katha', 'Satyapirer punthi') as well as in stories about the deity contained in other ballads, the deity first appears in the form of a Muslim fakir. But he soon becomes a protean character, changing easily and swiftly into the four-armed Hindu god Vishnu, into a sannyasi and back into a fakir.

The early eighteenth-century poet Rameshwar Bhattacharya in his 'Satyanarayaner bratakatha' describes him as 'of young age, finely dressed, with a sweet smile on his beautiful face, a turban around his head, and his body decorated with shells, tiger-skin, his neck garlanded with a necklace of brilliant pearls, and bells ringing around.'[10]

When he advises the poor Brahman to offer him shirni, the Brahman refuses saying that he will not behave like a *yavana* (a non-Hindu barbarian). The fakir, in the twinkling of the eye, changes into a Brahman, and then reveals to the awestruck poor Brahman his real identity—Vishnu holding in his four arms the familiar symbols of conch, disc, club and lotus. He then tells the Brahman:

Makkaye Rahim ami, Ajodhyaye Ram
(I am Rahim in Mecca, and Ram in Ayodhya.)

A contemporary Muslim poet describes the deity as a Hindu sannyasi:

Sarbangey tilak tar kapaley jora phonta,
Hatetey japanmala matha bhara jata.[11]

(His body is decorated with sandal paste marks, his forehead stamped with a pair of dots; in his hands there is a
rosary of beads and his head is shaggy with matted hair.)

Another Muslim poet of the same period describes the religious duality of the protean deity:

Galaye jahora doley Satya-narayan,
Hatetey matir mala hoiloy Baman.[12]

(A garland of precious gems hangs around his neck, and
he is Satyanarayana. He turns himself into a Brahman
when he takes a rosary made of earth).

It is interesting to note that the Muslim poet here uses the
term 'Satyanarayana' to describe the deity's incarnation as a
Muslim pir. It seems that the terms 'Satyanarayana' and 'Satyapir'
were interchangeable in the oral narratives, and had nothing to do
with the religious faith of the individual composers. In fact, of the
hundred-odd manuscripts found so far, there are quite a number
attributed to Hindu poets like Ballava, Shankaracharya or Krishnahari Das (belonging to the seventeenth–eighteenth century) who
have described the deity as Satyapir all through their narratives.

In order to understand this folkloric conception of the religious
duality of a popular deity, and belief in the deity's capacity to appear
in different incarnations, we have to place it in the context of historical developments in rural Bengal. Contrary to one view of
looking at the history of rural society as 'l'histoire immobile'
(unmoving history)[13] Bengali rural society did not remain passive
recipients of the political and social waves that swept over it
through successive periods of Buddhist rule, followed by domination by the Brahmanical orthodoxy, to be succeeded by Turkish,
Afghan and then Mughal invasion. In order to adjust themselves
to the succeeding sets of religious values and norms introduced by
the respective rulers, the Bengali rural lower orders had to rework
their inherited beliefs and folklore (from an animist past). They

did this in their own way, using their traditional resources to piece together a picture of reality and explain it in their own terms of reference. Their folk poets and preachers played an important role in this evolution of a belief system that could provide a secure base for their society. In the process, they infused their traditional folklore with different layers of meaning, retaining some of the past features and adopting some from successive religious and cultural forces. These layers were expected to appeal to the different levels of the multireligious community inhabiting Bengal rural society.

'Satyanarayana-cum-pir' had his predecessors as well as successors—in different incarnations. This brings us to the popular attempt to explain changes in patterns of political domination (over which, just as over natural disasters, the common people had no control) by resorting to the imaginative concept of incarnations. After the failure of the initial resistance to the new forces (whether religious, cultural or military), there was the popular tendency to reconcile themselves to the forces which had established domination over their economic and political existence. To rationalize their acceptance of this domination, they tended to mythologize the reality by depicting the new political rulers or dominant cultural forces as incarnations of past divine protectors. In order to illustrate the continuity of this popular tendency of evolving a sociocultural defence mechanism to adjust to political changes, we shall quote two pieces of folklore—one preceding Satyapir, and the other suceeding it.

Around the eleventh–twelfth century, a popular religious cult known as the Dharma cult developed in Bengal, primarily among the lower-caste people. Originally Buddhists, they were facing persecution from the rising Brahmans of the new ruling dynasties, particularly the Senas, who from the early eleventh century onwards extended their rule in Bengal. When the Muslims conquered Bengal (in the early thirteenth century), and began to persecute the Brahmans, these followers of Dharma welcomed it as divine justice. In a treatise called *Shunya-purana* which describes the rituals of Dharma-puja, there is an extraordinary narrative entitled 'Sri Niranjaner Rusma' or the 'Wrath of Lord Niranjana'. It tells us how the god Dharma in his abode in Vaikuntha arrived on earth in the incarnation of Khoda (the god of the Muslims) in a village in Bengal:

> Dharma hoilo Jaban-rupi
> Mathayete kalo tupi
> Hatey shobhey triruch kaman.

> (Dharma assumed the form of a *jaban*—a Muslim—with a black cap and a bow and arrow in his hand.)

The other members of the Hindu pantheon followed suit:

> Brahma hoilo Mahammad
> Vishnu hoilo pekambar,
> Adampha hoilo Shulapani.
> Ganesh hoiya gaji
> Kartik hoilo kaji
> Fakir hoilya jato muni.

> (Brahma became Muhammad, Vishnu the paigambar, and Shiva became Adam. Ganesha became a *gaji* and Kartika a *kaji*, and all the Hindu hermits became Muslim fakirs.)

All these gods entered the village and destroyed all the temples to punish the Brahmans.[14]

The entire poem suggests the vicarious thrill of the persecuted lower orders, watching the humiliation of their erstwhile rulers, the Brahman aristocracy. But those who carried out the vengeance (the Muslim rulers) had to be made acceptable to the popular imagination in the traditional framework of references. They therefore became incarnations of the old gods of the Hindu religion.

The second illustration is a verse-narrative from around early nineteenth-century Bengal—following the British conquest. Composed in 1813 by a village poet, Ramprasad Maitreya of Pabna in north Bengal, it celebrates the year 1765 as a watershed in the history of his country since the East India Company on 12 August that

year received from Emperor Shah Alam the imperial grant of
dewani or revenue authority in Bengal and Bihar. Describing the
advent of the new rulers, the poet says:

> Apurba shuno he shabey swargeyr jatek debey
> Bilatey hoila saheb rup
> Chharila ahnik puja paridhan kurti muja,
> Hatey bet shirey dila tupi.
> Banglar abhilashey aila sadagar beshey
> Koilakata purana kuthi adi.
> Gatamal subhedari shubho san bahattori
> Angrej amol tadobodhi.[15]

(Listen to this wonderful tale. All the gods from heaven
came down to Europe and became white men. They
stopped their daily prayers, wore trousers and socks, put
on hats on their heads, and took sticks in their hands.
Yearning for Bengal, they came here as traders, and set up
factories and offices in Calcutta. They received the gover-
norship in the Bengal era of 1172 from which date the rule
of the English has begun.)

Although we cannot rule out the possibility of these lines being
written in jest, we can still discern a continuity in the popular belief
in theophany, or divine manifestation in the shape of a new generation of mortal rulers. While in the days of the post-Muslim
conquest, the new rulers were held to be incarnations of the old
gods dressed in Middle Eastern attire, 300 years later, after the
British conquest, another generation of rulers were similarly projected in folklore as avatars of the same old gods—dressed this
time in European clothes.

The innovation of Satyapir as an incarnation of a familiar god
of the past in the early modern folklore of Bengal can therefore be
seen as a manifestation of the consistent popular craving for a
divine protector and benefactor. In the oral narratives, Satyapir thus
helps the poor (the Brahman beggar) to get rich, and protects the
enterprising (the merchant) from adversities.

Although in orthodox Islam there is no religious sanction for incarnation, the Muslims in Bengal shared with their Hindu brethren the same faith in the avatar of Satyapir. According to some critics, this can be traced to the Sufi influence in Bengal which introduced the theory of 'Hulul', propounded by the famous Persian Sufi thinker of the tenth century, Mansur-ul-Hallaj. In the Sufi sense, it means 'infusion of divine spirit into the body of man, transforming him into a god in the form of a man.'[16] In fact, a few literary historians, while interpreting some of the Satyapir texts, have speculated that Mansur-ul-Hallaj's claims of divine manifestation in mortal shape (preached by Sufis in Bengal) could have inspired the story of Satyapir and its acceptance among Muslims in Bengal.[17]

While such philosophical legitimization of the idea of incarnation could have satisfied the Muslim educated elite, among the Muslim lower orders it seems that the pre-Islamic common cultural heritage that they shared with the Hindus in Bengali rural society led to the shaping of the folklore and rituals surrounding Satyapir or Satyanarayana. As Bangladeshi Muslim scholar Muhammad Enamul Huq has observed about the Bengalis who converted to Islam in the medieval era: 'Converts cannot all of a sudden turn out to be totally different men—different in customs, habits, nature, temperament, thought, popular beliefs and culture . . . Thus by fresh recruitments of the Indians, Islam unconsciously had to make room for a considerable part of Indian environment in its own fold.'[18]

Apart from the assumption of the forms of a fakir and Narayana alternately, there is another duality in the role of Satyapir. In folklore, he appears as a benign benefactor as well as a vengeful power. Anyone who forgets to pay him his tribute or despises him, is punished immediately.

In his meting out of rewards or punishment, there seems to be a consistency in folklore. The popular poets make Satyapir favour the poor devotees who always remain faithful to him, while his punishment is reserved for the arrogant rich who forget him after they get some wish fulfilled through his grace. In the main story, the poor Brahman before whom the deity first appears remains steadfast in his devotion to him. Soon after his initiation, a group of poor woodcutters arrive at his door seeking water and food. Learning the story of his turn of fortune, the woodcutters offer shirni to Satyapir, and become his devotees. But unlike the Brahman and the woodcutters, the rich merchant ignores the deity after gaining his objective, and as a result, he is punished. In Shankaracharya's *Sri Sri Satyanarayan-er Panchali* traced to the six-teenth–seventeenth century, after their release when the merchant and his son-in-law set sail for home, Satyapir appears in the guise of a fakir at the wharf, and begs the merchant for alms. The merchant abuses him, taking him for a poor beggar, and continues his journey—only to find in the middle of the sea that all the goods that he had acquired had turned into charcoal.[19]

The contrast between Satyapir's treatment of his poor devotees and the rich (particularly the merchants) becomes more pronounced in an eighteenth-century text—'Bara Satyapir O Sandhyabati Kanyar Punthi' by Krishnahari Das, who was believed to have belonged to the syncretistic cult of Bauls. In this narrative, the deity arrives in the guise of a fakir before Heera Muchi, a poor cobbler, who although ignorant of the real identity of his guest, goes through all sorts of travails, just to procure some food for him. Impressed by his hospitality, Satyapir finally reveals himself to him, and offers him 'two jars filled with gold.' But,

> Heera Muchi boley—saheb, dhoneyr nai kam,
> Bhiksha koria ami labo tomar nam.[20]

> (Heera Muchi says—my lord, there's no use for gold. I prefer to beg and invoke your name.)

In the same narrative, when a prostitute, Shashi, tries to seduce Satyapir, the latter assumes various forms and finally compels Shashi to accept defeat and repent. Taking pity on her, Satyapir lifts her from her ostracized status and rehabilitates her as Josi Fakirani—a female fakir.

This generous act of Satyapir stands in sharp contrast to his vengeful role towards the merchants. Jasmant Sadhu promises to offer him one boat full of all the commodities he will acquire during his voyage. He comes back with ample treasure, but refuses to keep his promise to Satyapir, who punishes him by sinking the biggest boat of his fleet. Another merchant, Shundi Saodagar, propitiates Satyapir, who blesses his wife saying that she will have two sons, but extracts a promise from the couple that the youngest son must be offered to Satyapir as a servant. After the birth of the sons, Satyapir comes to reclaim the younger. But the merchant tries to cheat him by dressing the child as a girl. An enraged Satyapir calls up Pavana, the wind god, who generates a gale that blows off the clothes of the child and reveals his sex. Satyapir takes him away from his parents.

The Voyage and the Shirni

The repeated references to the misfortunes of the merchant on his journey in different versions of the folktale give rise to the speculation that the folklore and the rituals could have developed as a protective rite to shield people from natural disasters and other calamities during their sea voyages.

The shirni became the magic agent to influence this malevolent maritime world, and the narration of the deity's life and exploits became a sort of verbal amulet to protect the traveller.

Folklore thus absorbed elements of contemporary socioeconomic life. The hazards of sea voyages in a merchant's life figure prominently in other Bengali folk narratives of the early modern age, like the popular series about the travails of Chand Sadagar who was punished with calamities at sea because he dared to defy the snake goddess Manasa.

Apart from natural disasters like norwesters and cyclones (quite common in the Bay of Bengal), there was also the fear of pirates. From the early sixteenth century onwards, Portuguese buccaneers had begun their raids. The Arakan pirates were also a menace on the eastern coast. Traders and sea-faring people therefore travelled under the shadow of a hostile environment and sudden attacks.

The fear comes out clearly in the utterances of the merchant in Faizullah's *Satyapirer panchali* (recorded in manuscript form in the eighteenth century). The merchant has come back home after suffering a series of disasters, including a long spell in the dungeon. Meanwhile, in his absence, his son has gone on a voyage in search of his missing father, towards the south. Hearing this from his wife, the merchant exclaims:

Dakshiner katha more kohitey pran phatey.
Pakshitey taroni ney, hangorey manush kathey.
Abola chhaoaley tumi diley pathaiye.
Konkhaney machhey tarey phelilo giliye.[21]

(Don't ask me to speak about the south; my heart trembles!
Birds swoop down to carry away ships, sharks kill men.
How could you have sent my innocent son to that place?
Surely, he must have been swallowed up by some big fish!)

The votive offering of shirni is usually associated with the worshipping of Muslim pirs. It is, however, another common form of the long ritualistic tradition of dedicating food to, or seeking grace from, god, before partaking of it among members of many religious communities (e.g. breaking bread among Christians; offering 'bhog' and eating 'prasad' among the Hindus). In the Satyapir ritual, the shirni usually consisted of flour, molasses or sugar, milk and bananas mixed into a porridge. Betel leaves and nuts also form part of the offering. After offering this to the deity (accompanied by the incantation—'Namo Satyapiraya'), the devotees, both Hindus and Muslims, used to eat the shirni.

As in the main text of the narrative, in the paraphernalia arranged for worshipping the deity, we find the same coexistence of Hindu and Muslim traditional symbols. A low square-shaped wooden stool without legs was placed in a courtyard, with four *tirs* (arrows or posts) fixed at each corner of the stool. The top of the stool was decorated with an *alpana* (design painted in white rice paste). The pir was supposed to be residing in the midst of this, although there was no image of the deity. Sometimes however, a *shalagram shila* (black stone representing Vishnu) used to be placed on it. A knife, a chopper, or a shining sword, was an essential part of the accoutrements.[22]

An essential component of the oral narrative that followed the worshipping, was the *vandana* or the invocation at the beginning. The poet or the narrator began by invoking the blessings of Muhammad, all the members of the Prophet's family, the numerous pirs and their wives, the gods and goddesses of the Hindu pantheon, all the folk deities spread over different parts of Bengal, and finally Satyapir.[23] It used to end with the self-introduction of the composer, where again in similar fashion, both the Hindu and Muslim deities were brought together. Thus, one eighteenth-century scribe, Haranarayan Das, who recorded a manuscript of the original narrative composed by Krishnahari Das, wrote:

> Haranarayan Dasey likhey, rachey Krishnahari,
> Musalman boley Allah, Hindutey boley Hari.[24]

> (Haranarayan Das is transcribing what was composed by Krishnahari. He who is called Allah by the Muslims is called Hari by the Hindus).

This tendency to bring together both Hindu and Muslim customs and expressions in one ritual, was also evident at the end of the narrative. Thus, the Hindu poet Shankaracharya ended his composition by requesting his listeners: *Atohpar baloe sabey Amin, Amin!*[25] (Let everyone now say—Amin, Amin, i.e. so be it!)

The popular innovation of the concept of 'Satyapir-cum-narayana' in the early modern period of Bengal thus appears to be in line with the contemporary vogue in folk religion of adapting newly arrived beliefs and customs and grafting them on to earlier rituals that were meant to protect the community from calamities and promise them prosperity. An eclectic body of beliefs drawn from the animist past, Buddhist thought, Aryan Puranas and Islam, created the hybrid god Satyapir. As a modern Bangladeshi scholar points out: 'Satya Pir neither resembles the Puranic Hindu god Narayana nor a real darwish in any description. He is rather an idealized creation of Hindu and Muslim minds, which were in the fifteenth century, eager to meet with each other on a common platform of cordiality and unity.'[26]

Survival through Changes

What is of interest from the viewpoint of 'historical ethnology' is the survival of the practice of worshipping the folk-deity even today in Bengali households.

There have, of course, been changes that reflect an increasing tendency to split the deity into separate Hindu and Muslim images, and to conform strictly to their respective religious rituals when worshipping Satyanarayana and Satyapir in separate congregations. As one modern historian observes: 'the noble idea behind this common worship was lost, when the Muslim in their own congregation offered worship in the name of Pir in their own mosques, and the Hindus though begging in the name of the Pir performed a Brahmanical Puja in which Pir became translated into Satyanarayana.'[27]

The dichotomy seems to have developed by the end of the nineteenth century, when we find references to separate Hindu and Muslim versions of the worship of the deity in some places. The Hindus brought in a Brahman priest to preside over the rituals, while Muslims invited a mullah to do the job, although the rituals (like the use of the wooden stool with the arrows, the preparation and distribution of the shirni and the narration of the folk tale) remained the same.[28]

The division could have been brought about by pressures from the orthodox sections from among the two communities. In fact, the cult of Satyapir drew the ire of the Brahman clergy soon after its emergence. Kanka, a folk poet of Mymensingh in east Bengal (who is usually traced to the sixteenth century) was born a Brahman, but was brought up by an outcaste couple after the death of his parents. He came under the influence of a living Muslim pir and was inspired to compose a ballad to pay homage to Satyapir. The ballad was very popular in eastern Bengal. But when his admirers sought to restore Kanka to his Brahman caste, the orthodox Brahmans of Mymensingh opposed the attempt on the ground that he was brought up by outcastes and received spiritual instruction from a Muslim. They burnt all copies of Kanka's work on Satyapir.[29]

After the end of Muslim rule, following the assumption of power in Bengal by the British, the Brahman orthodoxy reasserted their supremacy over Bengali Hindu society. The Brahman pundits sought to purge un-Hindu beliefs and practices which they feared had contaminated pure Aryan religious customs. But while other similar syncretistic deities were worshipped by the lower orders mainly (like Ola-bibi) or were confined to particular localities (like Badakhan Gaaji, the protector of the Sunderbans villagers against tigers) and could therefore be left undisturbed, Satyapir-cum-Narayana had invaded the space of the respectable Bengali Hindu middle classes, where the Brahman aristocracy was now attempting to devise different systems of religious norms and behaviour on the plea of restoring Hinduism to its pristine glory. It was necessary for them therefore to trim and tailor the popular cult to suit their purpose. The deity was thus stripped of Muslim traces, and became pure Satyanarayana. In the incantation, 'Namo Satyapiraya' (as found in the old texts) was replaced by 'Om Satyanarayanaya Namoh'. Instead of the term shirni, the offering was described as *naibedya*. It is in this style that the deity is worshipped in Bengali Hindu middle-class homes even today.

As for orthodox Muslim preachers, their offensive against the syncretistic popular god assumed more organized, and even violent, forms, in the nineteenth century. The socio-religious reform movement known as the Feraizi movement, which started in Bengal in the early nineteenth century, and rapidly spread in the rural areas, denounced and abolished rites and ceremonies like the worship of pirs, and Hindu customs and superstitious beliefs that had crept into Islamic practices. Followers of Sufist cults were quite often physically assaulted by the puritans. Although the offensive could not completely drive out the pirs from the Bengali Muslim belief system, it probably forced the Muslims (who still worship Satyapir and other pirs) to turn him into a pure Muslim saint and placate the puritans by inviting a mullah to preside over the function.

Whatever transformations might have taken place—usually at the upper levels of Bengali Hindu and Muslim society—the rural poor in various parts of both Bangladesh and West Bengal still continue to worship Satyapir. As one Bangladeshi scholar points out: 'the belief in him as 'Pir' seems to be lingering still among the people of some parts of Bengal, such as Dinajpur, Rangpur (in Bangladesh), Maldah, Midnapur, Burdwan, Howrah and 24-Parganas.'[30] Indeed, in a village called Kalsara in north 24-Parganas, there is a *dargah* (shrine) erected to commemorate Satyapir, where both Hindu and Muslim villagers light lamps and offer fruits and sweets and distribute them.[31]

The survival of the syncretistic ritual and folklore in the Bengal countryside suggests a structural constancy in the popular faith in the protective role of a syncretistic avatar with supernatural powers of rewarding the faithful and punishing the impenitent, despite several metamorphoses that took place during the period in the content of the folklore (through the various incarnations from Dharma-thakur to Satyapir and the latter's interchangeability with Satyanarayana). The enormous staying power of the belief and rituals testifies to the tenacity of an old view of the world. This image of the world under the sway of their popular deities (each ruling a particular area of their living experience—birth, disease, occupational hazards, etc.) as seen from below by the common folk, does not conform to the universe of meanings stipulated either by the established religious authorities, or by modern science. 'Hagiography', as the French scholar H. Delehaye said, is the 'obedient echo of popular tradition.'[32]

Conclusion

The Satyapir cult combines folklore and rituals. This inseparable combination was born in the early modern age out of the popular need to adjust to emerging social and religious changes. Its persistence today, however, poses challenges for modern scholars who venture to analyse folklore in their attempt to reconstruct the popular history of the past.

In trying to make sense of the beliefs and practices that were associated with the cult in early modern Bengal, we have suggested the possible underlying 'rational' purposes (i.e. accommodating the religious ideas and customs of a dominant political power, creating a common identity, maintaining social solidarity, continuing past belief systems, etc.) But then, if the birth of the cult was peculiar to a particular historical juncture, how do we explain its continuity—albeit with changes—till today?

It is in this context that 'historical ethnology' assumes importance—in order to understand the continuity of certain belief systems that appear to acquire an autonomous momentum independent of their historical origins.

Through this shift in interest toward the life of ordinary men, historical ethnology leads naturally to the study of mentalities, considered as 'that which changes least' in historical evolution. Even at the heart of industrial societies, archaism becomes evident as soon as collective psychology and behaviour are examined. Mental time being 'out of joint' with other historical time scales, the historian is compelled to become an ethnologist.'[33]

It is true that certain beliefs in the 'collective psychology and behaviour' of the people resist change. Yet, even in our tradition-bound society, we have seen how strongly embedded beliefs and their accompanying rituals died out (e.g. human sacrifice). Why do certain religious practices disappear, and other practices survive?

Keith Thomas in his *Religion and the Decline of Magic*,[34] argues that the crucial factor in the decline of magic and the widespread dissemination of a more scientific and rational approach to the natural world in seventeenth-century England was the growth of a notion of self-help, in both the religious and economic sense. The idea of self-help, in the context of England, meant increased economic opportunities for people of the lower classes and their greater assertiveness in directing their lives.

Following this argument, one could state that in our rural society where such opportunities and assertiveness are lacking, the common man in his daily struggle with adversities can hardly be expected to draw comfort from scientific discoveries and approach hurdles with what we call rationality. Attempts to demonstrate the marvels of technology or to enthrone science in the place of familiar popular beliefs may mean for him no more than the replacement of one vague and mysterious explanation of phenomenon with another.

Even when an individual in such a society rationalizes the adversities on a scientific basis and endeavours to act upon such rationalization, surrounding social pressures or personal psychological problems may quite often compel him to participate in a collective mythologization of the adversities and observance of rituals in an attempt to overcome them. Such rituals claim an ancestry that is older than modern science and hence enjoy a wide and deep-rooted popularity. The individual's rational approach to socioeconomic problems is thus overcome by the collective's faith in supernatural powers and magic, and hegemonic injunctions to follow the traditionally ordained rituals. Listeners to the narrative of Satyapir's exploits during the ritual in a rural environment cannot therefore be compared to the individual reader of a ghost story, who after a 'temporary suspension of disbelief' derives thrills from the other world. The meticulousness with which the devotee observes the ritual, suggests faith in the supernatural powers that are described in the narrative.

The supernatural, which has been the anchor for a whole system of peasant beliefs in our society for ages, may also be held to be crucial to the sustenance of certain moral values in a fast-changing rural environment. Superstitious beliefs in the supernatural powers of the deity serve as personal and moral explanations for misfortunes or success that an individual might experience. But they also tend to reinforce time-tested ethical values, since those who break traditional norms fear that supernatural retribution will follow.

Do we seek the roots of the survival of Satyapir—or for that matter, other similar folk deities—in this complex 'collective psychology' of the rural poor?

This thrust of our enquiry can be countered with the argument that superstitious rituals and belief in the supernatural are not peculiar to the economically deprived and educationally backward rural society, but are also common among sections of the urban elite both in India and the West. While agreeing with this argument, we may point out that the recent proliferation of godmen', 'gurus' and 'swamis' can be traced to a different 'collective psychology' altogether. This new breed of 'avatars' has emerged in response to the needs of an elite class—the nouveau riche, the politicians, the bureaucrats—who are perpetually gripped by a sense of insecurity and are anxious to preserve their privileges. The prophesies and assurances meted out by these 'godmen' are disguised appeals to their followers' cupidity.

To come back to the survival of popular faith in Satyapir—and similar other syncretistic cults in West Bengal and other parts of India—we should examine its implications for, and relevance to, two major pursuits in our present society. The first is, maintenance of harmony in inter-religious relationships. The second is what our Constitution describes as the fundamental duty 'to develop the scientific temper.'

As for the first objective, in the present context of violent communal hostilities, the continuity of a syncretistic tradition in our distant villages where both Hindus and Muslims participate in a common rite, should surely serve as a sane reminder of popular desire to live in harmony and overcome religious differences. It reveals a different dimension of religiosity in our country, the origins of which may be traced to a past when the organization of religious beliefs into watertight compartments of rigid doctrines had not yet taken place.

It may be tempting to use the survivals of such syncretistic traditions as serviceable weapons in the critical contest with communal forces. But, dislocated both from their historical context of the past and from the present rural social milieu in which they survive today, these folk religions when transplanted into the arena of a political combat, may be reduced to exploitable commodities— their idiom becoming empty shells without the culture-specific living spirit that sustains these religious traditions.

Besides, to turn the arena of today's anti-communal struggle into a battlefield of two contending religious traditions—the syncretistic on the one hand and the orthodox, divisive on the other (often corresponding to the popular 'little' and the elitist 'great' traditions in our culture respectively)—would be to miss the basic political objectives of the communal forces. The selective use of religious traditions by the latter to gain popular sanction in their search for political power cannot be countered by a strategy of a similar selective use of syncretistic religious traditions—for the simple reason that the two traditions are unequal contestants. While the 'great' traditions of orthodox Hinduism, Islam or Christianity had become powerful mainly through sustenance by, and orientation towards, state power, the 'little' traditions of popular syncretistic religions in India developed in nooks and corners of civil society primarily from the needs of the common people in their daily struggle for survival as well as spiritual salvation, rather than for intervention in the polity. It is unwise therefore to pose the two traditions in an encounter on a political arena where the rules of the game are dictated by concerns about capturing political power. In the contest between the communal forces and those opposing them the idiom will have to be fashioned from within the political arena by demystification of the religious rhetoric being resorted to by the communal elements, and by restoring the language of a political discourse, rather than by borrowing the etymology of syncretistic religious traditions.

But there is another dimension to it also—which has major implications for the second pursuit that we mentioned earlier. The faith in Satyapir as protector and benefactor, the belief in the shirni as the magic cure, the observance of rituals, indicate the continuity of a behaviour pattern that counters all attempts at developing the 'scientific temper' which is aimed at emancipating people from a fear of gods and dependence on irrational beliefs. Satyapir is not a mere metaphor in popular folklore, but a godhead around which certain practices are followed. At the level of thinking, such a belief system is seen to cripple the spirit of enquiry and reform. At the level of practice, let us remember, it is such beliefs that drive the rural poor in our country to shun immunization and seek the blessings of local godlings to cure cholera or small-pox, or in extreme cases to burn so-called witches in order to protect a sick person from the 'evil eye'.

Yet, while the development of a 'scientific temper' is aimed at motivating the people to approach relationships from a rational viewpoint without allowing religious differences to disrupt them, here we find a popular belief system woven around the religious godhead of Satyapir which does not prima facie conform to our standards of logic and scientific temper, but nevertheless brings together the Hindus and Muslims.

How do we shape our attitude towards a situation that appears paradoxical by our standards? How do we deal with what to us at one level seems sensible and necessary, and at another level bizarre and unreasonable, what seems progressive and yet archaic?

There are no simple answers. Let us first accept the fact that the survival of the Satyapir cult is embedded in a different culture. The criteria for evaluating it can be sought within that culture. In that culture, terms like 'irrational' and 'superstitious' may appear misplaced and their use by us to describe certain practices in that milieu may sound pejorative and suggest a patronizing inclination to list them as backward.

In order to avoid such a position, we have tried all along through the present discussion to understand the belief in Satyapir, and its continued acceptance in the milieu of rural folk culture, by identifiable yardsticks conditioned by a state of mind contemporary with the deity. This state of mind is born in social structures of a rural society which have different historical speeds, and which cannot be aligned simultaneously on the same position as structures in an industrial society. People inhabiting these structures can quite legitimately ask: has science provided answers to all our problems?

But while we should surely reject scientism—another variety of superstitious belief that science alone can solve all the problems of humanity—we cannot reject scientific enquiry, which promises expansion of the areas of freedom of humankind. We cannot deny that the man who recognizes that thunder and lightning, the tides and the behaviour of all external nature, proceed not according to the caprices of the gods, but according to certain laws, can liberate himself from the fear of, and dependence on, the gods.

When a state of mind that believes in scientific enquiry encounters another state of mind that adheres to a different conception of the world, it becomes necessary to test and shift the boundaries of the meaning of terms like 'irrationality' and 'superstition.' In such an encounter, the life experiences, beliefs and customs of a peasant community should be recognized on their own terms. But if they are given a privileged epistemological status and embraced without challenge or criticism, the conclusions that emerge from such an evaluation may be flawed. The syncretistic tradition of Satyapir and the beliefs and rituals associated with it, therefore, need to be mediated through conceptual and critical categories, if we are to build up a critical theory about popular perceptions of the rural masses and their culture.

III
RADHA AND KRISHNA
IN A COLONIAL METROPOLIS

I

The mythological story of Radha and Krishna had been explored
and exploited in Bengal by both the theologians of the 'great' tradition, and the practitioners of the 'little' tradition.[1] As a result, the
Radha-Krishna romance, on the one hand, had formed the basis
of a highly complex philosophical system and an institutionalized
religion of beliefs and practices known as Gaudiya Vaishnavism
that was formulated in the sixteenth century by the disciples of the
famous Bengali religious reformer Chaitanyadev. On the other
hand, it had also inspired a wide variety of folk songs and dances
in Bengal that predated Gaudiya Vaishnavism,[2] and an equally
extensive range of popular religious sects and practices in Bengal
(which were as philosophical, but less institutionalized) that post-
dated Chaitanya's death.[3]

This abiding popularity of the Radha-Krishna story among all
classes in the Bengali religious and cultural milieu had also led to
its enrichment and transformation through embellishments and
interpretations in the hands of religious scholars and imaginative
artistes over the ages. The romantic pair had had a long history of

metamorphosis in India's religious and cultural traditions. From their humble origins as the cowherd prince and his milkmaid lover of the folk tales of the pastoral Abhira community of north India, they graduated to membership of the Hindu pantheon in the Puranas.4 The couple found their way into popular religion and culture of other parts of India, including Bengal, where they were transformed into religious icons. They re-emerged as romantic lovers—more human than divine—described in highly erotic terms in the popular lyrics of Chandidas and Vidyapati in Bengal in the medieval era. Still later, they were elevated as symbols of the symbiotic relationship between god and the devotee by the theologians of Chaitanya's Gaudiya Vaishnavism. They reappeared in the religious and cultural environs of a colonial metropolis—nineteenth-century Calcutta—attired in entirely modern urban metaphors and imagery.5

In the long history of the transformation of this romantic couple in Bengali culture and religion, Chaitanya played an important role by putting a novel interpretation on the traditional fable. Born in 1485 in Nabadwip, Nemai (who later came to be known as Chaitanya) rebelled against the suffocating syllogism of the Nayayik logicians who dominated Nabadwip at that time, and the repressive moral order of the Smarta authorities. He came up with his message of 'bhakti' asking people to express their devotion to the Supreme Being (i.e. Krishna who was a manifestation of Vishnu) in a spontaneous display of love and affection, and opened the doors of his creed to everyone, irrespective of caste, religion and sex. In order to spread his message, he chose the popular Radha-Krishna story and interpreted it in such a way as to uphold Radha's intense longing for Krishna, her death-defying determination to be with him, and her experience of bliss in her complete surrender to him, as the ideal qualities to be cultivated by the devotee who wanted to be in communion with god. In other words, Radha became the symbol of the ideal devotee. But in this interpretation, the image of Radha underwent a dramatic change. She was divested of all the erotic attributes of physical passion that marked her representation as a romantic and adventurous heroine

in the old Bengali folk songs and the lyrics of the medieval poets
Chandidas and Vidyapati. Instead, in Chaitanya's sanitized representation of Radha, her devotion to Krishna was emphasized to the
extent of reducing her to the role of a subservient female as a symbol of the devotee's total submission to God.

In Vaishnavite philosophy, the *bhavas* or states of mind in
which the devotee can relate to Krishna are five: (i) *santa* where the
worshipper views Krishna as the supreme being while s/he remains
in a placid and passive state; (ii) *sakhya* where the devotee and
Krishna are on an equal footing as friends; (iii) *vatsalya* where the
devotee looks upon Krishna as a child much in the same way as
Krishna's foster parents did in Vrindavana; (iv) *dasya* where Krishna
is the master to be served like a slave by the worshipper; and (v)
madhurya where Krishna is considered as a lover, as Radha and the
gopinis did in the idyllic environs of Vrindavana. Chaitanya, in his
interpretation of the Radha-Krishna fable, appeared to tilt more
towards the *santa* and *dasya* moods of devotion, which stressed the
deferential and submissive role of the devotee (symbolized by the
female lover). In fact, according to his contemporaries, Chaitanya
quite often experienced Radha-*bhava,* a mood of total surrender to
the Supreme Being—when he imagined himself to be in the role
of Radha as a faithful slave to her master Krishna.[6]

This later paved the way for Chaitanya's six disciples, the six
Goswamis, to recast Radha in a new form, that of a 'dasi' or slave
to Krishna, rather than as a lover in the mood of *sakhya* where she
approached Krishna on equal terms, or that of *madhurya* where
her passion came to the fore. Of the six, Rupa Goswami (1489–
1558) in his *Shri Radha-Krishna Ganoddeshadipika* and *Ujjalaneelamani* shaped the new concept of Radha. When one compares the
pre-Chaitanya lyrics (of Chandidas, for instance) with the works of
Rupa Goswami and his colleagues, one detects a change in the conceptualization of Radha. While in the former, Radha's relationship
with Krishna is marked more by the *sakhya-bhava,* in the latter
there appears to be a bias in favour of the *dasya-bhava.* In *Sri
Radha-Krishna Ganoddeshadipika* for instance, Radha has been

elevated from the milkmaid to the royal consort of Krishna, but she waits upon Krishna, behaving more like a servant than a lover.[7] In his *Ujjalaneelamani*, Rupa Goswami, while describing the qualities of Radha, stresses her modesty, compassion, bashfulness, devotion to elders and other deferential attributes. When talking about the three types of *rati* (the term literally meaning lovemaking, but used as a metaphor for the devotee's communion with God), Rupa upholds the *samartha* type, where the devotee, while in intercourse with Krishna, is totally devoid of any personal desire for pleasure, and only consecrated to pleasing Krishna. According to Rupa, the *gopinis* of Vrindavana—and Radha being the highest among them, was eminently suitable for the role—were the best exponents of the *samartha* type of *rati*.[8]

There is a historical background to this new conceptualization of Radha by Rupa Goswami and his colleagues among the disciples of Chaitanya. Before his death in 1533, Chaitanya chose the six Goswamis (including Sanatan and his brother Rupa, and nephew Jeeba) and sent them to Vrindavana with the objective of establishing a centre there so that his message could be given an organized theological shape and be made acceptable to the religious scholars outside Bengal. All these six came from the nobility and upper castes. Most of the available texts composed by them in the seclusion of Vrindavan were in Sanskrit (suggesting the gradual distancing of the Goswamis from the indigenous Bengali popular idiom in which Chaitanya and the Vaishnavite poets spoke to the people). In these texts, they often re-asserted the tenets of the old Brahmanical order (e.g. caste distinctions, elaborate and expensive rituals, etc.).[9]

Significantly enough, one can detect that this gradual transformation of Radha into a female slave of Krishna's by Rupa Goswami and his colleagues coincided with a similar attempt made by the Brahman and upper-caste Vaishnavite leaders in post-Chaitanya Bengali society to reduce the role of the under-privileged sections who had hitherto enjoyed to a certain extent moments of emancipation in the Vaishnavite movement. From one of assertive participation, their role was now to be reduced to that of passive submission to the authority of institutionalized Vaishnavism. Those from the depressed castes who were drawn to the movement by Chaitanya and his comrade Nityananda, and enjoyed equal status within the Vaishnavite fold, were now downgraded and came to be known by the term *jaat*-Vaishnav (which in a pejorative sense implied that they had become Vaishnavites after having lost their *jaat* or caste identity, as distinct from the upper-caste Vaishnavas, known as Goswamis, who maintained their caste-based customs and rituals). Conversion of lower-caste people to Vaishnavism began to be looked down upon by the Goswamis. When Birabhadra, the son of Chaitanya's colleague Nityananda, initiated about 2,500 Buddhists from the lower castes, he was chastised by the Goswamis.[10] The revival of Brahmanical rituals also alienated the Muslim devotees of Chaitanya. The position of women—a major component of Chaitanya's followers during his lifetime—also changed. With the repeated stress on Radha's role as that of a female devotee who was required to surrender herself completely to Krishna, unscrupulous Vaishnavite gurus in Bengal, taking advantage of this message from the Goswamis of Vrindavan, began exploiting women. Under the garb of the spurious theory that every man and woman could respectively represent Krishna and Radha, they initiated women into Vaishnavism and used them as sevadasis (maids-cum-mistresses), assuaging and elevating their sentiments with the assurance that they were enacting the role of Radha! This trend increased in Bengali society in the later period. Nineteenth-century Bengali farces, as well as the folk paintings of Kalighat of that period, provide ample documentary evidence of such behaviour among Vaishnavite priests. Their lechery and hypocrisy were butts of popular ridicule, as in the following couplet: 'Magur machher jhol, jubotir kol; Mukhey Hari bol, Hari bol' (Fond of fish curry and the lap of a young girl while chanting 'Hari! Hari!' all the time).

Thus, the tenets and rituals constructed by the six Goswamis in Vrindavan which were institutionalized in the form of Gaudiya Vaishnavism, ultimately led to upper-caste hegemony over the masses of the socially and economically depressed followers of Chaitanya, who had earlier broken down the traditional order of social taboos, and could have posed a further challenge to the ruling Brahmanical establishment. It was necessary, therefore, for this elite to impose a religious symbol on these masses which they could internalize and which would enable them to play the required role of submissive followers. What could serve this purpose better than the newly reconstructed image of Radha in the texts of the Vrindavan-based Goswamis? Thus Radha was turned into a symbol of servility, all her attributes of unquestioning subservience to Krishna (no longer her *sakhi* or friend, but her Lord) upheld as the ideal qualities. When translated into the required norms of social behaviour in the post-Chaitanya Bengali society, the new idealized form of Radha could only abet the subordination of the deprived and underprivileged masses to the religious and political authorities in late sixteenth–seventeenth century Bengal.[11]

The restoration of the upper-caste dominance in the shape of Gaudiya Vaishnavism in Bengali Vaishnavite society after Chaitanya's death, and the consequent marginalization of the lower-caste devotees, led to the gradual departure of the latter from the mainstream of the Vaishnavite movement. They set up their separate orders by converting members from their own castes and claiming to carry on the original message of Chaitanya. This led to the emergence of a large number of syncretistic sects during the seventeenth–eighteenth century in Bengal, which could be described as representing popular Vaishnavism as distinct from Gaudiya Vaishnavism. Overriding caste and religious barriers, these sects also provided space for the equal participation of women, which they had enjoyed for a brief period during the early years of Chaitanya's movement. Some of the major sects of this nature, which are still functioning in various parts of Bengal, are Karta-bhaja (in Ghoshpara), Shahebdhani (in Chapra), Balarami (in Meherpur), and Lalanshahi (after the famous Baul singer of the late eighteenth-early nineteenth century, Lalan Shah, based in his birthplace in Kushthia, now in Bangladesh).[12]

This history of the schism in the post-Chaitanya Vaishnavite movement in Bengal had an important bearing on the reinterpretation of the Radha-Krishna fable in the popular culture of
nineteenth-century Calcutta. It is necessary in this connection to
remember that the folk poets and singers of the colonial metropolis
then mainly consisted of migrant labour—uprooted peasants and
artisans as well as traditional folk artistes dispossessed of their
lands and occupations by the new colonial economic order who
came to Calcutta in search of a living. These composers and
performers derived their inspiration from the orally transmitted
rural tradition of Bengali folk ballads and songs (in which the
Radha-Krishna story occupied a major space). Coming from the
lower castes and labouring classes they were more inclined towards
popular Vaishnavism than the scriptures of Gaudiya Vaishnavism
written by the six Goswamis.

This rich corpus of Bengali rural literature and popular religion harked back to a more domesticated and romantic image of
Radha and Krishna as a pair of lovers who, like many other human
couples, were aroused by physical desires, and torn by infidelity
and betrayal. Most of the poets and singers of this oral tradition in
the post-Chaitanya period of sixteenth–seventeenth century Bengal
were from the lower orders, and quite a few were literate enough
to preserve these compositions in the shape of manuscripts. The
eminent historian Dineshchandra Sen, who collected these manuscripts from their descendants and other sources in the early
decades of the twentieth century, names some of these writers,
indicating their humble origins—like Madhusudan Napit (a bar-
ber), Bhagyamanta Dhupi (a washerman), Ramnarayan Gope and
Kalicharan Gope (both milkmen).[13]

Interestingly enough, in Calcutta of the late eighteenth–early
nineteenth century, some of the most prominent kobi-walas (folk
poets and songsters) who reinterpreted the romantic tale of Radha
and Krishna in the popular culture of the metropolis, also came
from the same lower-caste and labouring-class background as their
predecessors in sixteenth–seventeenth century Bengali folk literature. Thus we come across the names of Gonjla Guin (from a

lower-caste agricultural community), Keshta Muchi (a cobbler), Raghunath Das (variously described as a blacksmith or a weaver), and Bhola Moira (a sweetmaker) among others, who dominated the scene of Calcutta popular culture in those days. While some among these kobi-walas composed their own poems, others sang the traditional poems.[14]

II

In the songs of this first generation of kobi-walas, and the oral compositions and visual performances that flowed from succeeding generations of poets, songsters, dancers, actors and actresses in the colonial urban milieu of nineteenth-century Calcutta and its suburbs, the Radha-Krishna fable underwent yet another change in the continuous dynamic process of reconstruction and reinterpretation that this mythological couple had been passing through for ages, acquiring certain new dimensions in these songs and performances.

These new dimensions were influenced to a great extent by three major factors: changing social norms and cultural tastes in the contemporary socioeconomic environment of nineteenth-century Calcutta; the allegory of the conventional narrative structure of the Radha-Krishna story which allowed for flexibility of interpretation and the introduction of various suggestions in the literary compositions of the poets; and the continuity of the long tradition of the domestication of deities in Bengali folk culture, which helped in the transformation of Radha and Krishna into urban heroes and heroines of contemporary Calcutta culture.

In the changed socioeconomic environs of the colonial metropolis, the folk poets who migrated from their villages to Calcutta found new masters, patrons and audiences, spread over a wide area of contemporary Bengali society. They included the Bengali grandees of the late eighteenth–early nineteenth century (who still retained some links with their rural roots and the Vaishnavite cultural tradition); the new generation of the foppish parvenu (known as babus) of the mid-nineteenth century; the middle-class professionals; and the vast masses of the urban working population. In the course of this sociocultural interaction between the rural religious and cultural tradition and the urban social structures of nineteenth-century Calcutta, Radha and Krishna developed into new urban icons. They acquired features from the contemporary surroundings and responded to a variety of popular expectations and cultural tastes that had emerged at various layers of Calcutta society during that period.[15]

Urban poets and poetasters, singers and songsters, performers in the jatra (folk theatre), and composers of panchali songs, women Vaishnavite kirtan-walis and dancers of jhumur (a style of dancing accompanied by singing), who entertained both the middle and the lower classes of Calcutta society, all these artistes contributed to the construction of a new image of the divine couple that was often at variance with the one being worshipped by the orthodox Vaishnavites and the educated gentry of that period. The latter usually dismissed and disparaged this image as a cheapened, falsified and fragmented variant of the sacred image of Radha and Krishna that was found in the written scriptures of the Gaudiya Vaishnavite theologians, which were held to be sacrosanct.

But then one could counter this by reminding these critics that the Vaishnavite theologians who wrote those scriptures were also selective in choosing only certain aspects of the original folk legend of Radha and Krishna, interpreting them at a certain historical juncture to suit their particular ideological objectives, and underplaying various other dimensions of the legend.[16]

In history, there had always been a transaction between 'great' and 'little' traditions, each borrowing from the other whatever was needed, and rejecting whatever it found unsuitable for its respective religious and cultural requirements at a particular time of history. Each had its own sieve to separate the grain from the chaff. What might have been considered poison for the practitioners of the 'great' tradition could have been meat for those of the 'little' tradition.

In this two-way traffic between the traditions, the treatment of the Radha-Krishna legend in Bengali popular culture of nineteenth-century Calcutta reflected the tensions that developed at different levels in the contemporary urban society. This new urban version of the divine pair can thus be viewed as a natural adaptation to the changing needs of a new type of listener and patron, especially since the mythological fable of Radha and Krishna had lent itself to a series of transformations over ages.

When we examine the flexibility of the narrative structure of the Radha-Krishna fable which makes way for a number of innovative allegorical interpretations, we find that the conventional model of narrating the story was retained by the urban composers and performers. But the events and characters, particularly its heroine Radha, went through perceptible and marked changes, suggesting almost a new allegory.

The inbuilt structure of the traditional Radha-Krishna narrative, as found in ballads and pala-kirtans, follows a set pattern. It starts with *poorvarag* (the beginnings, where love is born at first sight—or even at the first sound, e.g. of Krishna's flute); and then *sambhog* (the consummation) followed by the familiar developments that mark 'dangerous liaisons'; *abhisar* (the journey to the secret rendezvous); *daan-leela* (where Krishna demands toll from the *gopis* or milkmaids, including Radha, in the form of love); *nauka-bilash* (when Krishna as a boatman takes Radha and her friends across the Jamuna river and tries to seduce her); *biraha* (Radha's anguish at her separation from Krishna); *mathur* (Krishna's departure for Mathura where he becomes the king and forgets Radha, who, left behind in Vrindavan, pines for him and sends her messenger to him).

In Vaishnavite theology, this narrative is read as an allegory of the tortuous relationship between the devotee and the deity—the latter testing the former's love and loyalty at every stage of his/her spiritual journey. Each of the episodes mentioned above in the Radha-Krishna narrative is supposed to symbolize the different phases in the devotee's search for the ultimate communion with

the Supreme Being, who is described in human terms as the
beloved in the narrative.[7]

In the songs of the popular poets of nineteenth-century Calcutta, the narration of the Radha-Krishna story quite often became
an allegory of contemporary social trends—complexities of the
man–woman relationship in the new environs of an urban metropolis. The kobi-walas and other performers followed the same narrative structure, but described the various episodes in such a way
as to suggest in unmistakable terms the contours of the social life
of their times, seeming to treat Radha as a metaphor to describe
the plight of a forsaken and betrayed woman in contemporary
Bengali society. Such allegorical reconstructions and readings of
fables and myths are quite common in Indian religious discourses,
and have been made possible in Bengali folklore in particular by
the long tradition of the domestication of deities.

This brings us to the third factor that influenced the reconstruction of the Radha-Krishna fable in the popular culture of
Calcutta. The 'little' tradition had usually adopted the divinities of
the 'great' tradition by imagining them as its own kith and kin.
For instance, the poets of the medieval Bengali folk ballads called
Mangal-kavyas looked at the mythological story of the divine
couple, Shiva and Parvati, from their own contemporary social
perspective. It became their own story, through which they narrated both the sad and the humorous facets of the life of a rural
couple in the garb of the Shiva-Parvati legend: the poverty and
unemployment of Shiva, his addiction to hemp and his gauche
behaviour, Parvati's fights with him, the sufferings of the young
bride at her lazy husband's home, the few fleeting days of reunion
between Parvati and her mother, the distance between the home
of the bride and that of her husband which made such reunions
difficult. All these experiences, which were familiar to the Bengali
villager, turned Shiva and Parvati into next-door neighbours. The
verses of the Mangal-kavyas were thus quite often a transparent
cloak for describing the contemporary domestic experiences of a
rural people. The religious signification of the original myth was
relegated to the background by the down-to-earth reconstruction

of the story by medieval Bengali rural poets like Mukundaram Chakravarty, Rameshwar Bhattacharya and others.[18]

While the deities Shiva and Parvati were domesticated as a typical rural Bengali married couple in the Mangal-kavyas, Radha and Krishna were shaped into the image of young adventurous romantic lovers in the other Bengali folk cultural genre called padabali-kirtans—lyrical ballads. The pastoral romance of Radha and Krishna occupied a special niche in the psyche of the common masses of Bengal who even today flock to performances that celebrate the loves of this divine couple. This is because of the human touch that went into their domestication in Bengali folk culture. The recital describes in minute detail typical feelings common to lovers in the mortal world—the intensity of longing, the passion in the consummation of love, the anguish at parting, the wounded pride at desertion, the forgiveness at the time of reunion, etc. In the popular cultural performances in Bengal, like 'pala-kirtan' singing, or 'kathakata' narrations, or the rural jatra theatrical presentations, even today it is these romantic episodes that prevail over any didactic moralizing.

These basic ingredients of a conventional love story were further embellished in the Radha-Krishna mythological narrative in Bengal by the introduction of a secret relationship that was considered illicit by society. In the narrative, Radha, being a married woman, is not only involved in an adulterous relationship with Krishna, but is also entangled in an incestuous bind with him, since her husband, Ayan Ghosh, is also Krishna's uncle. Such liaisons which defied social norms, although not widespread, were not unusual in Bengali rural society. Taboo relationships such as secret affairs between young widows and their lovers, incestuous relationships within the home, adulterous entanglements outside the family, were kept under wraps. But the rural people listening to the woes of Radha as narrated by the kirtan singers (who usually painted her as a typical Bengali housewife) could easily identify them with familiar emotions and events in their daily existence.

Clearly, such a story eschewed all possibilities of a moral message, putting generations of Vaishnavite scholars to test, embarrassing and forcing them into pedantic convolutions to excavate a moral from what still continues to be condemned as 'immoral', adulterous and incestuous by society in general. Different Vaishnavite theologians have conceptualized the adulterous relationship between Radha and Krishna in the theory of *parakiyavad* (literally meaning the love of a man for a woman who legally belongs to another man). Chaitanya's direct disciple Rupa Goswami sought to explain away the adulterous relationship as Krishna's *prakata-leela* (sport in his manifestation as a human being) and insisted that in his *aprakata-leela* (in his role as the unmanifested deity), his devotees were *swakiya* (possessed by him alone) and not *parakiya* (belonging to—or married to—someone else). Chaitanya's biographer Krishnadas Kaviraj, while subscribing to the theory of *parakiyavad*, tried to dissociate it from any worldly practice by stating: 'Brojobina ihar anyatra nahi bash' (It has no place outside Braja—the divine playground of Krishna).[19]

The theological concept of *parakiyabad* suggests the possibility of a hidden dialogue between the official Vaishnavite doctrine and the folkloric traditions which threw up the image of Radha. In fact, *parakiyabad* can be traced back to much earlier traditions—its roots probably embedded in pre-monogamic societal norms which were later developed into the popular religious concept of *sahajiya* by Buddhist Tantrik theologians, to be followed by various Vaishnavite cults, which legitimized the role of the woman as an equal and essential partner of the male, whether his own or someone else's wife, in sexo-yogic religious practices.[20]

In the Bengali Hindu intellectual circles of nineteenth-century Calcutta, further efforts were made to come to terms with the popular appeal of this particular episode of the adulterous relationship in the Radha-Krishna legend, which was a perennial source of embarrassment for the newly educated Bengali bhadralok. A leading Bengali intellectual, Bankim Chandra Chattopadhyay, in an effort to sanitize Krishna, sought to excise the entire subplot of his amorous escapades from the legend by describing it as unhistorical, fictitious and baseless. More of this later.

But to go back to the folk tradition of narrating the Radha-Krishna allegory, it yielded a certain secular direction both in the songs and compositions of the popular poets of nineteenth-century Calcutta, and in the responses of the urban listeners and readers. The complex relationship between the spiritual idea and its material embodiment—basic to the structure of allegory—created a wide space between the original religious signification of the Krishna legend as presented in the *Srimad Bhagavata*, and its final materialization in literature. This space allowed the play of a variety of imaginative interpretations through which the contemporary social reality shone through.

In nineteenth-century Calcutta, some songs viewed Radha through the lens of a lingering medieval Vaishnavism, while others stripped her of the halo of piety which the Vaishnavite scriptures had bequeathed her, and twisted her traditional image into that of a harridan. Other oral compositions and visual performances occupied an intermediate zone, invoking the classical image of Radha, retaining her historical accoutrements, but moulding her into the image of a typical middle-class Bengali housewife.

Such domestication of the deities in folk culture also led to their demystification. Thus, in Bengali folklore the mighty Shiva of mythology is turned into a corpulent and indolent hemp smoker, a delightful eccentric, while in innumerable folk songs and stories the heroic warrior Krishna of the ancient religious legends becomes a charming but philandering cowherd, an ever-popular romantic hero.[21] In a similar vein, the popular poets and singers of nineteenth-century Calcutta transformed Radha into a multi-dimensional contemporary urban heroine. Her image ranged from that of the neglected wife of a profligate babu to that of a street hoyden openly asserting her love for her paramour. One can notice a steady progress from domestication to demystification, often leading to the desecration of the image of Radha.

It is necessary to add, however, that neither the earlier domestication of Hindu deities in Bengali folk culture, nor the later urbanization of Radha in the popular culture of nineteenth-century

Calcutta, detracted in any way from the religious faith that the people had in these divinities. They would laugh at the depiction of an utterly stoned Shiva's hemp-inspired gaucheries, or at the humbling of Krishna by Radha and her *sakhis* while listening to folk songs, but at the same time they would solemnly offer prayers and seek their blessings at temples during religious festivals or rituals. They apparently separated their cultural choices and responses from their religious needs.

While this may look like a contradiction to outsiders, it was actually the attempt of the common people to reconcile a wide range of feelings with regard to their deities—respect and fear from a distance, as well as a need to bring down the ethereal to the material level so as to make it more accessible. The tendency to desecrate sprang from their impulse to overcome their fear of these powerful deities, an assertion of the victory of laughter over the fear and awe imposed by the religious orthodoxy of the upper castes and classes regarding the so-called superhuman powers of these deities. While fearing and respecting the powerful, the powerless masses seek an opportunity to find a chink in their armour, so as to be able to reassure themselves that the high and the mighty are just as vulnerable as themselves. The desecration of deities in popular culture therefore was inspired by those lapses of the gods and goddesses which resembled all-too-human frailties—Shiva's indolence and addiction to drugs, Krishna's infidelity and promiscuity, Radha's jealousy and fits of pique.[22]

III

As mentioned earlier, the main forms of musical and visual performances in the popular culture of nineteenth-century Calcutta emerged partly from the folk cultural tradition that was brought to the city by migrant labour from the villages. But they were adapted to the needs and demands of the urban environment and patronage. Partly also they evolved as original innovations born of the new sociocultural milieu, and the professions that dominated the city's streets and marketplaces.

A closer examination of the songs of the first generation of popular poets or kobi-walas who flourished in Calcutta during the late eighteenth and early nineteenth century[23] would reveal that they concentrated only on certain episodes from Krishna's life, and particular moods of Radha, as listed in the traditional narrative. In selecting these few episodes from the 'great' tradition they were following in the footsteps of their ancestors in the 'little' tradition. If we examine the songs of the 'little' tradition in Bengal, we find that the poets usually preferred Krishna's romantic exploits to his military triumphs as described in the Puranas, or his role as a guide-philosopher in the *Gita*. They had chosen those episodes from his life which were exclusively devoted to his relationship with Radha and his frolics with the *gopinis* of Vrindavana, and his final betrayal of these friends when he leaves for Mathura and the title of king. Was it because they found in these episodes echoes of human experience they could relate to? The Radha-Krishna episode from the ancient Puranas offered an ideal opportunity for Bengal's folk balladeers to use it as a model for expressing the various situations and moods of lovers.

The Calcutta kobi-walas selected particular episodes of the story, the choicest being *nauka-vilash*, *viraha* and *mathur*, which provided them with the maximum opportunity of weaving in innuendos and allusions to contemporary social habits and customs. Of the eight moods of Radha as delineated in classical Vaishnavite literature, these folk poets primarily chose *bipralabdha* (when Radha feels anguished at Krishna's failure to keep his tryst with her), *khandita* (when she is hurt by signs of Krishna's infidelity) and *proshita-bhartrika* (when she is left behind by Krishna who departs for Mathura).[24]

Nauka-vilash (literally meaning 'the pleasure of a boat-ride'), as built into the conventional narrative by earlier poets, offered ample scope for erotic descriptions. Thus, the medieval Bengali poet Bodu Chandidas in his *Srikrishnakirtan*[25] narrates the plight of Radha the milkmaid who, in a hurry to sell her milk, wants to reach the market on the other side of the Jamuna river. The boatman is Krishna, who, taking advantage of her helplessness, demands concessions of a sexually compromising nature. During the crossing, a storm threatens the boat, and a frightened Radha pleads with Krishna to save her. Krishna tells Radha that his boat is overburdened by her generously endowed body, her swelling breasts, her enormous thighs, her massive hips and also her ornaments and garments. He then asks her to shed the latter so that the boat might become lighter, and Radha obliges by throwing them into the river![26]

An interesting variation on this episode can be found in a kobi-gan by the well-known nineteenth-century Calcutta kobi-wala Ram Bosu (1787–1829). He makes Radha describe the boating expedition in the following verses:

Tuley taronir upor
Natobar karey kato chhal;
Baley dekhichho ki Rai, Jamuna prabal.
Tumi porechho Rai, neel basan.
Megh bhebey badey paban.
Baley taranger majhey, ulango hotey,
Eki lajja, ai go ai.[27]

(Taking me into the boat the rake started all his tricks; He said, 'See, Rai! The Jamuna is turbulent. You are wearing blue clothing. Mistaking it for the clouds, the wind is getting excited.' In the middle of the river, he asked me to strip. Alas! Where am I to hide my shame?)

The above account is typical of the kind of pleasure trip popular among the nineteenth-century Bengali rich, who used to hire barges, steamers or boats for joyrides along the Hugli river to Mahesh, near Calcutta, on the occasion of the bathing festival (held in honour of the Hindu god Jagannath in May–June). Women dancers—khemta-walis, baijis[28] or ordinary prostitutes from the red-light areas of Calcutta—were an essential component of these excursions. Kaliprasanna Sinha (1840–70), a perceptive observer of the manners of nineteenth-century Calcutta citizens, who wrote in the local Calcutta patois under the pseudonym Hutom Pencha (the owl who keeps his eyes open at night) in a series of sketches on contemporary Calcutta, gives an amusing description of these pleasure trips: 'Some of these babus strip the women and make them dance the khemta. In some places, unless they [agree to] kiss, they don't get their due remuneration.'[29] The behaviour of Krishna from the mythological tales thus meshed with those of the contemporary Bengali babus in the eyes of the popular poets.

While the *biraha* section of the traditional Radha-Krishna narrative is taken up with Radha's complaints about an elusive Krishna dallying elsewhere with his mistresses, *mathur* deals with Radha's wounded pride after Krishna deserts her to become the king of Mathura, where he takes the hunchback Kubja as his consort. In this episode, Radha sends him a messenger who hurls rebukes at him. In the kobi-gan, the *biraha* episode quite often becomes a transparent cloak for the bitter admonitions of a Bengali housewife against her profligate husband, a subject which was the staple of numerous social novels, poems, plays and farces in nineteenth-century Calcutta. With the growth of Calcutta as a metropolis, the city became the centre of a variety of thriving professions, prostitution being one of the major ones. Along with uprooted peasants and artisans, poor and destitute women also streamed into the city and ended up in brothels. Their main clientele consisted of members of the Bengali upper and middle classes—pampered sons of rich landlords and commercial agents known as banians, upstart fortune seekers, their flunkeys and hangers-on, and employees of the expanding tertiary sector. They formed a distinct urban group of pleasure-seekers with new social habits. The city's prostitutes offered them a readily available avenue for their extramarital adventures. It became a fairly common practice among these Bengali babus to spend their nights in brothels, and rarely visit their wives, tucked away in the zenanas (women's quarters) of their ancestral households in Calcutta or neighbouring villages. In the Bengali plays written during the nineteenth century, the plight of these abandoned wives was frequently juxtaposed with the pleasures indulged in by their husbands in brothels. In his play *Sadhabar Ekadoshi*, the well-known author Dinabandhu Mitra (1830–73), encapsulated these in brilliantly conceived sequences appealing to the various layers of contemporary society—the lonely wives pining away for their deviant husbands, and the latter revelling in carousals with their favourite prostitutes, their philistine flunkeys and cynical intellectual friends. In the play, Kumudini complains about her husband Atal, son of a rich Calcutta family, who spends his time with the prostitute Kanchan. Atal's sister, while taking pity on Kumudini, gives her a detailed description of her brother's debaucheries, which rubs salt into her wounds, and Kumudini rues the day when her father married her off to a rich family. 'What's the use of money to me?' she asks, and adds: 'I wish I were dead!'[30]

Let us compare this with a contemporary *biraha* song by the Calcutta kobi-wala Horu Thakur (1738–1808). Like the sister-in-law in *Sadhabar Ekadoshi*, in this song too, a *sakhi* of Radha's expresses pity at her being deserted by Krishna, and then—again to rub salt into her wounds—proceeds to describe how Krishna has spent the night with Chandrabali, another *sakhi* of Radha's:

> Achhey Chandrabalir gharey.
> Dekhey elem tomar Shyam chanderey.
> Shuye kusum shajyapore.
> Nishir sheshehero alosey achetan,
> Karo sangey nahi basano bhooshano
> Bhuje bhuje bandha, jukto adhorey adhorey.[31]

> (I've just come back after having seen your darling Krishna in Chandrabali's room. Both of them were lying on a bed of flowers, lost to the world in the languor of the end of a long night. None had any clothes or ornaments on them. Their arms were entwined, their lips glued together.)

Both the urban housewife Kumudini in *Sadhabar Ekadoshi* and the mythological heroine Radha in the kobi songs share the same sentiments of betrayal and humiliation. To Calcutta's Bengali listeners of Horu Thakur's *biraha* song therefore, Radha's complaint rang a familiar bell.

It was not only the similarity of certain episodes, but also the metaphors and images chosen by the kobis, which brought the

Radha-Krishna story down to the level of real-life situations and almost turned it into a narration of the hopes and desires, the pains and the tensions experienced by men and women in the Calcutta Bengali society. The traditional Vaishnavite allegorical reading of the story as a narrative of the trials and tribulations of a devotee's spiritual journey was soon replaced by its alternative reading in the urban social milieu which secularized it in a large measure, through the help of familiar images of contemporary society that were used by the popular poets of Calcutta.

Quite often, the imagery of the flesh trade in Calcutta's commercial transactions was boldly borrowed by the kobis of this period to describe Radha's exploitation by Krishna. Radha is frequently painted as an ingenuous peddler selling her youth who is cheated by a crafty purchaser, Krishna, who seduces and then deceives her. The following verses by Ram Bosu play on the term *rasika* or *rasikey* (which in Vaishnavite terminology stands for Radha, as well as a female devotee). He describes Radha as a *rasika* who appears rather like a vivacious woman looking for love and a good time (the same term *rasika* is used for such women in common Bengali usage), instead of a devotee in search of love in the form of communion with Krishna:

> Madano rajaro, premero bajarey,
> Eley prem labho hoy.
> Rashikey ramoni, elem ami shey ashoye.
> Agey ke janey, shoi, ey biboron
> Kapat mahajan hetha amon,
> Nutan byaboshaye ramoni peley,
> Pherey pharey korey chaturi.[32]

(The market of love is ruled by the king Madan. Whoever comes here gains love. Being a *rasika* woman, I came here looking for love. Who could have known, my friend, that there are such deceitful traders here? If they find women entering a new trade, they cheat them at every opportunity.)

There is also a double meaning implied in the term *mahajan* in this song. While in common usage it means a trader, in Vaishnavite terminology it is often used to describe the composer of the *padas* or devotional verses. Is Ram Bosu suggesting that the *pada*-composers are using Radha in their verses to serve their interests in the same way as the market traders use women to reap profits?

The *mathur* episode of the Radha-Krishna narrative lent itself to still further recasting of the divine couple in the mould of contemporary characters. In the traditional *mathur* song, Radha's messenger (*dooti*) arrived in Mathura and abused Krishna for forgetting all about Radha. She reminded him of his humble days as a cowherd in Vrindavana, and his frolics with the milkmaids. She then ridiculed his rise to the kingship of Mathura and his liaison with the hunchbacked Kubja, a one-time maid in the royal household there.

The nineteenth-century Calcutta poets reconstructed this image of Krishna in a manner that bore unmistakable signs of a typical Bengali parvenu who had left his village home and disowned his past after making a fortune in the metropolis. In the version of the *mathur* narrative as recited by these poets, the listeners could decipher suggestive allusions to the prevailing trends in contemporary Calcutta society—the rise of the babus, often from humble rural origins, to the status of the 'nouveau riche', their desertion or ill-treatment of their wives, and their habit of establishing new liaisons with the city's prostitutes, perceived by them to be more urbane and sophisticated.

The abuses hurled at Krishna by Radha's messenger in the *mathur* recitation in these popular songs of Calcutta, while recasting Krishna in an urban mould, also gave voice to the complaints of a neglected Radha, who became identified with the ill-treated wife. Some of the best examples of this urban reading of the *mathur* episode are to be found in another folk form which became popular in nineteenth-century Calcutta, the panchali. Panchalis were basically songs interspersed with the recitation of short rhymes, and were composed around the Hindu mythological characters. The leading exponent of this form in nineteenth-century Bengal was Dasharathi Ray, or as he was more popularly known, Dashu Ray (1805–57). Although he was not a resident of Calcutta, many of his panchalis on the Radha-Krishna story were sung in Calcutta, and were laced with satirical allusions to the social customs of the metropolis.

In one panchali, Dashu Ray makes Radha's messenger address Krishna, who is installed as a king in Mathura, in terms which lampoon his preference for Kubja as consort over his earlier milkmaid lover Radha. Kubja is depicted as an ugly hag, beautifying herself with the cosmetics and ornaments which were in demand in the Calcutta markets in those days: huge pendant nose-rings (to hide her snub nose), a wig (to cover her bald patch), and *diamon-kata* jewellery (a contemporary hybrid term derived from the word'diamond', to describe ornaments with faceted decorative patterns):

> Tumi banka, Kubja banka, dui bankataey milechhey.
> Tomar jamon banka ankhi, Kubji temon kotor-chokhi
> Khanda nakey jhumko nolok duliechhey.
>
> Mathar phankey taaker upor parchuletey gherechhey.
> Bhalo bhalo gaahona ganta, tatey abar diamon-kata.
> Porey jano bhangon buri sejechhey.[33]

> (You are crooked, so is Kubja. The two of you match each other in crookedness. Your eyes are bent in sidelong glances, while those of Kubja's are sunken in their hollow sockets. She has huge pendants on her snub nose . . . She has covered the bald patch on her head with a wig. The decrepit hag has made herself up with beautiful ornaments—and they are diamon-kata to boot!)

There is a play of words on the term *banka* (meaning twisted, or crooked) to describe Krishna and Kubja. It is a reference to Krishna's twisted torso as Tribhanga-Murari, the familiar image of Krishna playing the flute with his body bent in *tribhanga* or three curves: his head turned sideways while playing the flute, his waist bent in the opposite direction, and his two legs crossing each other. To a jilted Radha, this once-beloved *tribhanga* pose of Krishna's has now become a symbol of his crooked double-crossing nature. Like Krishna, Kubja, his new consort in Mathura, is also *banka*, being hunchbacked.

According to the *Srimad Bhagavata,* however, Krishna touched the back of the hunchbacked maid Kubja, curing her of her deformity and turning her into a beautiful woman. But, significantly enough, Bengali popular poets, from the early fifteenth-century Chandidas to the nineteenth-century Calcutta singers and composers, chose to ignore this transformation and preferred to retain the image of an ugly old woman.

This is a familiar characteristic of popular culture. As mentioned before, its poets and listeners, artists and audience, are selective in their approach to the 'great tradition'. They accept and reject according to the demands of popular imagination. As Peter Burke observes: 'The minds of ordinary people are not like blank paper, but stocked with ideas and images; new ideas will be rejected if they are incompatible with the old.'[34]

What could have prompted generations of poets to reject the beautified Kubja and repeatedly make her a butt of ridicule? Although Radha herself is not present in *mathur*, her voice comes through in the vitriolic comments made by her messenger. We should remember that whereas, in *biraha*, Radha competes for the love of Krishna with rivals from her own peer group (like her friend Chandrabali), in *mathur* she has to contend with the maid-turned-queen Kubja of the Mathura royal household. Popular sympathy for Radha required that Kubja be turned into a decrepit hag—the antithesis of their beautiful heroine. This is in continuity of the folk cultural tradition of setting virtue against vice, good against evil, the hero against the villain, the fairytale princess against the wicked witch. It was this tradition that re-asserted itself in the oral culture of nineteenth-century Calcutta.

The language of some of the songs evoked the ambience of a contemporary lawsuit, as is evident from a 'dhop-kirtan', a form of kirtan developed by Madhusudan Kar (1818–68), a folk poet whose songs were popularized by women kirtan singers in Calcutta who were fond of the alliteration and play on words that marked Madhu Kar's compositions. Among these women singers, the most famous were Jaganmohini, Gurudasi, Thakurdasi, Bama and Shyama. In one of these dhop-kirtans, in a *mathur* scene, Radha's messenger confronts Krishna with his *daskhat* (bond of slavery) which he executed through his *dastakhat* (signature) on Radha's sole (a footprint of which is brought by the messenger as a *khat*, a promissory note, to demand Krishna's return to Vrindavana). The alliterative use of the word *khat*, and the play on its different meanings when used as an affix to words, were borrowed from contemporary juridical terminology. The secularization of religious idioms becomes more explicit towards the end of the song, when Radha's messenger threatens Krishna's courtiers in Mathura:

> Khat loye jai rajar hujurey, tabey amra pabo decree,
> Toder rajar daphaye hobey decree, jodi korbi adalat.[35]

> (If we go with our *khat*—promissory note—to the royal court, we'll get a decree in our favour. But if you approach the court, the decree will be the ruin of your king.)

The increasing tendency among Calcutta's popular poets to choose metaphors and imagery from contemporary urban situations and institutions tended to undermine the sanctity with which Radha's image was enshrined by the orthodox Vaishnavite scholars in their scriptures. The narration of the Radha-Krishna story by the Calcutta poets and singers quite often slid into parodies of the original story. Some of the best examples of such parodies can be found in the compositions of Rupchand Das (1814–90), better known as Rupchand Pakshi (or Rupchand, the Bird).[36] A favourite with both the fashionable Calcutta aristocracy and the city's common populace, Rupchand composed songs in a light satirical vein, reflecting the social reality around him. One such song deals humorously with the *mathur* episode in a jargon of mixed Bengali and English

words, in vogue among sections of the educated Bengalis in the
early nineteenth century. Rupchand makes Radha's messenger
address the guard at the gates of the Mathura palace in the
following words:

Let me go, *orey dwari,*
I visit to *Bangshidhari.*
Eshechhi Brojo hotey,
Ami Brojer Brojo-nari,
Beg you door-keeper, let me get,
I want to see block-head
For whom our Radha dead.
Ami tarey sarch kori.[37]

(Please let me enter, oh guard! I want to see Bangshidhari
[Krishna]. I have come from Brojo [the neighbourhood of
Mathura]. I am a woman from Brojo. I beg of you to let
me get in. I want to seek the blockhead [Krishna] for whom
our Radha has been pining away and has nearly expired. I
am searching for him.)

The concluding lines of the song are a humorous commentary
on Krishna's exploits in Vrindavan:

Moral character *shuno ore*
Butterthief *noni-chore,* blackguard *rakhal* poor
Chore Mathurar dandadhari . . .
King black nonsense very cunning,
Fulutey korey sing,
Majayechhey Rai Kishori . . . [38]

(Listen to his moral character. He used to steal butter, and
was a scoundrel ['blackguard'] who came from a poor
cowherd community. This thief has now become the ruler
of Mathura. This dark-skinned stupid ['nonsense'] king is
very cunning. He played the flute ['Fulutey'] and seduced
our young Radha.)

Here is the 'world turned upside down', as is often found in
the popular culture of the world. What is upheld as sanctimonious

in strictly ordained religious terms and practices, is often found suffocating by the people, who on occasion try to break out by parodying the omnipotent deities.[39] Thus, while at one level they worshipped Krishna as the mighty warrior of the epic Mahabharata, at another level they chose to turn him into a butt of laughter and derision by selecting episodes about his romantic exploits from the Puranas. In this popular world of inversion in nineteenth-century Calcutta street culture, even Radha often appears deromanticized. The romantic glamour built around her by Chandidas and Vidyapati in their verses is replaced by a kind of uncouth directness that marks the behaviour and utterances of the Radha of the Calcutta street songs. An interesting illustration of this trend can be seen in a jhumur song[40] sung by a woman singer Bhabani, who had her own troupe and moved around Calcutta and other parts of Bengal in the late 1850s. One of her songs plays on the *abhisar* episode of the Radha-Krishna story—Radha's frequent trips to the river, ostensibly to bathe and fetch water, but actually to tarry there for a glimpse of Krishna. As in Vrindavana, where she used to call her milkmaid friends to accompany her to the Jamuna river, in Bhabani's song also the heroine asks her companions:

> Chal soi, bandha ghatey jai,
> A-ghater jaleyr mukhey chhai!
> Ghola jal porley petey
> Gata omni guliye othey,
> Pet phenpey ar dhekur uthey heu heu heu![41]

(Come on, friends, let's go to a well-laid out bathing place. Fie upon the waters of out-of-the-way river banks! As soon as I take in the muddy waters, I feel like throwing up. My belly aches and I start belching—heu, heu, heu!)

By describing in these stark, earthy terms the physical hazards involved in a romantic rendezvous, Bhabani actually makes a parody of the famous lines of Chandidas, where Radha uses the bathwaters as a metaphor to describe her agonizing immersion in her love for Krishna, her hopes dissolving into regrets:

Amiya-sagorey sinan koritey
Sakoli garole bhela.[42]

(As I dipped into the ocean of nectar for a bath, everything
turned into poison.)

In Bhabani's song, a defiant Radha deglamorizes her given
role, and comes up with a down-to-earth rendering of the *abhisar*
scene.

This trend of deglamorization becomes more explicit as we
move into the streets of nineteenth-century Calcutta. We find
Radha shedding the traditional attire of religious sanctity and
romantic grace that had marked her appearance in the earlier texts
and songs. She is appropriated by various sections of the lower
orders of the city—prostitutes in their songs, for instance. In one
such song, a prostitute when describing her harassment by her
greedy landlady, ingeniously weaves in the *abhisar* motif to draw a
parallel with the domestic plight of a harassed Radha waiting to
escape and meet her cowherd lover, Krishna:

Amar bhalobasha abaar kothaye basha bendhechhey,
Mashey mashey barchhey bhaara,
Baariulee dichhey taara,
Goylaparar moyla chhonra praney merechhey.[43]

(My love has built a nest again in some other place . . . The
room rent in this place is being hiked up every month. The
landlady is hustling me into quitting the room. Meanwhile, my soul has been smitten by that dark lad from the
milkmen's colony.)

The singer's surrender to the charms of the 'dark lad from the
milkmen's colony' is a reconstruction of the Radha-Krishna fable
in her own localized version.

The fable underwent a further comic transformation in the
popular jatra staged by the working people in nineteenth-century
Calcutta. Primarily aimed at entertaining the masses, these jatras
elaborated upon the sportive aspects of the traditional narrative,
and turned the Radha-Krishna romance into a rollicking session

of lilting songs and dances. A contemporary observer describes a jatra mounted by the milkman community of his neighbourhood in north Calcutta, in which the famous jatra performer Gobinda Adhikari (1798–1872) was invited to act. Well-known for his ability to move the audience with his intense rendering of the *mathur* episode, Gobinda Ahikari, however, chose a humorous approach to entertain the milkman audience. According to the observer, Radha appeared in the role of a dancer cavorting to the rhythm of doggerel about the Radha-Krishna story![44]

Dancing indeed became an integral part of the jatras which were performed by the popular artistes of the city. As one highbrow Bengali bhadralok sarcastically commented in a contemporary journal: 'In the jatras today, the dance is the main thing; everyone dances . . . Krishna dances, Radha dances, Ravana dances, Sita dances, Kaikeyi dances, perhaps old Dasaratha would have also danced, but for the fact that the old man is usually cast in the role of the violin-player in all the jatras . . .'[45]

Such was the popularity of the dancing Radha of the jatras that she became a household character in a common Bengali saying: 'Sat mone tel-o purbey, Radha-o nachbey' (literally—'wait for tonnes of oil to burn to watch Radha dance'). The reference was to night-long jatra performances lit by oil lamps. The saying implied a wait for a miracle to happen, like 'If the sky falls, we shall catch larks!'

This final metamorphosis of Radha in the street jatras and jhumur dances of Calcutta can be seen as the ultimate antithesis of the Radha image as fashioned by fifteenth-century Bengali bards like Chandidas and later by the disciples of Chaitanya in their theological treatises. Far from celebrating Radha as the ideal of youthful grace and desirable beauty, the songs of the prostitutes and the street dancers show the wrinkles in an ageing Radha's soul, a battered soul that has suffered a long history of agony and humiliation: as the docile Bengali housewife neglected by the profligate husband, as the khemta-wali dancing to the tune of the upstart babu, as the prostitute hounded out from her shack, waiting eternally for her lover to make a home with her, or as the rustic ingenue left behind in the village, and forgotten by her fortune-hunting husband obsessed with the lure of the metropolis.

Radha appears in all these roles in the panorama of popular culture that unrolled in nineteenth-century Calcutta. Her metamorphosis, often comic and bawdy, in the city's streets and marketplaces is a typical instance of a system of representation that characterizes popular culture in many parts of the world, namely the 'world turned upside down.'[46] Inversion (of the respectable into the commonplace), laughter (at the discomfiture of the superiors), and derision (of the sacred values of the scriptures, or the romantic norms of traditional songs) were the essential ingredients of the oral culture of the Calcutta streets, which turned the given 'world' (as accepted by the Establishment, or powers that be) into its opposite in its songs and dances. Drawing upon the rural oral tradition of the Mangal-kavyas, the nineteenth-century Calcutta poetasters and songsters turned the Radha-Krishna fable 'upside down' first by making Krishna into a prince of rogues, and then by casting Radha in the role of an assertive and often aggressive member of the demi-monde.

IV

The treatment of Radha and Krishna in the popular culture of nineteenth-century Calcutta can be seen as an attempt to explore relationships of power against the background of both traditional religious and contemporary social hierarchies. The discrimination by the powerful of the weak re-appeared in urban society in a variety of forms: the upper-caste ostracization of the city's lower-caste people in religious matters; the bhadralok's disdain for the chhotolok (the abusive Bengali term for the unlettered poor); the injustice meted out by the males of this bhadralok society to their wives; the harassment and persecution suffered by the city's commercial sex workers at the hands of their male clients and employers.

All the unequal relationships of this urban society peer through the Radha-Krishna narrative as reconstructed by the city's popular raconteurs, the kobi-walas, the singers of the panchalis and dhop-kirtans, the jatra performers, and the jhumur dancers. In these various forms of the urban oral and visual narrative, we notice a running thread in the behaviour, utterances, dialogues and songs put in the mouth of Radha. It reflects the desire of the weak to get even with the strong, either by outwitting them, or by humiliating them. It is significant that the urban folk poets selected mainly those sections of the Radha-Krishna narrative that served this purpose, namely *abhisar*, *nauka-bilash* and *viraha-mathur*.

It would be interesting at this stage to examine the attitude of the contemporary Bengali bhadralok towards these popular cultural performances dealing with the legend of Radha and Krishna. Many among these English-educated bhadralok carried on a sustained campaign against the representation of the Radha-Krishna story in popular culture. Their disparagement flowed out in angry letters and writings in contemporary newspapers. A letter by a bhadralok in an English journal for instance, objected to the dancing scenes in a Radha-Krishna jatra in the following words: 'Who that has any pretension to a polite taste, will not be disgusted with the vulgar mode of dancing with which our play commences; and who that has any moral tendency will not censure the immorality of the pieces that are performed?'[47] An article on jatra published in a Bengali journal complained that 'anyone from among the illiterate fishermen, boatmen, potters, blacksmiths, who can rhyme' were composing jatras, and then added: 'Thanks to the present type of jatras, Krishna and Radha look like goalas (milkmen); in the past, the qualities of a good poet made them appear as divinities.'[48] Another bhadralok, in a book written in English, described the jatras in the following words:

> The plays most frequently acted, treat of the amours of the lascivious Krishna and of the beautiful shepherdess Radha ... It is needless to say that topics like these exercise a baneful influence on the moral character of the auditors [*sic*] ... The gesticulations, with which many of the characters in these yatras recite their several parts, are vulgar and laughable.'[49]

About the jhumur-walis who used to dance to songs about Radha and Krishna, one bhadralok made his views even more explicit when he wrote without any qualms: 'They were chhotolok, dark skinned wenches who stank when they passed by . . . Their language was extremely coarse'.[50]

These views of the educated Bengali bhadralok of nineteenth-century Calcutta reflected the cultural tastes that a new generation was imbibing under the British educational system. Their English teachers had taught them to look down upon their divinities and the literature that celebrated them as defiled by grossness and indecency. This led many among them not only to dissociate themselves from their folk cultural heritage, but also to reject the Hindu religion itself.[51]

To meet this challenge, some among the Bengali Hindu intellectuals tried to reinterpret Hindu religion in a way that would make its divinities stand the test of judgment by the European standards that they had acquired. The novelist Bankim Chandra Chattopadhyay (1838–94), took up the challenge of rehabilitating Krishna. While in the pages of *Bangadarshan*, the journal he edited, articles appeared denouncing the depiction of Krishna as a profligate in popular cultural performances, he himself undertook the task of reinterpreting the Hindu god in a different light. In *Krishnacharitra*, published in 1892, he dismissed the legend of Krishna's dalliance with the milkmaids and Radha as unhistorical: 'the stories about Krishna—his habits of stealing and adultery—all these are baseless and fictitious'.[52] Thus, in order to make Krishna acceptable, he had to reconstruct the divinity, by cutting out all those acts of his described in the Puranas and folk culture, that were considered unpalatable according to the cultural norms that Bankim had imbibed from his education. Looking back at Bankim's reinterpretation of Krishna, Rabindranath Tagore commented: 'Bankim had tried to make Krishna stainless and beautiful.'[53] Much later, a modern Bengali historian probably hit the nail on the head when he observed: 'He (Bankim) accepted Krishna as an incarnation of the Deity. No arguments are offered in defence of this faith except that his Western education had reinforced his belief in this regard.'[54]

A few years after the publication of Bankimchandra's *Krishna-charitra*, Rabindranath Tagore wrote a piece on the songs of the kobi-walas. He had listened to these songs as a young boy, and remembering them now, he accused the songsters of ignoring the 'beauty and depth of Vaishnavite poetry', choosing instead mainly those sections that were 'extremely unworthy' (of literary presentation). He added: 'The favourite topics of the kobi-walas are scandal and deception. Again and again, Radha and her friends make use of Kubja, or some one else, to bitterly abuse Shyam (i.e. Krishna) through spicy jokes.'[55]

Accurate in his description of the typical attitude of the kobi-walas in their choice of episodes from the Radha-Krishna legend, Rabindranath however failed to delve into the deeper motivations of the kobi-walas, as well as the demands of the popular audience, which led to the preference for 'scandal and deception' and 'spicy jokes' against Krishna in these songs and performances. The choices that these performers and the audience made about the Radha-Krishna narrative were prompted by their own experiences in real-life situations in nineteenth-century Calcutta. Being at the bottom of the socioeconomic hierarchy, constantly subject to oppression and humiliation by the powers that be, the urban poor and labouring classes had only a few avenues of relaxation through which to let off steam: leisure activities like watching and listening to jatras, kobi-gans, panchalis or jhumur dances. The boundless world of fantasy and imagination that these offered helped them to escape from an increasingly depressing environment, also offering them the weapon of laughter against the rich and the powerful.[56] Salacious gossip about Radha and Krishna was a form of vicarious enjoyment of scandals in high society. The ribaldry and jokes at the expense of the divine couple often found in kobi-gans or jatras were frequently an expression of the commoner's desire to thumb his/her nose at the sanctimonious platitudes of the religious elders of society. At a more serious level, there were also opportunities for identification of the distraught Radha and the unfaithful Krishna with the neglected wife and her promiscuous husband in contemporary Bengali society.

In close empathy with the popular mood, the poets and singers adapted the inherited theme to the needs of listeners and audience so that the specificity of time and place showed through the universality of the traditional story. The urban narration of the Radha-Krishna fable against the background of the growth and development of Calcutta society in the nineteenth-century, involved a switching of codes, rhythms, and language from the given tradition through a multi-dimensional process—from the allegory of Vaishnavite theology to the romanticizing of the fable in the popular kirtans, to its clothing in contemporary kobi-gans and panchalis, and finally to what was disparaged by the Bengali bhadralok society as the profanation of Radha's image in the marketplace jatras and street jhumur performances.

We must hasten to add, however, that this process of secularization was not a rejection of religion. It was an expression of fears and fantasies, and assertion of grievances in increasingly worldly terms. Aron Gurevich's explanation of the apparent desecration of divinities in the popular culture of medieval Europe bears some relevance to what we are discussing: 'the lowering (of the divinities) assumes neither denial nor disregard, but a temporary overcoming of it (ecclesiastical culture) through an inclusive inversion'.[57]

The popular artistes and their audience in nineteenth-century Calcutta borrowed the image of Radha for their repertoire, and transformed it to the extent of 'inclusive inversion'. Romanticization of the religious myth in lay terms; inversion of the roles of the powerful and the weak (the latter represented by a Radha who 'overcomes' the submissive role typecast for her in Vaishnavite theology); laughter and derision at the expense of Krishna, the king of Mathura—all these can be read as defence mechanisms (sometimes becoming subversive of the established religious and social norms) developed by the common people to cope with the repressive and mystifying forces of urbanization in a colonial setting.

At the religious level, Chaitanya's message of bhakti could no longer be a healing balm for the distressed citizens. Besides, much of the respect and adulation that Chaitanya's followers and Vaishnavite priests used to enjoy in the past was getting eroded in nineteenth-century Bengal, where, by popular perception they were often guilty of lechery and hypocrisy.[58]

In the urban re-reading of the religious myth, therefore, the popular mood often tended to shift from faith to scepticism, as reflected in the selective stress on particular episodes of the Radha-Krishna narrative, which allowed both the narrators and the listeners to temper their devotion with a large dose of healthy cynicism. At the level of human relations, personal associations and values were undergoing dramatic changes in the urban milieu. The concept of romantic love itself, as perceived in the past, was under a cloud. In the songs of the medieval poet Chandidas, Radha, even though her love was unrequited, still hoped for Krishna's return. But in the songs of the nineteenth-century kobi-walas, that hope disappears, and Radha reconciles herself to a secluded life, wanting only to be relieved of the remnants of her lost love. In the totally cynical environment of the streets, love, like all other ideals, is held to be corruptible, and is often reduced to caricature in street songs.

Having already undergone several metamorphoses in the past, Radha was poised for urbanization in the colonial metropolis of Calcutta. She thus became a woman of the city—a sad and dangerous city which undermined traditional family relationships and opened up new liaisons and associations based on bargaining powers in a market economy. She learned the city's language and acquired knowledge of its customs and skills while emerging in her urban incarnation, to be able to meet the needs of new social structures and the cultural tastes of a colonial metropolis.

IV

FROM AULCHAND TO SATI-MA:
THE INSTITUTIONALIZATION OF THE
KARTA-BHAJA SECT IN
NINETEENTH-CENTURY BENGAL

As mentioned in the previous chapter, in the post-Chaitanya period in Bengal—during the seventeenth and eighteenth centuries—popular interpretations of Vaishnavism bore exceedingly diverse fruit in the form of a variety of syncretistic sects. In their mode of worship, their hymns and rituals, their living style, the followers of these sects represented a radical deviation from the established norms of Gaudiya Vaishnavism (which by then had become institutionalized and hegemonized by the upper-caste Goswamis).[1]

Most of these sects were founded by members belonging to the depressed castes among the Bengali Hindu and Muslim population who were disappointed by the replacement of the original egalitarian idealism of Chaitanya by the old caste-based hierarchy of his Brahman and upper-caste devotees.[2] In fact, some of their songs harked back to Chaitanya's idealism, and most of their rituals reasserted the message of equality between castes, religious

communities and men and women that marked the initial phase
of Chaitanya's movement.

According to a nineteenth-century Bengali scholar, there were
at least 56 Vaishnavite or semi-Vaishnavite sects still flourishing
in Bengal during the 1870–80 period, with a large number of them
tracing their ancestry to the seventeenth–eighteenth century. While
some among them were centred around individual preachers and
developed into personality cults, many floated around as amor-
phous groups sharing certain common beliefs and rituals.[3]

Among the personality-oriented sects, the major ones were:
Lalanshahi, followers of the famous Baul singer Lalan Shah, based
in his birthplace in Kushthia, now in Bangladesh; Shahebdhani,
after a Muslim hermit of that name who lived in Shaligram in the
Nadia district of today's West Bengal; Balarami, founded by
Balaram Harhi, who came from the so-called 'untouchable' community, and operated from Meherpur in Nadia; and Karta-bhaja,
traced to the late seventeenth-century mystic, Aulchand, whose followers established their centre in Ghoshpara in Nadia.

There are a few interesting aspects that need to be noted in
this context. First, all the above-mentioned major sects originated
in villages located in one particular area of Bengal—Nadia, where
Chaitanya initiated his movement of socio-religious reforms. But
like Chaitanya's Vaishnavism in the sixteenth century, these sects
also soon spread their influence all over Bengal, drawing members
of the Hindu lower castes, outcastes and Muslim atraps, converts
to Islam from the lower orders. Secondly, today in Bengal, most of
these sects remain somewhat diffused as isolated families of devotees here and there in the countryside, following the rituals of their
respective sects, like the Shahebdhanis, Balaramis or nomadic Baul
followers of Lalan Shah, who gather once a year at his birthplace
in Kushthia for a festival.[4]

Unlike the other sects, the Karta-bhaja sect—which is the subject of our present investigation—succeeded in emerging into a
well-organized institution even by the nineteenth century, and continues to maintain that character till today. The institutionalization

was marked by (i) specifying a particular spot as the permanent headquarters of the sect; (ii) a dynastic succession of 'gurus' who claimed that the authority of the first 'guru' was bequeathed to them; (iii) organized priesthood consisting of a network of preachers in different villages and towns in charge of the converts whom they had proselytized; (iv) collection of money on a regular basis from the converts by the headquarters; (v) a repository of written texts (mainly in the form of songs) explaining the religion of the sect and the rituals to be practised.

The pattern of development of the Karta-bhaja sect over the last 200 years or so poses a whole series of questions. What are the catalytic agents—religious, or socioeconomic—that encourage the institutionalization of heterodox sects that started their journey as rebels against the similar institutionalization of their parent religions (Vaishnavism in the present case)? Is it the continuity of the charismatic image of the founder of the sect, credited with superhuman authority and turned into yet another god by his immediate pupils who, in order to perpetuate their own personal authority over his devotees, build up an institution? Is it the collective memory of the local people (of Ghoshpara in Nadia and the neighbouring areas, in this case) of the legends that had grown around the founder of the sect, Aulchand, who arrived at Ghoshpara sometime in the early eighteenth century, that unwittingly collaborated in the process of institutionalization?

While searching for answers to these questions, in our investigation we may recall Arnold Toynbee's observations on the felt need for institutions among the people, and how at the end, institutions built upon these popular needs freeze into structures far removed from the initial requirements: 'Institutions . . . enable Man to satisfy social needs that cannot be provided for within the narrow range of relations attainable through direct personal intercourse'. He then added:

> One generic evil of an institution of any kind is that people
> who have identified themselves with it are prone to make
> an idol of it . . . The true purpose of an institution is simply

to serve as a means for promoting the welfare of human beings . . . yet, in the hearts of its devotees, it is apt to become an end in itself, to which the welfare of human beings is subordinated and even sacrificed if this is necessary for the welfare of the institution. The responsible administrators of any institution are particularly prone to fall into the moral error of feeling it to be their paramount duty to preserve the existence of this institution of which they are trustees.'[5]

The history of the Karta-bhaja sect's institutionalization partly conforms to this pattern traced by Toynbee in his approach to religion as an historian. But it raises another set of questions relating to the entire concept of 'popular religion' (as represented by the Karta-bhaja sect and its practices, which apparently enjoyed a popular base, particularly among the lower orders in Bengal in the nineteenth century). Is popular religion a product of popular spontaneity, independent of and unaffected by the received precepts of the dominating religious establishment? Does it trace its origin to the days preceding the institutionalization of the dominating religion—in the European context, to pre-Christian pagan rites and practices, and in the Indian sub-continent to pre-Brahmanic animist cults? Or, is it a 'popularized' version of the precepts preached and institutionalized by the established religious organizations? Or—yet another possibility—can popular religion be defined as something quite plastic, including all forms of assimilation and contamination—both from the past and the contemporary era, from the localized spontaneous roots and the centralized dictates of the religious establishment?

The history of the Karta-bhaja sect offers a rich and interesting quarry for explorers trying to dig up answers to these questions— relating to the circumstances accompanying, firstly, the birth of a popular religious cult, secondly, its gradual institutionalization, and finally, its continuity in the present era.

This chapter intends to explore the history and development of the Karta-bhaja sect through these main stages of its odyssey

during the last 200 years in Bengal—and in between, the author
hazards a few explanations!

History and Legend

Like the origins of most of the seventeenth–eighteenth century
Bengali syncretist preachers, those of the founder of the Karta-
bhaja sect also are shrouded by a haze in the twilight zone between
recorded history and oral legends. From the various accounts,
handed down from one generation to another, and later recorded
(in the nineteenth century) in printed texts, a vague outline of sorts
emerges.[6]

It seems that Aulechand, or Aulchand, the founder of the sect,
was born sometime in the eighties of the seventeenth century, and
died in 1779. He was discovered one day, as an eight-year-old
foundling of unknown antecedents, by a betel-grower called
Mahadeva in his plantation in Ula village in Nadia. Mahadeva
adopted him and named him Purnachandra (meaning 'full moon',
maybe because he was found on a full-moon night?). The surrogate
father, perhaps a Vaishnavite, sent the boy to a local Vaishnavite
teacher, Harihar, from whom he learnt the religious scriptures. He
stayed with Mahadeva's family for 12 years, and then moved out to
travel all over Bengal.

During his travels, he spent a lot of time in the eastern part of
Bengal, particularly in Srihatta and Dhaka—the two place-names
which frequently crop up in songs about Aulchand. Incidentally,
in these areas, during his visit (in the mid-eighteenth century), an
Aul preacher, Alak Shah was a popular figure among the Sufi
fakirs. It is speculated that Purnachandra became an Aul and
adopted the name Aulchand.[7]

Aulchand's next halt was Jagadishpur village in Nadia, where
he met Ramsharan Pal—a Sadgope (agriculturist caste originating
from the larger pastoral community of Gopes or milkmen and
cowherds), who was the manager of a local zamindar. Aulchand
cured him of his colic pain, and Ramsharan became his disciple.

According to another version, Aulchand cured Ramsharan's wife Sarasvati by applying mud and water from a nearby tank in Ghoshpara, in the Muratipur village where Ramsharan was living. Following this, Aulchand acquired the reputation of a miraculous healer, and Ghoshpara (literally, 'milkmen's colony') became a pilgrimage centre. The pomegranate tree under which Sarasvati was cured (known as Dalimtala), and the tank, the mud and water of which were used by Aulchand to cure her (known as Himsagar) are still there, worshipped every year by thousands of devotees. Sarasvati, in later years, was to become the apostolic head of the sect, to be known as Sati-ma.

To come back to Aulchand, after having settled down in Ghoshpara, he initiated 22 disciples into his religious sect. From the names, it seems that the majority came from the milkmen community. That there were no caste prejudices is evident from the fact that among these, there was a brass-smith named Shyama Kansari, and an untouchable named Panchu Ruidas.[8]

Since Ramsharan Pal was his first disciple, Aulchand probably preferred to stay at his house in Ghoshpara, which became the headquarters of his sect. According to legends, he wore a loincloth under a flowing cloak, with a patchwork quilt thrown across the shoulders, when he moved around. He used to preach in Bengali, and treated Hindus, Muslims, untouchables and everyone equally. He shed all caste prejudices and took food from everyone.[9]

Sometime in 1769–70, Aulchand left Ghoshpara for another village called Boalia, ostensibly to visit a disciple of his. He stayed on in Boalia, where he died in 1779. His disciples buried his patchwork quilt in that village, and buried his body in another village called Parari.

Curiously enough, neither the village Ula, where Aulchand was found, nor the two other villages—Boalia and Parari—where his remains were buried, are the main pilgrimage centres of his followers. It is Ghoshpara where all the devotees congregate for three days once a year, beginning with the Dol (or Holi) festival on the night of the full moon. The choice of the dates could

have something to do with the original name of Aulchand—
Purnachandra—or simply with the holiday mood of the spring festival. The three-day festival at Ghoshpara is marked by a fair with
entertainments like songs and circuses, merry-go-rounds and
magic shows, community feasts and jatras—which draw the general crowd from the neighbouring villages as well as Calcutta and
nearby towns. The famed Dalimtala and the Himsagar tank attract
a different crowd—those with ailments, who believe in the miraculous powers of these spots consecrated by Aulchand. There is a
third group—small in number—who are the initiates of the sect,
known as Karta-bhajas, who assemble at Ghoshpara during these
days for a reunion with their fellow-initiates and a collective
engagement in their rituals and songs.

But we shall deal later in detail with the Ghoshpara fair (or
mela as it is known in Bengal)—which is an important component
of the institutionalization of the Karta-bhaja sect. To come back to
its founder, Aulchand, as evident from the scanty details of his life-
story, we can hazard a few guesses as to his original message.

First, all the various legends revolve around the eclectically religious origins and development of Aulchand. While some legends
describe him as being an abandoned child (without any indication
of the religion of his parents), there are others which narrate how
he appeared in the plantation of the betel-leaf grower Mahadeva as
a full-grown fakir, with all the marks of a Muslim mendicant, the
patchwork quilt and a flowing cloak.[10] There are also other legends
which claim him to be an incarnation of Chaitanya, or the living
Chaitanya in disguise. According to these legends, Chaitanya did
not die in Puri (in 1553), but disappeared, and reappeared more
than two hundred years later in the shape of the fakir Aulchand—
because Chaitanya felt that 'an excessive stress on the ascetic ideal
had made the Gaudiya Vaisnavas extremely unpopular' and that
'fake Vaisnava orders . . . constituted a terrible threat to ethics and
genuine spirituality.'[11]

It appears therefore that the emergence of the semi-historical
Aulchand at the end of the seventeenth century was in continuity

of the popular tradition of inventing saints with common Hindu and Muslim characteristics that marked Bengali society following the Muslim conquest in the thirteenth century. As we have seen the traditional animist, Buddhist and Hindu beliefs on the one hand, and the newly introduced Islamic beliefs—mainly of a Sufist nature—on the other, quite often blended to give birth to a host of popular saints and pirs of a rather hybrid nature. Some were transformed from old local godlings, while some were new semi-historical figures. For example, the syncretist saint Satyapir, or Satyanarayana, who is worshipped even today in Bengali homes; or the Muslim pir Gorachand (retaining the old Hindu name) who is worshipped in Bardhaman and the 24-Parganas. A blending of two possible historical characters—a Hindu guru, Matsyendra and a Muslim warrior of the seventeenth century, Masnad Ali—led to the formation of Pir Manchandali in Medinipur.[12]

These saints continued to answer to the perennial need of the common people to believe in a superhuman power—not of an abstract and distant God—but of a mortal being, tangible enough for them to metamorphose him/her from semi-historical origins into an easily accessible form, either as an image, or as relics of the departed figure, or as a guru in the form of a living descendant of the original saint.

The fusion of pre-Islamic and Islamic religious beliefs in Bengal also led to the emergence of a large number of syncretistic sects without any particular individual saint as their focus. These were the Bauls, Auls, Fakirs, Darbeshis and numerous other wandering mendicants and minstrels who can still be found in the Bengal countryside.

Aulchand derived his origins from both the syncretic personality cults and syncretic sects. His religious creed—originally called Satya-dharma (the religion of Truth)—emphasized certain common features that characterized these contemporary cults and sects. First, there was a deliberate attempt to reject the Vedas and the elaborate Brahmanical rituals in favour of a simple mode of worship (e.g. chanting the names of deities, and singing of *bhajans*). Secondly, there was a firm commitment to the upholding of equality of all human beings—irrespective of caste, religion and sex. Thirdly, distinct *sahajiya* traces (originating from the Buddhist period) and Sufist influences (from the later Islamic sources), could be discerned in certain concepts like the body as the microcosm of the universe: 'Moner Manush', whose seat was the human heart; the important role of the guru (the murshid in Indian Sufism) or the spiritual guide as the mediator between this world and the next world. These concepts were common to the Baul, Aul and other similar wanderings sects all over Bengal.

Interestingly enough, it was this crucial concept of the necessity of a guru in Aulchand's Satya-dharma that to a large extent, in its later development, underpinned the institutionalization of the religious creed. It lost its original name and came to be known instead as Karta-bhaja (literally meaning, those who worship their master, the *karta* or the boss—suggesting here the guru).

One might ask in this connection: although the concept of the guru or murshid was also embedded in the thinking of other syncretist sects like the Bauls, why did they not get institutionalized? If one may hazard a guess, it could be because of the basic difference in the conceptualization of the guru or the spiritual preceptor in Baul thought. While Satya-Dharma (or Karta-bhaja in its later version) came to be built upon the personality cult of Aulchand (who was worshipped as the first guru in a dynastic succession) the Bauls and the unorganized sects did not have any personified guru as such. For many among them, the guru was ultimately God. As one historian of Sufism in Bengal observed: 'In many songs of the Bauls, the identification of Murshid or Guru with God (i.e. mysterious Being) and the invocation of his spirit at the time of spiritual distress, clearly show . . . that they believe in the invisibility of their Guru'.[13]

For these sects, the guru or murshid is someone who forever remains invisible, but who at the same time inspires the disciple with the eternal hope of final deliverance from this turbulent sea of existence. In the meantime, this hope—the faith in the invisible spiritual guide—acts as a security in the boundless heaving sea of existence—like a lamp in the abyss of darkness[14] for the mortal disciple who has to survive this voyage. A typical Baul song captures the thinking style of the sect in the following lines, which uses the familiar image of the boatman caught in the eddies of a turbulent river as the symbol of the human being tossed by the vortex of daily existence. He sustains himself through it all with his abiding hope for the arrival (or guidance?) of the murshid.

> Unur jhunur baje nao amar
> nihaliya batasere!
> Murshid, roilam tore ashey (refrain).
> Paschime sajila meygh-re, dyaoyay dila re dak!
> Amar-chinrila hailer panas, naukaye khaila pak re!
> Murshid, roilam tore ashey . . .[15]

> (My boat is quivering, tossed by the rough wind! But, Murshid, I remain here, waiting for you. The clouds are piled up in the West, and the thunder roars! The rope of my craft snaps, and the boat, alas, has been caught in a whirlpool! Murshid, I remain here, waiting for you . . .)

We should however note at the same time that members of these sects carried out—and still continue—intricate esoteric practices inherited from the old *sahajiya*–Tantrik tradition. Because of the stringent nature of these practices, the help of a guru is sought at every step. We therefore find disciples being initiated into these practices by a guru or preceptor. After having mastered the intricacies of *sadhana*, the disciples left the guru and were on their own. Thus, Aulchand was believed to have been initiated first by one Balarama, a Vaishnavite guru; he then set off on his journey. The well-known Baul poet, Lalan Fakir chose as his preceptor a Muslim called Siraj Sain, before starting on his own. But unlike Aulchand, other founders of sects, like Lalan, Shahebdhani and Balaram Harhi were not known to have appointed any successor.

Aulchand's decision to select 22 disciples (like Chaitanya's choice of the six Goswamis) and entrust them with the task of spreading his message, could have laid the foundation of the institutionalization of the Karta-bhaja sect.

Dynastic Succession of Gurus

After Aulchand's death, the first among his 22 disciples, Ramsharan Pal, took over his mantle. According to some, Aulchand himself desired Ramsharan to succeed him,[16] while others speculate that differences arose between Aulchand and Ramsharan, leading to the former's departure from Ghoshpara and the latter's assumption of the guru's office.[17] Whatever might be the origins of Ramsharan's succession, that it led to some sort of schism in the original band of disciples is evident from their gradual eclipse, with one or two among them setting up separate 'ashrams'.[18]

Ramsharan, who was born sometime around 1720 and died in 1783 or thereabouts, seemed to have organized his followers on a firm basis. Given the title Karta-baba by the followers, he proceeded to consolidate the hierarchical structure through a network of sub-gurus, called Mahashayas (the Bengali equivalent of 'Sir' in English, addressed to respectable gentlemen). They were spread over Bengal and they recruited disciples, who were called *baratis* (meaning those who were assigned to a particular Mahashaya). Ramsharan also reinforced Aulchand's directive that disciples had to deposit half of their annual income with Sarasvati. With the rise in the number of Mahashayas and their *baratis*, there was naturally a corresponding increase in the flow of funds to the establishment in Ghoshpara, which under Ramsharan's leadership was developing into a major pilgrimage centre. Writing in the early years of the nineteenth century, W. W. Ward described Ramsharan's rise to power in the following words: '. . . from a state of deep poverty he became rich, and his son now lives in affluence.'[19] The son referred to by Ward was Ramdulal, who succeeded his father as Karta during Ward's time.

Ramdulal (or Dulalchand, as he was more popularly known) was by far the most important among the 'kartas'. Born around

1775, he lived till 1833, and contributed in various ways to the expansion of the sect. He was the first to codify its doctrine in the form of songs (numbering about 500), which are known as Bhaber Geet. They help us to understand not only the philosophy of the sect, but also to some extent the life of Aulchand. He was apparently a well-educated person—known to have learnt Persian and English, along with Sanskrit.

This ability to spread the message through his songs drew an increasing number of devotees into the fold of the sect. It was no longer confined to the rural lower orders. It was from his times that the rich and the urban gentry began to flock to Ghoshpara. One of his important admirers was Jayanarayan Ghoshal (1751–1835), the millionaire Raja of Bhukailash, of Khidirpur in Calcutta.[20] In 1802, two famous Christian missionaries in Bengal, William Carey and John Marshman of Srirampur, were reported to have visited Ghoshpara, and engaged in a religious debate with Ramdulal.[21] Their colleague, Ward, a few years later reported that the sect had more than 400,000 followers.[22]

Ramdulal's fame spread to other parts of the world too—either via word of mouth through his disciples, or more likely by the contemporary accounts of Christian missionaries and European visitors to India, who evinced a keen interest in the Karta-bhaja sect in the nineteenth century. We come across the curious account of Ramdulal being invited, 60 years after his death, to the Parliament of Religions held in Chicago in 1893. The letter of invitation, appointing him a member of the Advisory Council of the Chicago Parliament, and requesting his attendance there, is still preserved by his descendants.[23] Evidently, the nineteenth-century organizers of the Chicago Parliament of Religions—like many among their modern Western counterparts today—suffered from the same communication gap that continues to produce faux pas in East–West relations!

But with regard to Ramdulal, to quote one modern sympathetic observer of the Karta-bhaja sect: 'It was he (Ramdulal) who consolidated the theoretical basis of this sect by composing the songs of

Bhaber Geet, and at the same time, it was also through his hands that the religious 'zemindari' was full established.'[24] The term 'religious zemindari' is the most appropriate expression to describe the institutionalization of religious sects in nineteenth-century Bengal, particularly of the followers of the seventeenth-century preacher Aulchand, by the gurus or Kartas.

Ramdulal, apart from being an erudite scholar, was apparently well acquainted with contemporary commercial practices. The frequent use of business terms in his songs—like 'company', 'merchants', 'agents', 'brokers', 'stockists', 'indigo trade with Arab countries', 'shares', etc. has given rise to the speculation that Ramdulal could have been associated with some trade or trade agency, like many contemporary Bengali banians of the early nineteenth century. Did he reinvest the income earned from his disciples in some trade? Did profits from this allow him to 'live in affluence', as described by his contemporary, William Ward?

It is significant that in the religious idiom of the Karta-bhaja sect, mercantile terms are frequently used as metaphors to describe its practices. Thus, one old song, after listing the names of the 22 disciples of Aulchand, concludes with the sentence: Erai koriloe aashi hater patton (These people came and opened the market).[25] Any religious hermitage is commonly described as ashrama in Bengali, and Vaishnavites describe their monasteries as akharas. But the Karta-bhajas have traditionally used the term *gadi* for their religious headquarters in Ghoshpara, which had seen a succession of Kartas occupying—and sometimes disputing over—the *gadi*. The term *gadi* (from the Hindi *gaddi*, meaning a cushion), beginning its humble journey from the comfortable seat of the local trader, graduated to the cosmopolitan world of nineteenth-century Calcutta to become a formidable epithet for the trading houses operating in the metropolis in those days. The choice of the word *gadi* to describe the Ghoshpara hermitage could therefore reflect the Kartas' desire to establish their headquarters as a religious ally of the Bengali commercial society that was developing in Calcutta and other trading centres under the colonial regime.

Ramdulal also invented a term for the mystic and enigmatic language in which he composed his songs, which codified the religious tenets of the Karta-bhaja sect. The language, marked by extensive use of metaphors, harks back to the old traditional ideas found in *sahajiya* sayings and Baul songs about the hazards of mortal existence in this world. But Ramdulal, significantly enough, termed his language as Tyaksali Boli or the language of the mint (*tankshala* in Sanskrit) suggesting again the contemporary commercial interest in the changing terms of business transactions— from the old mode of exchange through cowries to that of coins. The British had begun to manufacture copper coins in Bengal from the end of the eighteenth century, and set up the Mint in Calcutta in 1830—a few years before Ramdulal's death. In the world of commerce, the value of commodities was getting designated by the new coins. In the world of religion too, Ramdulal felt the need for a new coinage to describe the ideas of the Karta-bhaja sect.

Ramdulal was succeeded by his fourth son, Ishwarchandra (1813–82) who in the words of a contemporary journal, lived 'in the style of a Rajah.'[26] It seems that during his regime, the religious 'zemindari' of Ghoshpara acquired some of the distinctive features of a typical Bengali decadent feudal family. The correspondent of a Bengali newspaper visited the annual fair at Ghoshpara during the Holi festival in 1864, and this is how he described Ishwarchandra: 'Ishwar Babu is lying on a bed. There are a number of women surrounding him. Some are pressing his feet; some are massaging his body; some are lifting food to his mouth to feed him; some are applying sandal-paste on his limbs, while some are garlanding him with wreathes of flowers.'[27] From another source, we learn that Ishwarchandra was at one time arrested, and had to spend time behind bars—although we are not told what the offence was.[28] But from different contemporary accounts, it appears that by the time Ishwarchandra had become the Karta in the mid-nineteenth century, the leaders of the sect had travelled a long way from the days of the poor fakir Aulchand, at whose feet, a hundred years ago, their humble predecessors had taken the oath to lead an austere life in order to spread the message of Satya-dharma. The later policy of structuring the sect on the basis of the organized collection of a levy through the Mahashayas and other agents in a well-developed hierarchical network (initiated by Ramsharan), led to the accumulation of capital in the headquarters at Ghoshpara, which swelled over the years with the expansion of the sect through new recruitment of the urban rich (like Raja Jayanarayan Ghoshal, whose contribution to the central fund must have been enormous, compared to the paltry sum collected from the poor rural disciples), and the local Mahashayas who recruited them.

How was this capital used? While Ramdulal (who appears to have been the most enlightened among the Kartas) might have invested it in burgeoning commercial ventures in the new colonial environment, according to speculations, his son Ishwarchandra apparently dissipated it in what we today would term as 'conspicuous consumption'—pomp and luxury, womanizing, and perhaps some delinquency which landed him in jail!

The next generation of the Pals failed to produce any Karta as enterprising as Ramdulal, or as colourful as Ishwarchandra. The sons and grandsons fought over the earnings collected from the disciples and the pilgrims, and some among them set up separate *gadis*. In 1894, the poet Nabinchandra Sen (who was then posted as an administrative officer in Nadia) visited Ghoshpara during the fair. He found that the original *gadi* was occupied by two descendants, probably Haridas Pal and Birchand Pal, the two grandsons of Ishwarchandra. The sacred tank Himsagar was in disrepair, its stagnant water a source of cholera. A rich female disciple was willing to spend Rs 20,000 on the renovation of the tank, but the two Kartas refused to give permission. After failing to persuade them, Sen felt: 'Their intention was to get the money from her in their own hands. But the Karta-bhajas know that both of them are such gems that once they are given the money, they will appropriate the bulk of it.' He then ruefully added: 'They have not yet reached the end of the third generation. And yet, the descendants of Ramsharan Pal have fallen to such a state!'[29]

The transformation of the Kartas through a hundred years (from the end of the eighteenth to the nineteenth century) was in a sense a religious parallel to the changes that were taking place in the contemporary socioeconomic milieu of Bengal during those crucial decades of the eighteenth–nineteenth century.

Like Ramsharan Pal, many among his contemporaries in the commercial world of Calcutta rose from humble origins to become millionaires in the eighteenth century. Ratan, a washerman by caste, had the luck to be employed as an interpreter by the English, and became Ratan Sarkar, a member of the Bengal elite. Piritram Marh, who was born in a low caste family and traded in bamboo logs, made a fortune when the price of bamboos went up in 1780, and built a palatial mansion in Janbazar in Calcutta.[30] Like Ramsharan's descendants, the later generations of these families continued an affluent lifestyle, but much of the entrepreneurship of their ancestors was lost—just as the Kartas of the later generations lost their original religious zeal and candour. One early twentieth-century historian, observing the changes in Ghoshpara, commented:

> Alas! the sport of Time has led to the proliferation of 'gadis' and . . . improvement in many external paraphernalia. But, there is no more the piety of the past. There are no longer that devotion and love, that honesty, that beauty and grace . . . All that remain are the exhibition of pomp for money only and the futile pretence of power to cure ailments by the magic of religion.[31]

But whatever regrets and disapproval might have been expressed by such observers, Ghoshpara continued to draw crowds of pilgrims, and the Karta-bhajas remained devoted to the successive Kartas. Crucial to this continuing popularity was the role played by one particular woman, who symbolized the 'magic of religion', and around whose figure the sect institutionalized itself on a broad base.

While Ramsharan discovered the possibilities of turning the sect into a business enterprise, Ramdulal provided it with a theological scaffolding. But it was Sarasvati who created the popular base of abiding devotion through her widespread reputation as the archetypal mother goddess.

The Evolution of Sati-Ma

Sarasvati was born sometime around 1752 and died in 1839. She was the daughter of Govinda Ghosh, a landlord of Govindapur village. Ramsharan Pal married her after the death of his first wife.

As we have noted, Sarasvati was believed to have been cured by Aulchand, which catapulted the fakir to the position of a mystic healer, and later the founder of the Karta-bhaja sect. Sarasvati also basked in the reflected glory of her guru, and a number of legends developed around her. According to one such legend, she begged Aulchand for a son, whereupon the fakir promised to be reborn as her son, and this was how Sarasvati gave birth to Ramdulal (six years after Aulchand's death)—a reincarnation of the guru.

When Ramsharan died, Ramdulal was hardly eight years old. The dowager Sarasvati looked after the *gadi*, and brought up her son. She was reputed to have a strong personality, and to disciples and devotees came to represent the Adya-Shakti. Stories of her miraculous healing powers spread far and wide. She was supposed to have cured the blind, the deaf and the dumb, and made barren women fertile. One story relates how a barren woman obtained her blessings and gave birth to a son. But the son was born deformed, and the mother refused to keep him and gifted him to Sarasvati, who reared him up with care till his body became near normal. He was called Bankachand (literally meaning the curved moon—obviously referring to his deformity), and was adopted as a son by Sarasvati, who arranged for his education and marriage, and built a separate house for him near the ancestral residence of the Pals. Pilgrims who gathered at Ghoshpara came to regard Bankachand's house as a sacred spot for paying their obeisance, along with the rooms of the various Kartas.[32]

As her fame spread, Sarasvati soon came to be known as Sati-Ma. This could have begun as an abbreviation of her name in popular usage. Instead of addressing her as Sarasvati-Ma the common people shortened her name to 'Swati'. Thus, what was Swati-ma in oral usage was elevated to Sati-ma in the iconography of the sect.

Although it is difficult to disentangle myths from facts in the history of the sect, it would not be wide of the mark to suggest that Sarasvati could have learned some of the secrets of traditional healing from Aulchand, using locally available medicinal plants. (Aulchand, as we recall, used the mud from the local tank to heal Sarasvati). Working upon the popular faith generated by her initial success in treating patients, she (or her followers) later established her reputation as the mother goddess with magical powers.

While suggesting this possibility, we should bear in mind the close association between religion and the aetiology of disease in the perception of the rural masses. The rural healing system has two aspects—practical and magical. Common sense, or practical healing, involves the use of certain herbs and minerals of known utility. Although anyone can make use of these familiar herbs, villagers often go to a local healer who is known to have special knowledge of how to mix these herbs. The magical aspect of healing consists of spells, charms, touch and hypnotic gestures by a special person in whom the patient, or his/her relatives have full faith.[33] It is quite possible that practical healing (with medical herbs and plants) laid the basis for magical healing in a rural society, where disease was regarded as a foreign presence in the body caused by supernatural powers, or the curse of some god. Basic to this concept of disease was the idea of exorcism—the expulsion of the disease (i.e. the evil spirit, or the curse) from inside the body by prayers and the invocation of God's name.[34]

In this framework of beliefs, the exorcist-cum-healer becomes a privileged intermediary between individuals on the one hand, and the supernatural powers that are supposed to cause illness on the other, between the past, the present and the future, and above all between life and death.

Sati-Ma, having acquired the skills of practical healing, could have combined them with the rituals of magical healing (like charms and spells), and emerged as a magico-religious specialist with functions complementary to both a priest and a doctor.

Perhaps the most interesting aspect of the institutionalization of the Karta-bhaja sect is that over the years, popular interest in Ghoshpara has shifted from the egalitarian messages of Aulchand to the 'curative' rituals associated with Sati-Ma. It is not without significance that the annual fair at Ghoshpara is known as 'Sati-Ma'r mela', and not by the name of the founder of the sect, Aulchand, or even by the name of the sect itself. The mother-goddess has not only literally outlived her guru, her husband, and her son,[35] but also historically outshone all of them in popular tradition.

The Fair of Ghoshpara

Ghoshpara, headquarters of the Karta-bhaja sect, has played an important role in the institutionalization of the sect. Numerous sacred spots like Dalimtala and Himsagar and rooms preserving relics of the Pal family are concentrated in the village and have turned it into an important pilgrimage centre.

Although there are several ceremonies held throughout the year in Ghoshpara (to observe the death anniversaries of Ram-sharan and other Kartas), the main attraction is the annual three-day festival beginning on the full-moon night during Holi. Devotees from all parts of Bengal put up makeshift shelters called akharas in fixed spots, for which they have to pay tax to the *gadi* of the Pal family. Shopkeepers with stalls at the fair also pay a fixed amount to the Pals. Many devotees offer gold ornaments and other precious jewellery at the temple of Sati-Ma as *mannats* (gifts for fulfilling the devotees' pleas to cure a disease, or cause the birth of a child, among other such prayers). All these taxes, rents, and offerings in kind during the annual fairs are an important source of revenue for the *gadi* in Ghoshpara.

Descriptive accounts of the Ghoshpara fair are available in contemporary newspapers from the mid-nineteenth century onwards. All these accounts stress certain common features: (*i*) community feasts where people, irrespective of religious, caste and gender distinctions, sat together to eat; (*ii*) a carnival spirit that embraced a variety of people who congregated there—ranging from disciples to the masses of common householders from nearby villages and towns—who participated in the festivities that were marked by singing, jatras and other entertainments; (*iii*) a convergence of members of different religious sects (Shakta, Vaishnavite and Sufi in nature) who used the fair as a platform for their views and beliefs through a variety of songs (e.g. by the Bauls, the Fakirs and the Karta-bhajas), and sermons (mainly by the Mahashayas who brought their respective groups of recruits to the fair); and (*iv*) a number of exhibitionist rituals, mainly carried out by the pilgrims to beseech favours of Sati-Ma.

The community feasts and the carnival spirit in the pilgrimage centre were sanctified by the religious songs and discourse by village minstrels and preachers, and thus created a comfortable ambience for the pilgrims who thronged there. The community feasts in particular played an important role in the Ghoshpara congregations. The meal served was not a banquet, but the bonhomie of thousands sitting in rows had a mass appeal for the pilgrims. The food that was cooked was usually khichri—the familiar gruel of boiled rice and pulses—perhaps accompanied by a few pieces of fried vegetable. A nineteenth-century account of the fair describes how 'piles of rice are being cooked inside the house of the Karta to be served for the devotees . . .' and expresses surprise at the fact that Brahmins, Shudras and Yavanas (meaning Muslims), ignoring their respective food habits, eat and drink in this place, adding: 'We have never seen or heard of any such thing anywhere . . .'[36]

Another nineteenth-century report refers to the large number of women in the public gatherings at the Ghoshpara fair, and explains: 'According to Hindu scriptures and practice, women do not have any freedom. In all situations and at all times they have to remain dependent on their parents, husbands and sons. But in the Karta-bhaja religion, they enjoy a great amount of freedom'.[37]

Community feasts on special religious occasions had been a common feature through the ages, among members of most of the religious communities, whether Islam or Christianity. A modern historian, speaking of the early church festival of Agape ('Love Feast' held by early Christians) observes: 'Originally, it would seem, the early Christian Love Feast was celebrated either in connection with, or separately, from the Eucharist, as a church supper with the wealthy providing most of the fare for rich and poor alike.'[38]

In Ghoshpara, the 'wealthy' Pal family which occupied the *gadi*, provided 'most of the fare for rich and poor alike' during the three-day fair. What they spent on feeding the pilgrims on the occasion—judging by the reports of the humble menu—was little compared to what they earned from the taxes paid by those hiring stalls on the fair premises, or occupying akharas in the vast mango and lichee orchards, or from the offerings (in the shape of jewellery) by pilgrims at the altar of Sati-Ma's temple.[39]

But the most significant feature of the community feast at the Ghoshpara fair was the shedding of all caste, religious and sex discrimination—unlike feasts organized by the orthodox Hindu gentry on religious occasions, where Brahmans were allotted a separate row and served specially cooked food untouched by any Shudra, and women were barred from joining the menfolk in the public feast. The Ghoshpara community feast, on the other hand, provided the Bengali lower orders (from the depressed castes, untouchables, Muslim peasants and artisans), as well as another underprivileged section of Bengali society—women—with an opportunity of coming together. Almost all the contemporary records repeatedly stress the predominance of these sections of the Bengali population at the Ghoshpara fair. They obviously enjoyed for once the sense of equality with members of the more privileged segment. It was thus a sort of annual excursion for the pilgrims, a convivial gathering full of shared pleasure and friendliness, where they could let their hair down! The daily constraints of living in a highly stratified caste-bound society, the mandatory behavioural patterns laid down separately for the different castes, the fear of pollution among the Hindu upper castes, the discrimination faced by the Muslim peasantry both from their Hindu zamindars and the upper-class ashraf elite of their own religious community—all this was suspended for three days at Ghoshpara once a year.

The next important component of the fair was the repertoire of religious songs and sermons. The Karta-bhaja songs shared much in common with the mystic songs of the Bauls and other similar sects who also gathered at the mela. But there were certain specific characteristics of the Karta-bhaja songs which were coded in an enigmatic language that was understood only by the initiates. To be able to understand the message of these songs, one will have to examine some of the main canons of the sect.

One of the rules handed down from one generation to another among the members of the sect is conceptualized in the saying: *Loka madhye lokachar; sadgurur madhye ekachar*, which means—in public and in society the sect members should observe the prevalent social norms and customs, but in the company of their guru and fellow members they should observe the mode of worship and rituals laid down by the Kartas.

A latter day disciple of the sect who claimed to have acquired some knowledge about the basic principles and practice of worship of its members 'through intimate association', observes: 'the devotees and followers of this religion are publicity-shy and their worship is done in secret. They (however) observe, without any scruples, the generally prevalent customs and rules in society'.[40]

Thus, unlike the other heretic popular religious sects that were offshoots from the Vaishnavite mainstream—like the nomadic Bauls, or even the homebound Shahebdhanis, who are marked out for their conspicuously unconventional lifestyles, the Karta-bhajas did not opt out of the system. It was only in their own gatherings—held periodically either in their villages, or in the Ghoshpara fair—that they were required to observe the tenets of their faith.

Given this liberal and accommodating message of *loka madhye lokachar* for the Karta-bhaja disciples, we can assume that the upper-caste disciples of the sect, all through the year, might have

followed the conventional norms of treatment—like untouchability—towards their lower-caste labourers in the villages, but would
have spent the three days at the Ghoshpara fair every year sitting with the outcastes and others from the lower orders to partake
of a common meal. The permission of *lokachar* therefore seemed
to have suited the gentry which, we may recall, flocked to the
sect during Ramdulal's times. For them, the obligation to discard their caste prejudices for three days at the Ghoshpara fair
could be an act of penitence for their *lokachar* during the rest of
the year.

In fact, penitence was an important part of the Karta-bhaja rituals. Every Friday was set apart for a confession-session by the
members. Known as Daik-Majlish (the assembly of the indebted),
these sessions were prefaced by a song beginning with the words:
'Aparadh marjana karo, prabhu' (Forgive my crimes, O Lord.)[41]

This brings us to the possibility of Christian influence on some
of the rituals of the sect. While the Friday Daik-Majlish is strongly
reminiscent of Catholic confessions, the sect also follows a set of
ten rules like the Biblical Ten Commandments, divided into three
groups of physical acts, mental wishes and verbal expressions. The
disciples are required to refrain from three physical acts—adultery,
theft and murder; three mental wishes relating to the above three;
and four verbal utterances—falsehood, abuses, senseless talk and
raving.[42]

The Christian influence was noted by many contemporary
observers.[43] In this connection, certain observations made by a
Christian missionary, who came in touch with members of the
Karta-bhaja sect in the 1830s, make interesting reading: 'The
founder (of the sect) . . . is said to have . . . become acquainted with
the Scriptures by one of the first Protestant missionaries, either
Carey, Foster, or Thomas. The doctrines and precepts of Jesus
appear to have come home to his conscience; and possessing a considerable knowledge of the Hindoo shasters, he undertook the task
of preparing a new religious system . . .'(The writer was obviously referring to Ramdulal—although he was not the 'founder').

Continuing in the same vein, the missionary described the rituals
followed by members of the sect:

> They meet every Thursday (?) in certain villages, after sun-
> set, two or three hundred together, sitting cross-legged, in
> a circle on the ground. They sing hymns in praise of their
> Creator. Every distinction of caste ceases at these nightly
> meetings; the Brahmin is sitting in brotherly fellowship
> by the side of the Sudra and the Mahomedan. They break
> bread together, and a cup passes round the circle, from
> which all are drinking: doubtless this is an imitation of the
> sacrament of the Lord's Supper.[44]

Even making allowances for over-zealous claims being made
by the Christian missionary, we must acknowledge that there was
indeed an impact of the contemporary Christian proselytization on
the rituals of the Karta-bhaja sect. In fact, records of the nineteenth
century indicate that some of the converts to Christianity in the
1830–40 period in parts of Bengal came from among the Karta-
bhajas.[45]

But from the point of view of Ramdulal (who presumably introduced the semi-Christian rituals), he could have been carrying on
the same eclectic tradition of his predecessor, Aulchand, the
founder, who in his lifestyle combined the behavioural patterns of
a Muslim fakir and a Hindu sannyasi.

What, therefore, was perceived by an early nineteenth-century
Christian missionary as a sign of the hegemony of his religion over
the 'infidels' and their religious sects, could actually have been a
continuation of the tradition of eclecticism in the syncretistic religious sects of Bengal. This tradition was fashioned by the common
people, who, over centuries of invasions, learnt to adjust to successive religious doctrines—ranging from the Brahmanical onslaught
on the prevalent Buddhist religious practices (by the Sena dynasty
which took over Bengal in the twelfth century), through the arrival
of Islam (in the thirteenth century, represented both by the sword
of the Turkish invaders and the benign doctrines of the Sufi

missionaries who came to Bengal at the same time), and to the final domination in the nineteenth century by a Christian power which introduced yet another religious doctrine.

The Karta-bhaja sect differed from other contemporary syncretistic sects in still another way. Some of these neo-Vaishnavite popular religious sects resorted to a variety of sexo-yogic practices in which a female companion was necessary for every male devotee while worshipping. Following the *sahajiya* tradition, the female companion need not be the wife, but could be any woman suitable for the male partner.[46] The Karta-bhaja sect was, however, strictly against such practices, and advocated a sort of austerity in sexual relations. Although, as we have seen, the disciples were mostly married householders (Ramdulal had four wives!), the stress on continence was theorized in the extreme form of a metaphorical dictum which said: 'Meye hijrey, purush khoja; Tobey hobey karta-bhaja' (Only when the woman becomes a eunuch and the man castrates himself, can one be a Karta-bhaja).[47] One interpretation of this enigmatic message suggests that the disciples of the sect must not only annihilate their sensual desires, but also reach a state of ultimate indifference to the material attractions of their present surroundings—freedom from the physical bondage to this earth—to be able to meet their Moner Manush. The *hijrey* and the *khoja* are perceived as symbols—or models—of the physical abstinence (enforced, though) that was required of the Karta-bhaja disciples in their daily lifestyle.[48] A Karta-bhaja song elaborates on this idea—again in an enigmatic style—

> Marar shangey mara bheshey jaye,
> Jeyante dhoritey geley habu-dubu khaye.[49]

> (A dead body floats along with another dead body. If a living being tries to catch them, he will be out of his depth in the water).

The two dead bodies are the impassive *purusha* and *prakriti*, who have reached the state of bliss. Anyone daring to disturb them will get into trouble.[50]

The choice of the metaphor of emasculation could have had another significance also. It emphasizes—in an extreme way—the inherent imperfection and disability of human existence. Every human being is deficient in one way or another. One has to depend on, and share with, a companion, to make up the deficiency. The deliberate use of the terms 'meye hijrey' and 'purush khoja' suggests the prevalent idea of disability and incompleteness associated with the two sexes in their respective roles in the reproductive system. Without mutual participation, the woman is as good as a eunuch, and the man a gelding. In this interpretation, the dictum assumes a different meaning: both are imperfect creatures, and it is this imperfection that leads them to seek refuge at the feet of the Karta. A Karta-bhaja song captures this idea in the following words:

> Kalar shangey bobar katha koy,
> Kala giye sharan magey
> Ki pabey nirnoy.
> Aar andha giye Roop neharey,
> Tar marma-katha balbo ki?[51]

> (The deaf and the dumb converse with each other; the deaf seeks help to ascertain the Supreme Being. But it is the blind person who can see the 'Roop'—the ultimate beauty of the Supreme Being. What can I say of this hidden mystery?)

Both the deaf and the dumb are imperfect creatures, and depend upon each other. But the one who is totally blind—the most helpless among the physically disabled—is able to meet the Supreme Being, because, untainted by the overpowering visual distractions that may sway the deaf and the dumb, s/he is capable of comprehension in a purer form.[52]

The choice of images of the physically disabled in the songs of the Karta-bhaja sect, and holding them up as the best candidates for meeting the Supreme Being, could have been prompted by the fatherly desire of Ramdulal (who composed most of these songs under the pseudonym Lalshashi) to comfort and rouse confidence among the hordes of pilgrims who dragged their physically disabled relatives to Ghoshpara in search of a cure. One such song is about a barren woman. Ever since the circulation of the legend of Sati-Ma blessing a barren woman with a son, wives without children have been flocking to Ghoshpara. Ramdulal's song elevates a barren woman to the position of a helmswoman in the turbulent river of the human existence:

> Bandhya dosh khed nindita tar shei joriye royeche narey,
> Lalshashi koy she nauka chalay, hal thela pal gun danrey.[53]

> (She is condemned because the blemish and sadness of barrenness are entwined with her entrails. But Lalshashi says that she rows the boat, hoists the sail, sits at the helm and tows it to the landing place.)

But in spite of such elevation of the physically disabled to privileged positions in the songs of Ramdulal—the stereotyped blind person or eunuch was assumed to be less sensually inclined, and was therefore expected in the songs and saying to accept his/her fate as the best way to reach the Supreme Being—the pilgrims who had been flocking to the Ghoshpara fair for the past two hundred odd years appear to have a different attitude towards their ailments. They go there looking for a cure for the same disabilities—blindness or barrenness—which are symbols of proximity to the Supreme Being in the Karta-bhaja songs. The promise of a cure held out by Sati-Ma contradicted the philosophical message, and the popular faith in the supernatural prevailed over that of the philosophy.

The Rituals of the Pilgrims

Unlike the private—and often secretive—rituals of the initiated members of the Karta-bhaja sect, the rituals observed by the general run of pilgrims had always been of a demonstrative nature, and primarily with the hope of a cure for the various disabilities and diseases from which they or their relatives suffered.

Apart from the usual sacred spots (like the Sati-Ma temple, the rooms containing the relics of the various Kartas), the two most important centres for a mandatory obeisance by the pilgrims are Dalimtala, the pomegranate tree under which Aulchand sat, and the Himsagar tank from where Aulchand was believed to have collected the water and mud to cure Sarasvati.

If one visits Ghoshpara today, one will find the twigs and branches of the pomegranate tree hung with small clay images of horses and fragments of bricks or stone chips. These are the offerings made to Sati-Ma by the pilgrims as *mannat*. If the ailment is cured, the votary takes off these little symbols of *mannat* and replaces them with more precious offerings—like gold and jewellery by those who can afford it—at the temple of Sati-Ma.

But while the *mannat* at Dalimtala—a traditional ritual—is a quiet affair, the other ritual associated with the Himsagar tank has always been of a rather violent nature, involving both exhibitionist self-flagellation by some pilgrims, and physical coercion of the disabled by the Mahashayas and other agents of the Karta-bhaja sect.

This ritual is known as *dandikhata*. The devotee takes a bath in the Himsagar tank, and then crawls—lying prostrate and dragging his entire body—to the temple of Sati-Ma. The physically disabled pilgrims—the dumb, the crippled, the blind—are also forced to undergo this exercise.

Let me quote in this connection two eyewitness reports—one from the mid-nineteenth century, and another by an observer in 1982. The first report describes how at the steps of the Himsagar tank, the 'sinners stand with one foot on earth and another in the waters of the tank, and confess without any qualms their respective sins before the messengers sent by the Karta, and thus gain deliverance.' But, 'as for those who hesitate in confessing their sins, the messengers (of the Karta) assume the features of Yama-doota (the servants of Yama, or Death), and by raging and storming, dragging them by the hair, and boxing, they force them to confess their sins, and make them immerse in the waters of the said tank (Himsagar) to eradicate their bodies of sin . . .'[54]

A later report from 1982 describes a more horrendous scene:

> A seven or eight year old boy near the steps of Himsagar. He is dumb. A shaggy-haired man is standing in breast-high water, and holding the body by one of his hands is plunging him into deep waters, and after ducking him pulls him up again. The dumb boy, out of fear and pain, is groaning in a hoarse voice . . . This is repeated several times. After every few minutes, the boy is brought up to the steps of the tank, and withered flowers, mud (from the tank) and stone chips are thrust down his throat . . . accompanied by blows and slaps and the repeated command: 'Say Ma! You must say Ma'.

About the reactions of the crowd of pilgrims watching the scene, the same report observes: 'One asks another in a whisper: Did he utter "Ma"? He must have. After all, this is Himsagar . . . One indeed feels pity while watching all this, but then how can you cure a disease unless you inflict a little bit of pain?'

The correspondent who wrote the above report later found out that of the two persons who were forcing the boy to undergo the ordeal of *dandikhata*, one was his uncle and the other a neighbour. The boy's mother was dead, and his father who accompanied him to the Ghoshpara fair (obviously hoping to get his son cured) left the spot, unable to watch any longer (his son's torture).[55]

The rituals at Ghoshpara—which had been apparently observed since the mid-nineteenth century (as our records suggest)—are a far cry from Aulchand's benign message of equality and love for all, or Ramdulal's songs which sought to comfort the disabled by upholding them as symbols of the human potential for proximity to the Supreme Being.

V
BAMAKSHYAPA OF TARAPEETH:
THE DRAMATIST OF POPULAR ANGST

Popular hagiography is usually indifferent to the modern historian's concern for the exact birth and death dates of its saints, to fit neatly the chronology which ties events to segments of time like years, months and days of the Gregorian calendar.

Bamakshyapa, the late nineteenth–early twentieth century Bengali mystic of Tarapeeth in Birbhum, West Bengal, was born and lived at a time which straddled two time scales—that of traditional hagiography, and that of modern biography. In his lifestyle and his messages, therefore, he had to cope with two different worlds—one which harked back to a hoary and hazy past (of legends of miracles attributed to him in popular hagiography), and another which was made up of daily challenges from devotees who came to him seeking relief from the variety of physical ailments, emotional problems or financial difficulties that were emerging in the fast-changing socioeconomic milieu of nineteenth-century Bengal. He dramatized in a fascinating way both the conflict and the conciliation between the values and norms of a traditional, rural belief system on the one hand, and new articles of faith encouraged by colonial commercial needs, administrative requirements and belief in the invincibility of modern science and medicine (that often threatened traditional popular therapeutics) on the other.

Tensions between these two systems of thought belaboured Bengali rural society all through the nineteenth century, but more during the last decades when all the paraphernalia of the colonial administration and ideology had succeeded in penetrating the Bengali countryside with a network of agents in different spheres of civil society. Subordinate officials took over the role of the local village *mandals* who used to arbitrate over local disputes. There emerged a host of new professionals, like doctors who replaced the traditional village *vaids* and faith healers; schoolteachers who became substitutes for the old guru-mahashayas, who in the past used to teach the village children; and lawyers who were found necessary to fight the increasing number of litigations, mainly on land disputes, that were prompted by the newly introduced colonial laws.

This external world of socioeconomic demands intruded upon the internal space carved out by the anchorite Bamakshyapa, whose path of religious contemplation was a separate world in itself, one of deep philosophical questionings and a long struggle to maintain faith in Tara (the image in which the mother goddess was supposed to have revealed herself to him) in continuity of the tradition of the Shakta *sadhana-marga* (mode of worshipping) into which he was initiated as a youth.

In the available accounts of Bamakshyapa's life, we hardly find indications of the year or the month of the events with which he was associated. But the hagiographers never fail to mention the *tithi*—the exact lunar day or night—when an important event like death, or birth, or the acquisition of spiritual power, takes place. Thus, while they differ about the year of Bamakshyapa's birth (the Bengali year 1240 or 1241—roughly corresponding to 1833 or 1834 AD according to some, and the Bengali year 1250, or 1843 AD. according to others), almost all agree on the *tithi* of his birth, which is described as *chaturdashi*, or the fourteenth day of the full moon.[1]

It was the same *tithi* on which he attained *siddhi*, or spiritual power—but we are never told which year it was! There is no dispute, however, over the date of Bamakshyapa's death—2nd Sravana of the Bengali year 1318 (approximately sometime in mid-July of 1911)—since by then he had become famous and acquired a crop of disciples who recorded some of their guru's utterances and the important dates in his life.

Bamakshyapa was born as Bamacharan in a poor Brahman family in a village called Atla on the banks of the river Dwarka in the Birbhum district of West Bengal. His father, Sarbananda Chattopadhyay, was a devotee of Kali and led a rather bohemian life, totally unmindful of his responsibilities towards his family which consisted of his wife, Rajkumari, and their two sons and four daughters. Bamacharan was the eldest son. But Sarbananda was apparently a delightfully eccentric character in his village, as is evident from the fond reminiscences Bamakshyapa narrated to a disciple of his. Describing his childhood, he said: 'In our home, the want of food and clothing made our lives miserable. There was no end to mother's worries. But father was completely indifferent to the domestic problems. Most of the time, he used to sit quietly at Kali-tala (the precincts of the village Kali temple), and occasionally smoked hemp.' The father initiated the son into hemp smoking one day by offering him the *kalika* (pipe), addressing him in the following words: 'You are the eldest son and the best of the family—here's some hemp for you to smoke!'[2]

But Sarbananda was a talented poet and musician. He would dress up his two sons Bama and the younger Rama as Krishna and Balaram, take them around neighbouring villages, and sing songs about the exploits of the two mythical heroes while the boys enacted the stories. They were a great draw at village gatherings, where the villagers offered them rice, puffed rice, molasses and sweets, which they brought back home for the rest of the family.[3]

A non-conformist by the standards of those days, Sarbananda earned the wrath of his caste fellows, when he dared to marry off his widowed daughter. His neighbours rebuked him for disgracing his *kula* (family lineage). Bamakshyapa in his reminiscences described how his father remained calm and took up his fiddle and sang a song comparing his plight with that of Radha, who also had to face slander for disgracing her *kula* when she defied conventional social norms by choosing Krishna as her lover/god.[4]

In his choice of imageries and idiom when singing in praise of Kali, Sarbananda was unconventional to the extent of appearing to disparage the goddess. The stark poverty surrounding him seemed to shape his choice. Bamakshyapa in his reminiscences narrated an incident one year when the family was facing acute distress, and yet Sarbananda faithfully carried out the rituals of worship on the particular auspicious date in the Bengali month of Kartik (corresponding to end of October–early November) when the goddess Kali is worshipped ceremoniously all over Bengal. 'With whatever few ingredients he could afford, my father got made a mud image of Kali, and worshipped the Mother. He made us, the two brothers, offer oblation at the Mother's feet. And then, at the end of the puja, he picked up his fiddle and sang—

> Chokher jaley buk bhashiloy—
> Tui jemon Ma dhoneer beti, Baba temni dhoneer beta!
> Bura brisha, siddhir jhola—ei tomader punji-pata!
> Dhan dibi tor matha-mundu, Babar tarey bisher bhanda.
> Tomar sambal nara-mundo hate ekta, galaye kata.
> Bash-bina shmashan-bashinee, bastra-bina ulongini.
> Anna-bina Trishul-pani paye porey dekhaey ghata![5]

> (Tears pour down my breast. You, Mother, are supposed to be the daughter of a rich man; so is the Father supposed to be a rich man's son. But all that you have as your capital are an old bull and a sack of hemp! I can't make head or tail out of the treasure that you offer. As for the Father, he holds a vessel of poison. All that you have are a skull in your hands, and some more around your neck. Without a home, you have to live in the cremation ground; without clothes, you have to remain naked; and without food, the

wielder of the Trident can only make a show by lying flat
on his back at your feet.)

The words of the song hark back to the irreverent tone of
the eighteenth-century Bengali mystic devotee of Kali, the poet
Ramprasad Sen, whose songs were, and still continue to be, popular in the Bengal countryside. In the same popular tradition of
domesticating and demystifying the deities, Sarbananda in the
above song paid his tribute to Kali by reminding her of his own
poverty and the austerities that she and her husband Shiva had to
go through, according to the myths that are held sacred in Bengali
folk culture. Shiva, although a god, is depicted in this culture as a
lazy good-for-nothing, perpetually stoned on hemp. As for the
'old bull' referred to in the song, it is the bull Nandi who is Shiva's
vehicle on his wanderings. The 'vessel of poison' is a reference to
the legend of Shiva's collecting the poison that emerged from the
churning of the ocean by the gods and the demons, which he drank
to save the world.

When he grew up, and became popular as a mystic sage,
Bamakshyapa in his songs on Kali often expressed the same irreverent tone as his father. In his lifestyle and behaviour, he seemed
to be influenced by the outspoken artless ways and absentminded-
ness of Sarbananda. But, like Ramprasad, his mocking remarks
about Kali concealed a deep sense of hurt at the failure of his chosen goddess to set things right in an unjust world. He rejected the
mode of worship which placed the deity on a distant pedestal, and
chose instead a more intimate means of expressing his devotion
by treating her as a comforting and homely mother, combining a
variety of emotions ranging from a sense of wonder at her power
(the archetypal feminine Shakti), to a child's demand for indulgence, and disappointment at rejection.

After Sarbananda's death, Bamacharan with his mother and
younger brother faced acute distress. Sarbananda had left nothing
for the family's sustenance, and Bama having inherited his father's
habits, had little time to learn a skill that could have helped him to

earn money. A truant from his childhood, he spent most of his time in the environs of the cremation ground and the famous temple of Tara at Tarapeeth, in the company of the various sadhus who gathered there. By watching their mode of worship, preparing hemp for their consumption, drinking with them, and listening to their experiences of religious revelations, the child Bama grew up to be an ardent devotee of Tara, the goddess they worshipped, and he thus developed his lifelong roots in the sacred spot where she was believed to have manifested herself, Tarapeeth, near Bama's village Atla. Like Kali, Tara was one of the ten incarnations in which Sati appeared before her consort Shiva, according to the ancient Puranas.

Bama was forced to leave Atla after his father's death to seek a means of livelihood, first at his maternal uncle's home, and later at other places (in various roles as a cowherd, a cook, a flower-plucker), in all of which he proved to be a failure to the exasperation of his employers. Returning to his village after these unsuccessful attempts, he was reported to have told his mother and neighbours that the call of Mother Tara kept him restless wherever he worked, and so he could not be away from Tarapeeth.[6]

Once having returned to his village, Bamacharan settled down (with the blessings of his mother, we are told) to the life of an ascetic at Tarapeeth. Here, he came under the influence of two Shakta sadhus, Kailashpati (also known as Moni Gosain) and Mokshadananda, who were recognized as Kaulas,[7] according to the norms laid down in the Shakta scriptures. They initiated him into the intricacies of Tantrik *sadhana*. On the fourteenth day of the full moon, Bamacharan sat for his final test, in a session of austere contemplation seeking mystic communion with the object of his worship, Tara, the Mother. He finally attained *siddhi*, the ultimate state of fulfilment, one night, when, according to his claims, Mother Tara appeared before him in all her splendour for a brief moment.[8]

Thereafter, Bamacharan, or Bamakshyapa as he was commonly known (meaning Bama the eccentric, due to his unconventional manners and habit of speaking), gradually acquired fame as a mystic who was attuned to the voice of the goddess Tara (whose messages he claimed to receive every now and then). Among the general people, however, he was more respected for his interaction with the lifeways and problems of the laity, who came from different parts of Bengal to seek his blessing and obtain the miraculous cures for which he became famous.

The rest of Bamakshyapa's biography—as available from the meagre records left by his contemporary devotees—is replete with stories of his miraculous deeds. He succeeded his guru, Mokshadananda, as the chief Kaula or the head of the Tarapeeth temple, in which capacity he presided over the daily rituals and the annual community rites and festivities at Tarapeeth. As his fame spread, his circle of devotees grew beyond the laity of the neighbouring villages, and embraced members of the elite, like the Maharaja of Darbhanga, and Raja Jatindramohan Tagore of the Pathuriaghata family of north Calcutta. But unlike his contemporary, Ramakrishna, who also came from a humble rural background, but settled down in the idyllic setting of Dakshineshwar on the banks of the river Hooghly near Calcutta, where he gathered around him a galaxy of the urban Bengali bhadralok, Bamakshyapa remained essentially a rustic ascetic who rarely stirred out of his hermitage at Tarapeeth. His environment—the cremation ground on the banks of the river Dwarka, strewn with half-burnt human bodies and skulls, with vultures and dogs as his companions—was a far cry from the tranquil surroundings of Dakshineshwar. It was in this ghoulish atmosphere that Bamakshyapa lived, carried out his religious practices and died on a night (in the month of Sravana of the Bengali era of 1318) of heavy rain and storm. Although such foul weather (described as *durjog* in Bengali) was common every year during the monsoon, the coincidence of the outbreak of the *durjog* with the moment when Bamakshyapa died, inspired his devotees with imaginative explanations which evoke images of the powerful Tara. Thus the author of one popular tract on Bamakshyapa (which is still sold at Tarapeeth), describing the circumstances of his death, says: 'Mother Tara seemed to have sent an aerial chariot over the waves of the floods in order to take away her beloved son Bama.'[9]

The contours of Bamakshyapa's life as outlined above lead us on an exploratory voyage through the state of popular religion in Bengal at the end of the nineteenth century, at three different levels: (i) a rural religious tradition of a syncretic mixture of Brahmanically influenced rituals, older Buddhist concepts, and a still earlier, but yet surviving, popular belief in Shakti, or power as manifested in the image of the mother-goddess—all these finding expression in esoteric practices by heterogeneous groups of ascetics; (ii) the experiments of one such ascetic (Bamakshyapa) whose mystical experiences and interaction with society reflected a fascinating interlacing of individualized roots of mysticism, collective rural religious rituals and beliefs, and the secular concerns of the same collective laity—considered as mundane; and (iii) these mundane problems of the populace, dominated by the fear of diseases and death, and the concern for cures and salvation; and an overwhelming anxiety about future insecurity and a craving for relief from it.

This essay is an attempt to explore these three areas and examine the angst of both Bamakshyapa and the devotees who came to him seeking answers to a variety of questions ranging from paths to religious salvation to therapies for ailments.

Tarapeeth as a Shakta Centre

The rural religious tradition which was imbibed by Bamakshyapa was rooted in the past of Tarapeeth—celebrated in myths and legends, as well as both oral and written history. These mythological and historical records about Tarapeeth's past reflected in a large measure the primitive beliefs and customs surrounding the concept of the mother goddess that prevailed in that area, their later incorporation and embellishment by the Buddhist theologians in their preachings and practices, and their still later co-option and transformation by the Hindu Shaktas in their religion. Unlike Dakshineshwar, Tarapeeth may claim an ancient lineage among

Bengal's pilgrimage centres. Dakshineshwar was an obscure spot on the banks of the Hooghly till the mid-1850s when Rani Rashmoni of the Janbazar family of Calcutta[10] built a Kali temple there, and appointed as its priest Ramakrishna, whose charisma turned it into a cynosure of the Bengali urban gentry by the end of the nineteenth century.[11]

Tarapeeth has a different story altogether, and predates Bama-kshyapa's appearance there as a guru (almost at about the same time as Ramakrishna). Both local popular legends and historical records suggest that the spot had for a long time been associated with a variety of religious practices which could be traced back to the Buddhist era in Bengal, particularly in Birbhum where Tara-peeth is situated.

It was during the Pala dynasty from the eighth to the eleventh century, through political ups and downs, that Buddhism flour-ished in Bengal. Archaeological remains like monasteries, stupas and stone images of Buddhist gods and goddesses, as well as his-torical records of cultural exchanges with other Buddhist centres in countries like Tibet and Sri Lanka, bear testimony to the spread of the religion in different parts of Bengal.[12]

Although most of these Buddhist archaeological remains are to be found mainly in the northern and eastern parts of ancient Bengal (a large chunk of which comprises modern Bangladesh) on the eastern banks of the river Ganga which cuts through Bengal, historians have discovered traces of the Mahayana-Vajrayana Buddhist school (noted for its Tantrik practices) in the Bankura-Birbhum area on the western banks of the river.[13] Tarapeeth, as may be recalled, is situated on the banks of the river Dwarka, a tributary of the Ganges, in Birbhum.

Still later, Tarapeeth came to be regarded as a *peetha*, although it does not figure in the official list of 51 *peethas*. It was obviously, then, a later addition—and that too in the local Bengali popular religious belief—probably in the mid-fourteenth century, when the first temple to Tara was built there.[14] But the spot was perhaps associated with earlier Buddhist practices, as is evident from the discovery of relics of the Pala era (eighth to tenth century) found when the earth there was dug up for building a mausoleum in memory of Bamakshyapa after his death.[15]

A local popular legend has woven a history of Tarapeeth which traces it to a mythological past. It is born of a collective memory of a phase of local history in Bengal (probably during the Pala and Sena regimes) which saw a confluence of Buddhist and Hindu myths and deities, as suggested earlier. The legend narrates the travails of Vashistha, the son of the Hindu god Brahma, who worshipped Tara to attain salvation, but could not achieve it. A celestial voice then advised him to go to China and learn the mode of worshipping Tara. On arriving there, he found that the devotees were worshipping Tara, not with the familiar flowers and incense, but with wine and meat. Revolted by their religious customs, which he described as *tamashik* (grossly materialistic), Vashistha was about to depart, when the other god of the Hindu trinity, Mahadeva, appeared to him in the form of Buddha, and told him that the Chinese mode of worshipping Tara (which came to be known as Cheenachar in Tantrik scriptures) was the only way of achieving salvation. Buddha further advised him to go to Birbhum in Bengal, where, on the banks of the river Dwarka, on the completion of his worship, he would find a stone image of Tara. Vashistha readily agreed and arrived at the specified spot (today's Tarapeeth) where on a cremation ground, under a shimul (silk-cotton) tree, he began his *sadhana*, or the long and arduous system of devotion, according to Cheenachara. He prayed while sitting on a seat made of five skulls—those of a jackal, a snake, a dog, a bull and a human being. Finally, the propitiated Tara appeared before him, and granted his wishes. He received a stone image of hers, which he set up at the sanctified spot—and thus Tarapeeth came into existence.[16]

This legend is an interesting instance of the eclectic character of popular religion, which borrows different ideas and rituals from a variety of sources to satisfy the needs—social, cultural, economic and religious—of the community. This is how popular syncretistic beliefs and customs have developed outside the framework of the religious establishments, in different corners of India, mixing elements of Buddhist, Hindu, Islamic, Christian and other religious faiths. This particular legend about Tarapeeth is clearly a locally inspired one, since the available ancient Tantrik scriptures do not refer to any such story of Vashistha's arrival on the banks of the Dwarka river in Bengal. It therefore reflects the popular desire of those living then in what is today Tarapeeth and its neighbourhood, to elevate their cluster of villages to the prominent position of a pilgrimage spot that would attract people from all parts of the country. Such an elevation would make their locality not only a religious centre, but also a market for profitable economic and cultural activities that could thrive on the various needs of the pilgrims. In this endeavour of theirs, they were lucky enough to draw upon the different layers of a rich tradition of local Buddhist and Hindu myths and historical events that harked back to a hoary past, which helped them to establish the claim that Vashistha had arrived at their place.

Incidentally, in a similar vein, inhabitants of a village called Mahishi in Bhagalpur in Bihar, describe a spot there as Ugra-Tarapeeth, and worship it as a sacred venue. They claim that Vashistha came there to offer prayers to Tara.[17] Like Bengal, this Ugra-Tarapeeth of Bihar also is not listed in the original 51 *peethas*. This again suggests how local community needs shape popular religious aspirations, which claim descent from a mythical past, to be able to be a part of the prevailing and dominating socio-religious mainstream.

Interestingly enough, both Bengal's Tarapeeth and Bihar's Ugra-Tarapeeth claim that Sati's eyes fell on their respective sacred spots. Presumably to reconcile these competing claims, the Bengali legends assert that it was only the third eye of Sati (the eye of knowledge located on her forehead) which fell at Tarapeeth.[18]

When we move from local legends based on mythology to those based on history, Tarapeeth offers an impressive list of narratives. The first such story is about a merchant called Joychandra in the mid-fourteenth century, during the reign of Shamsuddin

Ilias Shah in Bengal. Joychandra sailed with his fleet of Mayur-pankhis (ships fashioned in the shape of peacocks) and reached the banks of the Dwarka river in Birbhum, where his son—whom he had brought along to be trained in his trade—died from snake-bite. He was miraculously revived by the waters of a tank in the area, and Goddess Tara appeared before Joychandra and revealed herself as the deity presiding over that spot. Joychandra became her devotee, and built a temple there in homage. Gradually, what was once a deserted spot became a popular pilgrimage place, with people from various parts of Bengal settling down there, building houses and setting up shops around the temple. The earlier settlers were mainly from the Kaibarta caste—boatmen and fishing folk—drawn to the place evidently by the prospect of ferrying pilgrims to and from the temple of Tara. The village which developed around the temple was known as Chandipur.[19]

The original temple was reconstructed and new shrines were added around 1740 by a local zamindar, Ramjeevan Sinha (of the neighbouring village of Dheka) during the reign of Nawab Alivardi Khan (grandfather of the more famous last Nawab of Bengal, Siraj-ud-daulah who lost to the British at the 1757 battle at Palashi, or Plassey), who awarded him the title Raja. Local legends spun around Ramjeevan describe him as an ardent devotee of Tara. He found the temple of Tara in a dilapidated state, and, anguished by the lack of drinking water in the area, he decided to rebuild the temple and dig a large tank. But Ramjeevan's fortunes began to decline from the end of Alivardi's regime (the 1750s), and Tara-peeth lost its important patron.[20]

It took a few decades for Tarapeeth to regain its importance. Around 1776, Raja Ramakrishna, the adopted son of the famous Rani Bhavani of Natore (now in Rajshahi, Bangladesh), took over the zamindari of Chandipur. Inclined towards asceticism and religious meditation, Raja Ramakrishna granted the village as Brahmottor (rent-free land given to Brahmans) to the Tarapeeth priests who could now earn from the land and carry on their rituals, including daily offerings of rice, fruits, sweets, milk and luchi, and, on auspicious days, special offerings of meat from sacrificed goats, which (at the end of the worship) were distributed among the visiting pilgrims as prasad.[21]

By the beginning of the nineteenth century, Tarapeeth had found another patron. The temple and the shrines—built more than 70 years ago, under the auspices of Ramjeevan—were in a decrepit state, battered by thunderstorms and floods which had ravaged the area during the period. A philanthropist called Jagannath Ray of the neighbouring village of Mallarpur, came forward to renovate the temple and the complex in 1813. After five years of meticulous work by architects, masons and craftsmen, the construction of a new temple dedicated to Tara was completed in 1818. It is this temple which today dominates the main complex at Tarapeeth, being the centre of attraction for devotees, with the adjoining shrines and memorable spots (like the shimul tree under which Vashistha was reputed to have attained his salvation) remaining as secondary objects of devotion. A tank in the middle, called Jiyat-kunda, is supposed to be the old magic tank, the waters of which brought back to life the dead son of merchant Joychandra.

Tarapeeth had had a succession of Tantrik sadhus as head-priests, important among whom were Anandanath who was appointed by Raja Ramakrishna in the late eighteenth century, and Mokshadananda who initiated Bamakshyapa to become his successor sometime in the mid-nineteenth century. After Bamakshyapa's death, the position of the head-priest was inherited by Taranath, a disciple of Bamakshyapa.[22] Incidentally, before coming to Tarapeeth, Taranath was a member of the Jugantar group of armed revolutionaries in Bengal, which played an important role in the first three decades of the twentieth century in the national movement against British colonial rule. According to some reports, the revolutionary Taranath came to Tarapeeth in order to be initiated into Tantrik practices and came in contact with Bamakshyapa, who took him under his tutelage. Later, Taranath was reported to have set up an ashram in his birthplace, Baharampur, where he came to be known as Tarakshyapa.[23]

Tarapeeth and Bamakshyapa

The chronology of Tarapeeth's development from myths and legends to modern historical records, suggests a succession of streams of pre-Buddhist, Buddhist, and later Hindu religious concepts and customs—as well as their coexistence and confluence. The motif of the mother goddess which was the running thread through all these streams, was also the motivating impulse behind the development of Tarapeeth as a pilgrimage centre. The mythological stories, and later popular historical legends about Tarapeeth, are marked by certain common features revolving around the worship of the mother goddess Tara. They continued to play a major role in the life and activities of Bamakshyapa in the later history of Tarapeeth.

First, the mother goddess Tara in Tarapeeth had been almost invariably associated with imageries of death—of a macabre nature. Death with its associations—cremations, half-burnt bodies, corpses, bones, skeletons, skulls—loomed large over the history of Tarapeeth, its legends, and later day records of the austere religious practices carried out by Bamakshyapa amidst the gruesome surroundings of the cremation ground there. It was on this spot that Vashistha, according to legends, meditated on a seat made of animal and human skulls. This was again the spot that was claimed by the local devotees and the priests as the place where a dismembered piece of Sati's body—her third eye—fell. It was here again, according to the mid-fourteenth century legends, that the merchant Joychandra arrived with the embalmed body of his dead son, to be resurrected by the presiding deity Tara. The later historical records of the *sadhanas* practised by Kailashpati, Mokshadananda and their pupil Bamakshyapa, again repeatedly describe the physically gross reality of death—the dead body itself, its rotting remains, the burning pyres which dominated the cremation ground at Tarapeeth that was chosen as the main retreat by these devotees for their meditation. According to a graphic account of Bamakshyapa's habits by an observer, who visited his hermitage one day: 'A black dog came up to him (Bamakshyapa) from the burning ghat with a piece of a carrion in his mouth. He pulled out the raw piece from the dog's mouth, bit into it, retained a part of it in his own mouth, and tore off the rest to feed the dog . . .'[24]

The second interesting feature that follows from the death-centred construction of the Tara image, and runs as another common thread through all the myths and legends about Tarapeeth, is the therapeutic role of Tara. The legend about the resurrection of Joychandra's dead son through her benevolence, canonized Tarapeeth as a hospital of sorts in the popular psyche. Tara as the presiding deity over the spot acquired the reputation of curing the sick and reviving the dead. Pilgrims flocked to Tarapeeth, seeking remedies for physical or emotional ailments, and offered prayers to the goddess. Ironically enough, over the years, it was the high priest of the Tarapeeth temple who replaced the goddess Tara as the object of the supplicants who came there praying for remedies. Bamakshyapa, inspite of himself, gradually came to be the mortal surrogate for the divine Tara. For the pilgrims who thronged Tarapeeth looking for nostrums, it was not the stone image of Tara (to which they paid their ritual obeisance in a perfunctory way), but the physical presence of Bamakshyapa they approached seeking guidance, medicines, advice, etc. The goddess Tara was replaced by the mortal godman Bamakshyapa, a role which he tried desperately to shake off.

Bamakshyapa's experiences as the high-priest in Tarapeeth were classic examples of the dilemma faced by the mortal mediator between the deity and the laity. He was caught up between his own priority on the one hand (pursuit of spiritual salvation through esoteric Tantrik practices in his lonely retreat in a corner of the cremation ground), and the immediate daily needs of the pilgrims who flocked to him on the other hand (expecting him to cure the sick, solve financial problems, mediate in domestic crises).

The third feature surrounding the worship of the mother goddess in Tarapeeth that suggests a sort of continuity from the myths, through the historical legends and down to the recorded reminiscences about Bamakshyapa, is the nature of the rituals followed by the ascetics who came there to meditate on Tara and commune with her in prayer. These rituals were cast in a mould which could be described as hedonistic, with stress on sensual and carnal practices. The mythological character, Vashistha, who was the first to come to Tarapeeth in order to seek salvation, propitiated Tara with meat and wine.[25]

Local legends narrate the story of a sadhu who used to worship the goddess at Tarapeeth at the dead of night with meat and wine during the patronage of Ramjeevan Sinha in the mid-eighteenth century. Ramjeevan's objection to this provoked the sadhu to curse him, as a result of which Ramjeevan was supposed to have lost his estates in the 1750s to a local Pathan collector, Ali Lakha.[26]

Bamakshyapa's memoirs about his teachers—Mokshad-ananda and Kailashpati (who lived in Tarapeeth in the 1830s)—as well as the reminiscences about Bamakshyapa left behind by his direct disciples—repeatedly point out that all the three (along with their acquaintances, the managers of the temples, the guides of the pilgrims, the Doms who burnt the dead bodies)[27] were addicted to liquor and hemp, and insisted on the consumption of meat as essential for their religious contemplation and living style. A visitor to Tarapeeth, a few years before Bamakshyapa's death, has left behind an interesting account of his first encounter with the mystic. The moment he was introduced to Bamakshyapa as a youth who had come to learn from him, the old man asked him: 'Have you brought any dakshina (fees) for me?' The flummoxed visitor was then told by one of the disciples surrounding Bamakshyapa that dakshina meant an offering of hemp to which Kshyapa-baba (the name by which Bamakshyapa was known among the laity in and around Tarapeeth) was addicted! When the young visitor pleaded his ignorance of the drug, Bamakshyapa took pity on him, and advised him: 'Then, take the name of Kali, the name of Tara. Her name is the last word. There is nothing else that you can do?' He then—probably trying to explain his unconventional conduct to the shocked young visitor—described his own lifestyle which he shared in common with his disciples and acquaintances: 'We drink liquor and smoke hemp, and lay ourselves down at the feet of the Mother—accepting whatever she wills'.[28]

These words both conceal and reveal a complex rustic mental world. First, let us remember, they were uttered by Bamakshyapa in a particular context. A young visitor comes to visit him for the first time, and Bamakshyapa, assuming that he is one of the usual pilgrims seeking some nostrum from him, demands his usual fee—a packet of hemp! But when his disciples tell him that this visitor is different—a bhadralok from Calcutta who may not be favourably inclined towards consuming hemp—Bamakshyapa tries to withdraw into his shell. He utters the usual rhetoric: 'Take the name of Kali', the nostrum that he distributes among all and sundry who come to him for salvation. But then, he also has to defend his habits (now that they have been revealed to this urban bhadralok), and therefore hastens to suggest that his addiction to liquor and hemp actually helps him to surrender his self to the Mother by lying at her feet (symbolizing the devotee's total sub-mission to the Adya-Shakti—recognized as the primeval female power, conceptualized as Tara). Bamakshyapa's defence of his lifestyle, which sounds almost self-deprecating (maybe, because of his having to justify it to the urban bhadralok visitor?) is, however, typical of the rustic culture of Bengal, where the villagers, encoun-tering an educated babu from Calcutta, would try to evade his curious queries about their habits and customs by glossing over their inner meanings and resorting to the posture of a country bumpkin, pretending to conform to the stereotype formed by the urban gentry of lazy drunkard and hemp addict. In his later encounters with the bhadralok, the rich and the privileged, which we shall have occasion to examine, Bamakshyapa quite often gave the impression of being a gawky sloucher, indulging in practices considered vulgar and uncouth by the gentry, like drinking in the company of the 'untouchable' Dom menials of the Tarapeeth cre-mation ground, or eating raw meat!

Were these acts of Bamakshyapa's mere personal gestures—to shock the dainty and the squeamish among the pilgrims who flocked to him to seek his blessings, so that they could be kept away, and thus prevented from intruding into the unconventional lifestyle of an ascetic who probably wanted to be left alone? Or, did they have some deeper implications—representing a long tradition of socio-religious beliefs and rituals, of which Bamakshyapa was a part?

It should be noted in this connection that there is a predilection for both the macabre and the sensual that runs like a thread from the myths and legends woven around Tarapeeth to the later historical accounts about the sadhus and mystics who chose its cremation ground for their austere religious practices. The stress on ideas and exhibits that relate to death and the rotting body (like the conception of Tara as a fearsome goddess garlanded with a necklace of skulls, or the Tantrik practice of contemplating while seated on a prostrate corpse, known as *shava-sadhana*) which we find in these narratives, is accompanied by an equally forceful emphasis on what looks like a celebration of the earthy needs of the living. This is exemplified in the accounts about the Tarapeeth Kaula head priests and other sadhus who associated their rituals with practices like consumption of liquor, hemp and meat—and even mating with women—ritualized as a part of the Tantrik concept of the *pancha-makar* or the five Ms.[29]

This paradoxical coalescence of obsession with death on the one hand, and indulgence in extreme forms of sensuality on the other, that marks the history of Tarapeeth, is in fact a legacy from a hoary tradition. It harks back to primitive socio-religious rituals that accompanied the worshipping of the mother goddess, and which were modified and incorporated by successive generations of Buddhist and later Shakta cults in different corners of Bengal.

The Body as a Site of Human Destiny

This tradition was rooted in the popular views of the human body, both as a site of sensual pleasures, and as a site of the body's degeneration and final end in death. A symbiotic relationship between these two views of the human body was worked out in the Tantrik texts and practices which ruled Tarapeeth, and the lives of ascetics like Bamakshyapa who lived there. The present discussion, needless to say, is not an exhaustive and comprehensive account of all Tantrik schools and their various ideas and modes of meditation. We shall be touching upon certain main characteristics of Tantrik thought and practice in Bengal as far as they conceptualized the popular concerns and anxieties about the body, revolving around birth, sexual pleasures, sensual delights, physical disabilities, diseases, death and the decomposition of the body, and how these concepts were explained to the people at the collective level, and followed in practice at the individual level, by ascetics like Bamakshyapa. We shall also be comparing the precepts and practices advocated in the extant Tantrik scriptures (traced to the sixth century, according to some scholars)[30] with their popular interpretation by these ascetics, Bamakshyapa in particular, which sought to meet the immediate concerns and questions of the contemporary audience (mainly the rural poor) in the late nineteenth and early twentieth century in Bengal.

The body had always occupied a crucial position in popular psyche and behaviour, provoking the cerebrally inclined among the educated elite to look down upon the proclivities of the plebs as 'earthy' and 'carnal'—and giving rise to the pejorative term *Shisnodar-parayana* (meaning one who is addicted to the needs of only the penis and the stomach) in Bengali literary discourse. The human body was the source of both delight and fear. The creative powers of the human body were paradoxically enough inextricably bound up with the same body's vulnerability to the destructive influence of ageing and disability, of sudden epidemics, or of natural disasters. The ever-persistent rationality of the rural collective mind—as already explained, rationality in the sense of seeking and finding answers, explaining cause and effect, according to the given levels and styles of reasoning prevalent among a certain community in a socio-historical context—led to the creation of a succession of myths and religious doctrines that provided a structured explanation of the contradictions that dominated human lives like birth and death, pleasure and pain, health and disease.

Tantrism offered the lay person a rationale for these daily contrasts, and invited the more daring among them to follow the prescribed practices through various stages of meditation to overcome their troubles and ultimately obtain spiritual powers.

The body as the microcosm of the world was, for instance, postulated by one school of Tantrism—the Kamabajrajan, which was popular in Bengal in the thirteenth century. It held that the universe was created by the union of the female spirit of Shakti (power) with the male spirit of Shiva (symbolized by the linga or phallus), just as in humans the male sperm activates the female womb which gives birth to life. Ever since the creation of the universe, the two spirits have been copulating constantly and creating various forms of life every moment—the process described as *bisrishti* (meaning discharge, connotating that the ejaculation of the male sperm into the female womb leads to *srishti* or creation). The Kamabajrajan Tantrik texts advocated a harmony of this universal *bisrishti* with the parallel act of physical copulation in human society, through which alone the mortals could create and attain salvation.[31]

This stress on sexual union, which is to be found in various Tantrik scriptures, was explained in earthy terms by Bamakshyapa in one of his conversations. When a visitor to his ashram wanted to find out from him how best to educate one's self to curb one's sexual cravings, Bamakshyapa lashed out at him with a string of abuses, and rebuked him:

> How can you suppress fire with education? Whatever you
> use to cover fire will be burnt. What are you talking about,
> you stupid ass? The erotic sentiment, which is primeval
> and the original power behind creation—how can you
> reverse it by education? Is this something to be cultivated
> or taught, like any other external thing? This is the live feeling of the senses. Nothing can hide it. You can teach many
> other things, but this alone is something which never
> needs to be taught.[32]

The sexual instinct was recognized as the charging battery, the main source of all powers in human existence, by the Tantrik theologians and practitioners. To quote Bamakshyapa:'It is because of this, the Muladhar, the root of all powers.'[33] According to the Tantrik scriptures, the Muladhar is located at the base of the spinal cord (in close proximity to the male and female sexual organs). Around this root of Muladhar there lies asleep like a coiled serpent, the latent power of every human being, known as Kundalini. Once roused, this Kundalini creeps its way up to the crown of the head, where through an aperture (called the Brahma-randhra), it enters the brain, when the human being reaches the stage of final beatitude. While generally sharing this common objective of rousing the Kundalini to attain this stage in human existence, the various Tantrik schools had come out with different sets of rituals and forms of austere meditation to activate the dormant Kundalini.[34]

Bamakshyapa in his discourses, mainly among the rural audience, interpreted these Tantrik concepts and recommended practices in a manner which reassured the lay persons that their daily living style, with their sensual delights, daily concern about material problems and moral lapses, could also be in conformity with a spiritual existence. According to him, for instance, Kundalini could arise within the bodies of a sensitive couple, after the happy fulfilment of their mutual sexual desires during their youth ('the time when quite spontaneously their souls become restless in search for partners').[35] At the same time, Bamakshyapa in his framework of human spiritual progress, was considerate enough to allot a space for the intemperate, whom he also promised Kundalini. There were male lechers in rural society who were notorious for over-indulgence in sex, who, as it were, honed their sexual instincts by endless repetition of the act! Bamakshyapa used a typical Bengali rural expression to describe their illusive hope for acquiring sexual prowess through such repetitive acts: *kiliye kanthal pakano* (trying to ripen a raw jackfruit by constantly beating it).[36] The meaning of the metaphor, with its phallic imagery, surely could not have been lost on the practitioners of the art of lechery! They knew through their own experiences—both delightful and frustratingly bitter—that total immersion in sensual delights could not offer them that peace of mind, and hope for salvation, which most of them usually sought at the end of their lives. Bamakshyapa empathized with the plight of these people (both male and female), and sought to explain their proclivities in a homespun theological structure that allowed them also a chance for salvation. According to him, with such people, Kundalini arises following utter jadedness at the end of a life of debauchery. To quote him: 'if you run blindly in one direction . . . At some place or other, you are bound to get knocked down and fall. And then your senses will wake up. That power (Kundalini) then cannot remain asleep, and will be aroused.'[37]

But then, if Kundalini can arise in everyone in the normal course, what is the special role of the Tantrik practitioners and gurus? To quote Bamakshyapa again: 'For the Tantriks, it is a different matter altogether—a long process of cultivation and meditation—to make the Kundalini (in another way) climb up through the various wheels or chakras that are situated inside the human body. There is great fun in it!'[38]

Bamakshyapa felt that by consciously meditating to rouse the Kundalini through these chakras, the Tantrik practitioner can sharpen his/her intellect and establish control over exercise of power.[39] As for the place of sex in this process, the power that lies at its root can be elevated upwards in a spiral movement through these chakras towards the intellect at the apex. 'It is that power which has been at the source of the development of the best talents'.[40]

From this stress, in Tantrik precepts, on the sexual force as crucial to creativity (exemplified by Bamakshyapa through popular idiom in his discourses), there followed invariably an exaltation of the role of woman in Tantrik practices—and in Bamakshyapa's messages for his lay followers. In the traditional collective consciousness of the people, the woman had been the source of creation—fashioned in the image of the mother goddess in tribal myths and practices, chiselled in more sophisticated terms in the theological concept of Adya-Shakti becoming the archetype of female omnipotence, both as the creator and the destroyer).

In the prescribed practices of Tantrism, male followers seeking salvation are required to meditate and observe the rituals in the company of a female fellow practitioner (described as Shakti, meaning power). As opposed to the Brahmanical socio-religious injunctions against women (who were debarred even from reading the Vedas), Tantrik theology not only recognized the important role of women in religious practices, but also appeared to allot them a superior position in society. According to a modern investigator into, and observer of, Tantrik theories and practices: 'The basic tenets of Tantrism not only enshrine equal rights of man and woman, but celebrate the authority of the woman as something which is predestined. The woman is known as the symbol of power, without whom the progress of human beings and society remains stagnant. Therefore, Tantrik practices can never be complete without the woman.'[41]

Bamakshyapa in his own rustic and earthy style explained the concept to a layman:

Just fancy—how these women are preserving life! How did you get to know a woman at the start? At first, she bore you in her womb as a mother, and then in the midst of this creation of the universe, she delivered you at the right place and moment suitable for you, and then reared you up on the life-blood from her breasts, and then you grew up. You acquired strength and power and became a youth and began to spin webs of fantasy. And then you felt as if it was no longer possible to live alone, as if in spite of everything around you, there was a sort of loneliness. So then she came along in the shape of your wife to satisfy all your longings, and your gaze turned towards the newer and newer mysteries of a home shared with her, you got drunk with pleasures—totally lost! You created so much in those moments of pleasure! In her company, you discovered, you came to know so many things about the world . . . After all that, when the time ends, if you pop off, you escape! But if she leaves before you, you'll be left with the burden of unravelling the mystery of what she was for you. Without her—the woman—was there any chance of your coming into existence, of your growing up—and all that you have done?[42]

Here is the archetypal image of the woman conceptualized as the source of creation, sustenance, companionship and continuation of the species, each role of hers given due recognition and respect in a well coordinated and harmonious structure of the Tantrik concept of womanhood. How different is it from the hegemonic Brahmanical concept that prevailed and ruled over Bengali society during the times of Bamakshyapa (and even today)? To quote a Tantrik practitioner who was a contemporary of Bamakshyapa's (living a few miles away from Tarapeeth, in another pilgrimage centre): 'In Tantrik philosophy, there is no difference between castes, communities, religions, etc., except between men and women. In this sense, it is a protest against the Vedic and Brahmanical religion.' Elaborating on the differences between men and women in Tantrik philosophy, he said:

All that is ordained as practice by Tantrism is a protest against the concept that man is superior to woman. Whether a man, or a woman—they can never achieve salvation while remaining alone. From the stage of prayers and meditation till that of attainment of spiritual power, the man and the woman will have to combine with each other to carry out every task.[43]

Disease

But the human body which is the source of procreation and sensual pleasures, as celebrated and conceptualized in Tantrik theology, becomes vulnerable to diseases, falls victim to the physically degenerating process of ageing, suffers agonizing pain and finally surrenders to death. This conflict between the human creative power bred and sustained by the fulfilment of the senses on the one hand, and its destruction on the other, haunted the troubled imagination of the common people. The macabre in their psyche was reinforced by the sight of the gradual decomposition of the body, with the worms from within the body devouring it. It was these people who crowded the environment in which Bamakshyapa was born and operated.

How did Bamakshyapa address these concerns about disease that led people to flock to Tarapeeth to seek his advice? Contemporary records suggest that he resorted to a judicious mixture of pragmatic remedial measures and faith healing, the latter buttressed by legends about his supernatural powers that were propagated by his disciples.

But the success of Bamakshyapa's therapeutic interventions and the cures claimed to have been made possible by him, should be examined in the context of the aetiology of diseases in the perception of the patients who came to him, and the prescriptions that they expected (and had faith in) within the framework of their aetiological understanding.

Let us recapitulate the historical background. All through the nineteenth century, diseases like cholera and malaria (particularly the devastating Burdwan fever in the mid-1870s) ravaged the countryside in Bengal. The constant threat and recurrence of epidemics like small-pox and cholera had driven the people to invent and fashion their own godlings as protective deities—Shitala and Ola-bibi respectively.[44] The perpetual presence of such debilitating ailments and diseases made the people conscious of their bodies, anxious to know how their bodies worked, and understand whether the vulnerability of their bodies to such ailments was due to any disorder in the external world during an era of widespread social and moral degeneration (pre-ordained by the Hindu scriptures as Kaliyuga, or described by contemporary popular Muslim poets as Akheri Jamana), or their own individual physical and moral lapses.

In this state of a popular psyche of uncertainty, diseases were quite often regarded as foreign elements that had invaded the

body.[45] Victims of epileptic fits for instance were thought to be possessed by evil spirits, and were thrashed by witch-doctors to exor-
cise them of these spirits—a violent remedy which may be
explained today in scientific terms as shock therapy. In the popular
aetiology of diseases there was a symbiosis between the concept of
an external evil spirit invading, or possessing, the human body on
the one hand, and the need for an equally powerful remedial external force—faith in their local godlings, or witch-doctors—on the
other.

The invading disease was credited with a soul by a popular
imagination which suspected the presence of living spirits behind
any inexplicable or alien phenomenon, whether a solar eclipse, a
strange animal, or unusual behaviour by anyone within the community. Such 'signs' were immediately feared as omens of disaster
threatening the entire community. Diseases, particularly epidemics, fitted well with the popular imaginary world, crawling with
demons and grotesque creatures always ready to pounce upon
unwary mortals. The fears and nightmares caused by the recurrence of endemic and wasting diseases in nineteenth-century Bengal were more overpowering in the popular psyche than the images
of a heavenly paradise promised by the ancient religious scriptures.

In popular medication, expulsion of these foreign invaders
from the diseased body depended largely on what was considered
magic. Belief in the healing touch of a saint, or in the curative powers of the waters of a sacred tank, or in sudden miracles, dominated
the popular psyche, which felt an overwhelming need to find an
explanation for sudden sickness, fatalities and disasters, which
could be attributed to some evil and mysterious power from which
the victim could escape through a counter-miracle. Here again,
Tantrism offered the common people promises of cures through
exorcisms and spells to counteract menacing forces.

This therapeutic aspect of Tantrism was a part of a wider set
of Tantrik practices, known as *shat-karma* (*shat* in Sanskrit meaning
six), which were primarily meant to satisfy the popular cravings for
material success (as distinct from the spiritual salvation through

the arousal of the Kundalini prescribed by Tantrism for those so inclined) and for immediate objectives, like relief from illness. According to Tantrik texts, *shat-karma* consists of six practices—*shanti-karma* by which one could destroy diseases, evil spells and the malignant influence of planets; *bashikaran* by which one could bring under control other people; *stambhan* by which the practitioner could stop all powers, whether natural or human; *bidweshan*, or creating enmity between friends; *uchhatan* or eviction of a person from his home or country; and *maran* by which one could bring about the death of one's enemy.[46] It is obvious that these six practices were mainly of a populist nature, ranging from the provision of relief from ailments (which were attributed to extraneous evil forces) to promises of retaliation against personal enemies. Bashikaran in particular had a widespread appeal, especially among young victims of unrequited love, who sought spells and drugs from Tantriks to entice the objects of their passion. Wishful thinking, fantasies and hallucinations cemented the undying faith of the laity in these magic spells and miracles.

Miracles as Therapeutics

To come back to Bamakshyapa, by the time he was established in Tarapeeth, his reputation as a Tantrik—both as a cognisant anchorite and as a thaumaturge who worked miracles—had spread far and wide. His popularity in Tarapeeth, to start with, seems to have followed legends about his miracles. One such act was attributed to him as a young boy, when he accidentally shook out embers from the pipe of hemp that he was smoking into a haystack, causing it to catch fire. The frightened villagers rushed to the spot and blamed Bamakshyapa for the conflagration. Stung by the insults heaped on him, Bamakshyapa decided to commit suicide by plunging into the fire. But as soon as he shouted 'Jai Ma Tara!' (Hail, Mother Tara) and jumped into the flames, someone pulled him out from the inferno and whispered into his ears: 'Run, Bama, run!' The crowd of villagers who saw him jumping into the fire went back convinced that he was dead, but, soon after, discovered him swinging from the branches of a tree a few yards away, unscathed, without a sign of burns. The young boy told them that it was the goddess Tara who had taken him up in her arms from the fire.[47]

The next important miracle associated with Bamakshyapa came after his attainment of *siddhi*. On the day of the funeral ceremony of his mother, as the guests were about to start eating in the courtyard of his ancestral house, suddenly a thunderstorm broke out, threatening to ruin the ceremony. Bamakshyapa drew a circular line around the spot and shouted 'Hail, Mother Tara!' with his eyes lifted towards the sky. Immediately the rains stopped.[48]

But despite his fame as a wonder worker, Bamakshyapa in his treatment of the patients who flocked to him seemed to avoid miracles, and depend instead on sheer luck (attributing both success and failure to the wishes of the goddess Tara), or the faith of his devotees (who accepted him as the intercessor between themselves and the goddess, and were prepared to interpret his lost labour also as Tara's will), or the herbs and earth from the soil of Tarapeeth (which were reputed to have curative qualities).

A few incidents, as narrated by observers, suggest a sort of enmeshing of all these various factors in Bamakshyapa's mode of responding to the physical ailments of his devotees. Some of these incidents can be examined in the context of the traditional popular beliefs in miracles, as well as the newly emerging scepticism about the possibility of curing the sick through miracles. Bamakshyapa had to contend with both these forms of the popular attitude that prevailed in Bengal at the end of the nineteenth century. He shifted from one position to another, depending on circumstances, trying to fit the contradictions within a holistic framework that would make sense to his devotees. Describing his patients, he used to say: 'No one comes to me, unless seriously ill,' adding: 'What can I do? Whatever happens, is according to Mother Tara's will. Am I a doctor?'[49]

One of his closest disciples, Nagendranath Chattopadhyay, left an account of an interesting and revealing encounter between

Bamakshyapa and a dying person, recorded by a descendant of Chattopadhyay's. A rich zamindar, Purnachandra Sarkar, of a village near Tarapeeth, was dying of tuberculosis. After all the expensive medical prescriptions had failed, Sarkar's relatives came to Bamakshyapa with an assortment of gifts that included, apart from rice and sweets, liquor and goat meat. Nagendranath persuaded a reluctant Bamakshyapa to visit the dying man and just utter a few reassuring words to satisfy the requests of the zamindar's family. But when Bamakshyapa finally arrived at the zamindar's house, the first words he uttered were: 'What a big house and hall the rascal has built!' When he was taken to the bedside of the sick man and saw him blinking his eyes, Bamakshyapa was even more outrageous and shouted at him: 'Still gawking? Get lost, you rascal! Die, and come to Shimultala!' (meaning the cremation ground at Tarapeeth) and immediately rushed back to the palanquin which had brought him to the zamindar's house. On his return to Tarapeeth, Bamakshyapa was confronted by an agitated Nagendranath, who complained that he felt let down by this uncouth behaviour after he had obtained so many gifts from the zamindar's family for Bamakshyapa. Bamakshyapa turned extremely contrite and said: 'Believe me, I tried to utter the words "Get well" as instructed by you. But whenever I made the effort, my tongue got tied. Finally, Mother Tara came to my help, and asked me to tell the guy, "Die, you fool".'[50]

The episode illustrates a canny side to Bamakshyapa. Experience with different types of ailments had no doubt taught him that a dying victim of tuberculosis was beyond recovery. Instead of making false promises as advised by his disciple Nagendranath, he chose to be honest in his own rustic fashion and predict the death of the zamindar (who did die ultimately).

In another incident, however, recorded sometime in 1890–91, Bamakshyapa was reported to have brought back a dying man from the doors of death by his voice alone. This was during a rare (or perhaps sole) visit to Calcutta, when he was taken to treat the son of a well-known musician, Shyamacharan Chakravarty. The son, who was an engineer with the Geological Survey of India, had come back to Calcutta from an assignment in the jungles of central India, with a strange disease which had reduced him to a bed-ridden, inert and decaying bag of bones. Western medical treatment had failed to cure him. When Bamakshyapa reached the house, he found that a crowd had gathered, with a bier lying ready to carry off the body of the dying man as soon as he expired.

He was taken to the room where the invalid was lying on a bed with his head on his mother's lap. After one look at the surroundings, Bamakshyapa was reported to have shouted the word 'Tara' in such a roar that it seemed to 'encompass all the three notes in music ranging from the 'udara' (the first), through the 'moodara' (the middle) to the 'tara' (the alto—the highest in the adult male pitch), and it reverberated all through the environment, waking up everyone from a reverie, as it were . . . The lifeless body of the son also showed signs of movement.' Bamakshyapa then came up to the bed, lifted up the face of the son and addressed him: 'Look, my child, look up at your mother's face.' At these words, the son opened his eyes, turned his gaze towards his mother, and uttered: 'Mother'.[51]

Looking back at the incident from today's perspective, we can hazard one or two guesses. Was it a sort of shock therapy? The sound waves created by Bamakshyapa's roar 'Tara' could have roused the weak man to wakefulness. Was it a temporary recovery? We are not told about later developments, whether he survived, or died after the spell of Bamakshyapa was over. In the absence of such evidence, the incident can either be dismissed as false propaganda (mounted by Bamakshyapa's disciples), or taken as a revealing case of religious vulnerability to wish-fulfilling hallucination (shared even today by both the rural masses and the urban gentry).

There is a description of another incident, where a couple came to Tarapeeth to request Bamakshyapa to save their ailing child. He asked the couple to cast the child into the cremation ground nearby! While the mother clung to the child, the father, apparently having more faith in Bamakshyapa's curative powers, carried out his orders and left the child in the cremation ground. After they had left, Bamakshyapa called one of his favourite pet dogs, a black one, called Kelo, and sent him to look after the child. According to the eyewitness account, the next morning the child was restored to the parents in good health. When they began to praise him for his miraculous powers, Bamakshyapa interrupted them and said: 'It is the Mother (meaning Tara) who has saved him. I do not have any powers.'[52]

The eyewitness narrative is silent about the intervening period between the casting off of the child at the cremation ground (to be guarded from predatory jackals and vultures by the well-trained dog Kelo) and the restoration of the sick child (at least in one piece, to the satisfaction of its parents). During this intervening period, Bamakshyapa could have left his hut (situated near the cremation ground) to visit the spot where the child was laid down. He could have applied the herbal medicines available nearby, or the alluvial clay of the cremation ground (reputed for its curative value), to cure the child. Or, was it the sheer exposure to fresh, open air that revived the sick child who had been confined all along inside a room? We cannot come to any firm conclusion that would satisfy our present day demand for a rational explanation of such events, observed and described as they are by people who believed them to be supernatural. Much of the contemporary narration of such events is described in a rhetoric that tilts towards total acceptance of miracles, and thus makes it difficult for modern historians to test their veracity.

The traditional faith in miracle cures coexisted with, and often prevailed over, the exploratory experiments with the new Western medication that were being introduced in Bengali society at that time. In popular aetiology, the concept of disease (unlike the contemporary Western scientific and secular explanation) was deeply rooted in personal fears of moral transgression, invasion of the body by evil spirits, or retribution by some disgruntled godling, which led victims to propitiate the appropriate gods, approach religious preachers like Bamakshyapa, or seek exorcisms from local shamans or witch-doctors (who even today carry on the legacy of the pre-Aryan tribal doctors in rural Bengal and offer types of medication which are attributed to their magical powers by the patients). This was the popular method of rationalizing, by making an attempt to link causes (sins, evil spirits, etc.) to effects (ailments, diseases, epidemics, etc.).

It was this concept of disease, part of the popular religious belief system, that could have sustained some sort of physiological and psychological dynamism in the bodies and minds of the sick (as well as their relatives) who derived hope from the rituals, exercises and medication (all recommended to be followed as a strict religious regimen by the shamans). For the victims, it was a 'touch-and-go' situation. If they recovered, they remained loyal for ever to the shaman. If they did not, the shaman could always tell them that it was some transgression in following the regimen that had led to failure.

Death

Closely linked with the concern about disease was the obsession with death, the decomposition of the body and images of the worms devouring the cadavers. Particularly during epidemics, when death conscripted en masse, these diseases appeared as levies imposed by unseen powers for some collective sin.

These sudden outbreaks of epidemics produced a general instability in social existence, giving rise to what today might appear as a morbid preoccupation with the dead among the nineteenth-century Bengali populace. But even in normal circumstances, the rural Bengali collective temperament—particularly the Hindu one—was made hypersensitive by its constant exposure to public spectacles and events involving death. A person on his or her deathbed drew the entire community, ranging from the local *vaid* trying to lessen the patient's pain, and the priest administering the last rites on the one hand, to the crowd of villagers gathered just to watch the process and the paraphernalia accompanying it (the staple of gossip and speculation later) on the other. The collective participation did not end there. Another spectacle was yet to follow. The crowd accompanied the dead body to the cremation ground, where another set of elaborate rituals was an exciting sight for the eyes—the accumulation of the logs for the funeral pyre, setting it alight, *mukhagni* (applying fire to the mouth of the corpse), stoking of the fire by the Doms, till all that remained of the body was the grinning skull! The sound of the cracking bones of the corpse was an additional bonus for the spectators!

Although it visited them again and again, and should have therefore produced indifference, or the contempt bred from familiarity, death continued to be a source of endless curiosity and almost demoniacal fascination among the common people. Since it struck at their bodily existence they wanted to watch with almost ghoulish interest the dying of the body and its decomposition and indulge in hallucinations about life after death. Unwilling to give up their attachment to the human body and accept its reduction to a heap of dust, both in their dreams and nightmares, they were haunted by visions of the dead, appearing in their mortal form, either as benefactors urging them to do some good deed, or as vindictive souls threatening them with terrible punishment for some offence committed against them when they were alive. There was thus a pronounced fascination for the macabre, accompanied by an equally conspicuous obsession with life after death.

This popular necrosis was heavily drawn upon by Tantrik theologians and practitioners who formulated a major part of their concept around death and the dead body. Through a variety of complex and grim yogic exercises, they seemed to look for a way to fight and overcome the fear of death—explaining it in different ways, and always trying as it were, to domesticate the phenomenon as a part of their *sadhana*. Their religion and practice, although too rigorous and frightening for the lay person to follow, nevertheless offered the latter an opportunity (often from close quarters) to recognize that it was possible to come to terms with death.

The body of the dead, *shava*, became an important element in Tantrik concept and practice. The classic image of Shiva, looking like a *shava*, or corpse, at the feet of the goddess Kali, provided the Tantrik theologians with the necessary plank to introduce the cadaver into one of their major religious practices, *shava-sadhana*. Kali's entire image is adorned with parts of the human dead body, her neck wreathed in a garland of decapitated heads, one of her hands carrying another such head, and her waist girdled with a string of severed hands.[53] Each item in this range of cadaverous ornaments decorating Kali, is explained in Tantrik scripture as a symbol of some cosmic law or other.[54]

As suggested by some historians, this image of Kali (or Tara in another incarnation) could have evolved from the pre-Aryan, tribal mother goddesses depicted as fearsome deities presiding over both birth and death in aboriginal societies.[55] The continuity of the macabre imageries associated with these deities from the tribal past, in popular religious beliefs and practices, was the backdrop for the Tantrik theological stress on the corpse as both a source of spiritual exploration and as an aid in Tantrik practices to reach spiritual salvation. There was an elaborate set of rituals accompanying *shava-sadhana*. First, the right type of corpse had to be selected. Bodies of infants, old women, Brahmans, and those who had died of starvation or committed suicide, among others, were prohibited. Then, there was the site to be chosen. The stress was on deserted spots[56]—on mountain tops, abandoned banks of rivers, and most preferably, cremation grounds. As for the time for *shava-sadhana*, the preference seemed to be for dark nights. Unlike most other socio-religious rituals inherited by rural Bengal from its aboriginal past, which continue to be of a collective nature involving community participation, *shava-sadhana* remained a solitary affair to be pursued by the initiated Tantrik in deserted surroundings. The rituals recommended in Tantrik texts lay emphasis on the individual's private responsibilities, like tying the corpse's hair and limbs, accompanied by a number of mantras (incantations), then sitting upon the corpse and praying for the appearance of the Devi, the mother goddess. The Tantrik texts warn that during this *sadhana*, the practitioner would face fears posed by demons, and temptations by seductive females appearing as agents of these demons. Only by overcoming these distractions, could the Tantrik sadhak or worshipper be assured a glimpse of the goddess.[57]

The Tantrik scriptures recommended, and the Tantrik practitioners deliberately chose, the most horrifying environs for their meditation. The funeral spot—*shmashana* in Tantrik texts—emerged as the main arena of their experiments. Incidentally, the term *shmashana* (which today is generally used for the Hindu cremation ground) in Tantrik scriptures had a wider connotation. According to one major Tantrik text, *Nirukta-tantra*, *shmashana* is the place where the human body becomes reduced to fragments, or dissolves—a signification which allows for its interpretation as any site where a dead body is left to rot away.[58] The burial ground, according to this interpretation, is also a *shmashana*.[59]

In fact, Bamakshyapa's body was not cremated, but *samahita* (buried) under the legendary shimul tree where Vashistha was supposed to have attained salvation. It is at this burial spot that the temple in his memory has been built.[60]

To come back to Tarapeeth, although known as a cremation ground, it could not really provide adequate services for a full cremation, because of the poverty-stricken area in which it was located. Dead bodies were quite often left half-burnt, to be devoured by vultures and jackals. A disciple of Bamakshyapa's left a graphic account of grim, macabre spectacles in the Tarapeeth cremation ground, which he traced to the dire economic distress of the neighbouring villagers.

It is this cremation ground where the dead bodies from all the surrounding villages are burnt. The people of this area believe that they will be blessed if they can cast off their skeletons at Tarapeeth. As a result, there is no dearth of corpses here. Every day, five to seven corpses arrive here. During the monsoons, when Yama (the god of death) opens his doors, the daily quota is 20 to 25.[61] Again, during epidemics, the daily number goes up to even 40 to 50.

Here (at Tarapeeth) the general custom is not to totally burn the dead body—maybe because of the prohibitive cost of the logs (needed to burn the body), or some other reason. The relatives of the dead carry out the funeral rites by arranging the burning pyre deep down on the sand banks of the river, applying fire to the mouth of the dead body, and covering up the half-burnt body with sand. Soon after this, the awaiting pack of jackals and dogs exhume the body . . . The jackals and the dogs tear at the body . . . The vultures devour the flesh of the soles and other softer parts of the body . . . One rarely comes across such a horrible-looking cremation ground. Skulls roll around. Skeletons and bones are scattered everywhere. The cremation ground and the paths leading to it are filled with remains of burning pyres, and quilts and mats that are used to cover the dead bodies and thrown away from the biers.[62]

Bamakshyapa spent his childhood and youth in this poverty-stricken cremation ground, was initiated by its local sadhus into the intricacies of Tantrism through rituals heavily oriented towards the concept of death and the body of the dead, and chose to remain and settle down in these macabre surroundings of Tarapeeth. It was here that people of neighbouring villages, and then distant places, dragged their diseased bodies to him for a cure. The omnipresent spectacle of death at Tarapeeth helped Bamakshyapa to remind these miserable creatures of the inevitable end of their bodies, and warn them to prepare themselves for it—if his cures failed them.

Bamakshyapa's approach to death as both an idea and a physical reality can be examined in the light of what Vovelle (while speaking of popular religion in medieval Europe) described as the 'counter-systems . . . which used death to overturn symbolically the hierarchy of power'.[63] In the Brahmanical order that dominated the highly stratified Bengali Hindu rural society, as well as the urban rich and middle-class psyche, in the late nineteenth–early twentieth century, those in power always used death as a source of fear to ensure the docility of the weak. They threatened them with death as a punishment for their misdemeanour, evoked visions of excruciating tortures in hell if they died as 'sinners' by violating the prevailing order, or warned them about their rebirth in the shape of some lower species. These hegemonic religious and socioeconomic forces used death to create an abyss between members of the privileged castes and classes (who were promised bliss in heaven after their death because of their good deeds) and those of the lower orders (who were doomed to eternal punishment in the inferno called Naraka in Hindu religion, because of their misdeeds).

Bamakshyapa, on the other hand, used death as a component of a 'counter-system' that put the privileged orders in their place, at par with their lower counterparts. His unconventional behaviour and outrageous utterances during his visit to the house of the dying zamindar, described earlier, is a revealing instance.

Bamakshyapa behaved in the same way—perceived as heartless and inhuman by many—towards dying people or their relatives who came from humbler socioeconomic homes, as evident from the incident, where he had the ailing child cast into the cremation ground. These accounts reveal and reaffirm an interesting side to Bamakshyapa's personality and his attitude towards dying people and their relatives. Always desisting from any promise of a miracle cure, he sought with his brusque and dismissive behaviour to help them face death with a certain equanimity, to treat it as a terminus of all human experience—without either any hope of heavenly bliss or any fear of punishment in hell. If they survived death, it was sheer luck—which he attributed to the blessing of the goddess Tara. If they happened to die, there was no hell or heaven, but the lap of Mother Tara which took them back from their earthly existence—the existence which was bequeathed to them by the Mother herself. It was the return of the body to its source, from dust to dust! As one song of Bamakshyapa's expressed it in terms of his own hope:

Kshyapa moribey aar jabey Brohmey milaye,
Deha-sukh bhog saar,
Dui chari pal ayu taar,
Tar beshi nahe rey,
Moribo, aar omni jabo shunye milaye.[64]

(Kshyapa will die and dissolve into Brohmo, the wide universe. Mere physical pleasures and sensual enjoyment last
for a few minutes, and not more than that. I'll die and soon
enough I'll get dissolved into empty space.)

While acknowledging the position of authority enjoyed by
death in the 'hierarachy of power' by its ability to put an end to
human life, Bamakshyapa deflated the power of death by reducing
it to the role of a partner in a game of dice as long as life survived.
His insistence on meditating in the cremation ground, surrounded
by endless reminders of death, was a sort of challenge which
turned the fear of death into a defiance of death. This was in the
tradition of the old Tantrik practitioners who tried to overcome the
fear of death by internalizing the gruesome images related to
death—living among the dead and hallucinating about encounters
with the spirits of the dead.

For the Tantrik theologians, the cremation ground is the mirror image of the human being itself. While in the cremation
ground the physical body reaches dissolution, the emotions, the
cravings and attachments inside the human being are also van-
quished and reduced to non-entities by the austere meditation of
the Tantrik ascetic. Thus, death is a partner of the ascetic's soul.
While death disintegrates the physical body, the human will
destroys the passions that keep the body attached to material interests—thus paving the way for the return of the human soul to the
mother goddess. So, the *shmashana* exists within the being of the
ascetic; and there resides the goddess (Tara) who offers salvation
to the devotee.[65]

A song which Bamakshyapa was fond of singing, summed
up in his typically irreverent and facetious style this process of

internalizing death and its appendages. The following excerpt from the song is illustrative:

> Bhuter rajye kori baas, bhut dekhey tai hoy na traas,
> E deha bhuter-i baas, sada bhutey bhutey larai karey.[66]

> (I live in the kingdom of ghosts. So, I don't get scared by ghosts. This body of mine is inhabited by ghosts. They keep on fighting among themselves.)

Drugs and Hallucination

Delight in sensual pleasures (a large part of which involved sexual procreation) coexisted in a tense relationship with fears about the ever-present predatory diseases and the haunting spectre of death in the Bengali rural psychology of the late nineteenth–early twentieth century. Although the same concerns may be dominating the minds of most people today, whether rural or urban, some among them can stave off diseases, or even death, for some time at least, thanks to modern medication. Such facilities were unknown, or inaccessible, to villagers in those days. They therefore sought both physical and emotional solace in another direction.

In Bengali rural society of the period, the strong interest in matters like sex and procreation, the collective neurosis about diseases and ailments, and the general necromancy surrounding death were supported by another obsession—addiction to alcohol and drugs. Contemporary narratives about Bamakshyapa and his environment might well suggest that rural life was ruled by the quartet of satyriasis, neurosis, necrosis and narcosis.

But intoxication—with either drugs or drinks—was an essential part of living among the poor. It could have had a two-fold purpose. One, as an escape from the toil, tedium and utter helplessness of their lives, from their physical weariness at the end of a hard day's work. It also helped them reinterpret reality through hallucinations—discovering mysterious meanings in some sudden happening in their mundane surroundings, taking flight from that into wishful dreams and visions, where the divinities were conjured up in human form to soothe them or bless them with promises. Artificial paradises were thus opened up to them, which they could inhabit as long as the intoxicants allowed them to fantasize, before the euphoria slowly sank into somnolence. Visions of the supernatural and miracles that are associated with the life of Bamakshyapa could perhaps be traced to the consumption of hemp and alcohol, both of which he and his followers were extremely fond of.

In fact, drugs were an age-old part of the Bengali rural psyche. The archetypal image of the god Shiva, as conceived by Bengali folk poets in the narrative balladic Mangal-kavyas invariably depict him as a corpulent and indolent hemp smoker, leading a bohemian life, spending most of his time in the cremation ground carousing with a Domni—a girl from the Dom community. Even today, anyone visiting a cremation ground anywhere in Bengal is sure to find a ragged hermit taking a long puff from a 'chhoto kolke' (the term for the small bowl used to hold hemp), or a group of Doms drinking 'deshi maal' (cheap, strong country liquor), offered to them by the relatives of the dead, whose bodies they are required to burn. While stoking the funeral pyre, they take off occasionally for swigs from the bottles of deshi maal.

In the poor peasant's life, intoxication and hallucination were thus tightly bound in an inseparable symbiotic relationship. Nor was drug-induced hallucination peculiar to the poor of the Bengal countryside. Writing about medieval Europe, one modern scholar observes: 'Oscillating between narcosis and neurosis, the poverty-stricken society of the past sunk into a fantastic universe of high potential. The nocturnal deliria were piled together with the daytime intoxications and obsessions in order to build a particularly adaptable dream machine'.[67]

This was the rural equivalent of today's television soap operas or glossy commercial advertisements which form the 'dream machine' in the urban metropolis. The difference, however, is that while the latter is manufactured by powerful commercial interests from outside who exploit their consumers for profit, the fantasies and visions dreamt and circulated by mystics like Bamakshyapa were part of a collective consciousness that hallucinated and invented phantoms, and believed in the supernatural. There was a collaboration between the guru or shaman and the consumers in the rural environment where Bamakshyapa operated, where both were more or less at the same economic level, unlike the huge gap that separates today's 'shamans' in the advertising world and their target audience.

Hallucination was necessary for the poor to remain human in the utterly inhuman and degrading circumstances in which they lived. Bamakshyapa recognized this popular need for a 'dream machine' among the starving and diseased poor who surrounded him—the Doms of the cremation ground who could escape the mental stupor and emotional insensitivity that resulted from their daily occupation of burning corpses only by drinking and dreaming; the disabled who had no hope of recovery from incurable diseases, and could only dream of miracles; the toiling peasants who could overcome their daily despondency only by fantasizing about a brighter future. Bamakshyapa, in his usual style, legitimized this space for popular dreams—a vast space which ranged from collective auto-suggestions, wishful thinking and make-believe on the one hand, to visual fallacies like individual hallucinations and frenzies on the other. The need for intoxicants to reach these various stages of imagination—already prevalent among the rural poor—was validated and given a religious sanction by Bamakshyapa in his *sadhana* and personal lifestyle. He made no bones about his addiction to intoxicants, both hemp and liquor.

As discussed earlier in the section on the development of Tarapeeth as a Shakta centre, liquor was one of the five items (*panchamakar*) required for Tantrik rituals, and had to be consumed during particular ceremonies. In Tantrik scriptures, *madya* is described as a liquor that delights the soul during the *sadhana*. According to these texts, ananda, or bliss, is the image of Brohmo, which is situated in the human body. *Madya* is necessary to express that

ananda—and that is why the ascetics drink *madya*.[68] The ancient
Tantrik texts also recommended the ways of making *madya* by dis-
tillation from a variety of materials ranging from date palm and
molasses to rice.[69]

Bamakshyapa fell back on this Tantrik tradition to justify his
lifestyle, and also to be able to address the various needs of those
who came to seek his advice. Judging from his demands made in
public for hemp or liquor from his supplicants it seems that he
needed these intoxicants to stimulate his imagination (and quite
often hallucinatory powers), which helped him to repose his faith
in Tara despite adversities. In this respect, he was a faithful representative of the rural poor who surrounded him. The latter
required intoxicants to create a mood that could compensate for
their material wants, and help them survive poverty. Similarly,
Bamakshyapa in all probability, depended on liquor and hemp to
overcome his nagging doubts about the justice of the divinity
whom he worshipped, and to re-inforce his faith in her. There were
indeed moments of doubts and scepticism in his life. In the highly
respected pilgrimage centre of Benaras (where the young Bamakshyapa was once taken by his guru Mokshadananda for a brief
visit), he was reduced to such a state of impoverishment, and was
so disillusioned by the mercenary character of the people around
him, that he broke into a song addressing the goddess Tara:

> Sadaanander ghorey thako go sadaa,
>   Key naam rekhechhey Annada?
> Anna bina deho kampichhey sarboda
> Ogo bhababhoy binashini.[70]

(You always live in the homes of the happy rich; why then
are you called Annada—the giver of food? Without food,
my body is shivering, oh you who are known to destroy all
earthly evils!)

Some of the verses in the Tantrik texts appear to encourage indulgence in unrestrained drinking among the ascetics (these,
of course, are interpreted by later scholars as metaphorical

expressions of ways to achieve spiritual bliss), while other such Tantrik tracts lay down strict rules against excessive drinking by the devotees.[71]

Bamakshyapa, being an extremely canny observer of human behaviour, knew where to draw the line between unbridled expressions of his alcohol-driven mood—which he could afford to indulge in among his rural followers—and the need for restraint when he was being patronized by the urban rich of Calcutta. Some among the latter, during the last decade of the nineteenth century, were gravitating towards him thanks to his reputation as a thaumaturge! There is one interesting episode described during his brief stay in Calcutta in the 1890s, when he was being hosted by Jatindramohan Tagore of the Pathuriaghata Raj family. While visiting the home of a Tantrik preceptor, Bamakshyapa was reported to have polished off three bottles of liquor at one go, and yet remained steady! When asked how he could continue to be sober, in his typical manner he replied: 'Why, were those three bottles tipsy with all that liquor inside them?'[72]

Apparently facetious, these words of Bamakshyapa's, however, hark back to old Tantrik precepts, which said that liquor inside the body led to the mental steadfastness that guided the mind in one fixed direction—the objective of the devotee's *sadhana*, to reach the goal.[73] Liquor indeed helped the Tantrik practitioners to firm up their minds and conquer fears and revulsion during the rigorous and macabre rituals they were required to carry out in cremation grounds. Like the bottles of liquor, the human body also could be the container of liquor that made the mind stand still, overcome fears and distractions, and devote itself to one single objective.

Alcohol and drugs, therefore, in the life of the Tantrik acolyte, served the dual socio-religious purpose of stimulating ecstasy on the one hand, and strengthening the regimen required for austere practices on the other. They helped hallucinate a paradise, achieve a euphoric state of mind that imagined communion with the mother goddess, and stiffen the nerves to remain steadfast in *sadhana* despite adversities and distractions.

From Maverick to Institution

Bamakshyapa combined in himself a number of roles that reflected the coexistence of several stages of religious development in contemporary Bengali rural society.

He was operating in an environment where animistic, polytheistic and monotheistic beliefs rubbed shoulders with each other. The Santhal tribals in the villages in the neighbourhood of Tarapeeth, endowed the inanimate objects around them—stones, trees, food, the weapons and ornaments they used—with souls, and worshipped them. The peasants who came from the lower castes, the middle-class farmers and traders, and the various artisan classes, worshipped a polymorphous assembly of deities and godlings, ranging from the established Hindu divinities like Shiva, Durga, Lakshmi, Saraswati, to those representing their professions (like Vishwakarma, the god of the artisans) or goddesses who had to be appeased to prevent diseases (like Shitala and Ola-bibi). Among these same villagers one could come across practising Vaishnavas, who would worship only Vishnu, or Shaktas devoted totally to the goddess Shakti (in the image of Kali), who could be described as approximating to a monotheism of sorts. What all of them held in common was the belief in spirits and supernatural powers. The construction of these beliefs was an attempt to anthropomorphize the world and elements in order to make sense of them, to explain unforeseen events like natural disasters or unexpected occurences in personal life, like sudden death or financial loss, and attribute them to unseen superhuman forces.

It was these villagers who primarily came to Tarapeeth to seek answers to their problems, whether physical, material or spiritual, from Bamakshyapa. He responded by trying to appeal to these different layers of their existence and consciousness. At one level, he acted as a shaman, the traditional religious maverick who is believed to acquire special powers of divination through his own initiative and to possess certain special gifts such as healing. The shaman is unlike the priest who is the officially appointed representative of a recognized ecclesiastical organization, who interprets religious laws and administers ceremonies according to its scriptures. The shaman acquires religious power over the community by going through rigorous and austere practices in his personal life, mostly in isolation, the reports and legends about which are spread far and wide by his devotees. It is this reputation as an austere ascetic and a miracle-making thaumaturge which Bamakshyapa gained through his solitary *sadhana* in the macabre environs of the cremation ground of Tarapeeth. His interpretation of Tara was a highly individualized and personal one. Like a shaman again, Bamakshyapa served as a therapeutic-religious leader in the community—a faith healer whose techniques were primarily rooted in a spiritual rather than a microbiological concept of disease. The rural people who believed in spirits and supernatural forces, which they felt were responsible for their ailments, looked upon Bamakshyapa as a demiurge who, on their behalf, would intervene to influence these forces, as he was supposed to have special powers to divine the will of Tara.

The position of a shaman in rural society provides a socially approved role for the otherwise eccentric personalities in that society, whose unconventional behaviour is pardoned because of the special gifts that they possess. Bamakshyapa, therefore, could get away with the most shocking gestures and utterances, some of which at times amounted to direct insults to the revered deities. During his (probably) only brief stay in Calcutta, he was persuaded to visit the famous temple of Kali at Kalighat. But the strict protective circle set up by the orthodox temple priests around the heavily bejewelled image of the goddess, that prevented him from approaching her, repelled him, and he was said to have shouted at them: 'I don't want your monstrous Kali! I'd rather go back to my simple and sweet Mother Tara!'[74] His reaction was that of the typical rural migrant to the city who, after the initial exposure to its affluence and restrictions, resorts to a systematic disobedience of those newfangled regulations, and, if he has a chance, finally withdraws to his village home.

Back home in Tarapeeth, Bamakshyapa represented the intermediate agent who in a semi-literate society intervenes between the quotidian anxieties of the illiterate laity and the spiritual concerns of higher religion, between the popular faith in magical cures and the modern medical claim of scientific treatment, between the demands of the common people and the requirements of the modern state.

We thus find Bamakshyapa explaining to his rural devotees, in their familiar language of rustic imageries and metaphors, the deeper philosophical questions of body and soul as found in the sophisticated belief system of the Tantras. We also find him often intervening in disputes between his disciples and the local administration, where he discards his role as a purely religious guru. Instead of trying to wield his influence as a godman (which he knew very well would not work in those disputes), he displayed the cunning powers of survival which he had to cultivate as a poor villager, by suggesting a judicious compromise. When his disciple Nagendranath Chattopadhyay was once arrested by the police on some charges, he advised him to work out a suitable arrangement that would save him.[75]

At the religious level of his operations, he had to cope with both the Vaishnava and the Shakta streams which coexisted in his milieu. Bamakshyapa tried to accommodate both in his religious discourses in a sort of syncretistic synthesis. We learn from one of his direct disciples that 'in order to prevent his devotees from being contaminated by the ill-effects of sectarianism, he used to sing Hari's (Vishnu's) praises before his Shakta disciples and Tara's praises before his Vaishnava disciples.'[76] This was in the tradition of the eighteenth-century Bengali mystic Shakta poet Ramprasad, who often tried to present the naked turbulent Kali and the flute-playing Krishna as one and indivisible, as in the following lines:

Natobar beshe Brindabaney
Kali holey Rashbehari

. . .

Chhilo bibasana koti   Ebe peetadhoti
Elo chul   chura bangshidhari.[77]

(In the garb of a dancer, Kali in Vrindavana becomes
Krishna, who sports amorously in the Rasa festival . . . Earlier there was no cloth around the waist, now there is a yel-
low loincloth. The dishevelled hair has been braided into
a plume on the head of the flute-player.)

By way of explanation, it may be necessary to point out
that these two powerful popular religious streams in Bengal—
Vaishnava and Shakta—had more often converged than engaged
in violent conflicts, as in some other parts of India. To both the
Vaishnava and Shakta traditions in Bengal, the central role of
woman was common: Radha in the former, and Kali/Durga/Tara
in the latter.[78]

The same disciple of Bamakshyapa's, whom we quoted earlier,
tells us: 'The Master never showed any hostility towards the
religions of Muhammad and Christ,' and adds that he narrated to
one of his favourite disciples, Chhoto Kshyapa, the intricacies of
the 'Muhammadi' religion. He used to call this disciple 'Mianji
Taslimat'.[79]

Bamakshyapa, therefore, was looked upon by those who
flocked to him as a sort of subordinate agent of the goddess Tara,
and a privileged intermediary between spirits and human beings,
between the past, the present and the future, between life and
death, between the mundane requirements of the individual and
the higher spiritual concerns of philosophy.

This symbiosis, at a certain historical juncture, between popular religious beliefs and expectations on the one hand, and the
interventionist capacity of a particular religious personality on
the other, was not peculiar to the life history of Bamakshyapa. It
has spawned innumerable stories (some authentic, some fictitious)
and legends about other such personalities, which make the stuff
of popular hagiography. Among the subjects of such hagiography, the most prominent contemporary of Bamakshyapa's was
Ramakrishna Paramhamsa.

Both Bamakshyapa (1833?–1911) and Ramakrishna (1836–86)
shared certain common traits. But the differences were more

striking. Both came from a humble rural background. In their religious careers, both were said to have shown propensities towards mystical ecstasy during childhood; both claimed to have had visions of the mother goddess Kali; both were initiated into Tantrik rites. Ramakrishna was guided by a woman Tantrik, Bhairavi, while Bamakshyapa almost at the same time was being trained and initiated by the two Kaulas of Tarapeeth, Kailashpati and Mokshadananda. The teachings of both were marked by a certain catholicity, drawing upon Shakta, Vaishnava and other faiths. But, while Bamakshyapa spent his childhood in and around the cremation ground of Tarapeeth, where he received his initiation and stayed for the rest of his life, Ramakrishna came to Calcutta at the early age of 16, grew up in urban surroundings, and was later appointed a priest at Rani Rashmoni's temple at Dakshineshwar, near the city, which was the main site of his religious experiences. Nothing could be farther removed from Tarapeeth than Dakshineshwar. Its beautifully laid out flower garden and orchard, in the midst of which the temple stood looking down upon the marble steps of the bathing ghat beside the quietly flowing Hooghly, was a far cry from the stark and gruesome environs of the cremation ground at Tarapeeth, with jackals prowling among grinning skulls, past which flowed the river Dwarka choked with half-burnt bodies. The contrast between Dakshineshwar and Tarapeeth still persists—albeit in a different form—as will be evident to anyone visiting those sites today.

The followers of these two contemporary religious preachers were also different in their socioeconomic habits—a factor which had major implications for the future historian's task of reconstructing the life stories of Bamakshyapa and Ramakrishna. Those who flocked to Bamakshyapa primarily consisted of the rural poor and middle-class farmers from neighbouring villages, and the semi-literate traders from the suburbs around Tarapeeth. On the other hand, although Ramakrishna attracted all classes of people, the core of his direct disciples and followers was formed by the Calcutta-educated and salaried Bengali middle-class bhadralok—government employees, clerks, teachers, lawyers, medical practitioners, etc. It was one of them—Mahendranath Gupta, headmaster of a Calcutta school—who became Ramakrishna's Boswell, and chronicled his sayings in a well-maintained diary which was published (much after Ramakrishna's death) as *Ramakrishna Kathamrita*. Besides, several disciples and contemporaries, all highly educated Bengali bhadralok, had left behind reminiscences about Ramakrishna in written records. They remain the main source for all historians of Ramakrishna's life and experiences.

When we come to Bamakshyapa, we face a problem. We do not have any 'Bamakshyapa Kathamrita', or collection of his sayings, recorded by any contemporary of his, which would be acceptable by modern historians as authentic sources. Most of the sources relating to Bamakshyapa's life and exploits are hearsay and legend, which are even today circulated orally among the unlettered and semi-literate populace of Tarapeeth. Among his direct disciples, to my knowledge very few seem to have put down their reminiscences in writing, with the exception of Haricharan Gangopadhyay whose *Sree Bam-leela* was published in 1934. The disciple who was the closest to Bamakshyapa was Nagendranath Chattopadhyay, who also acted as his agent and looked after his public relations, and whom Bamakshyapa used to fondly call Lagen Kaka (Lagen being a corruption of Nagen in the rural dialect of Birbhum). Nagendranath's grandson, Shambhukinkar Chattopadhyay has published books on Bamakshyapa (*Tarasharan Bamacharan* being the major one, which came out in 1972), based on Nagendranath's reminiscences handed down to his descendants. These oral and written sources, while more or less corroborating the main events in Bamakshyapa's life and highlighting his idiosyncracies, often tend to be hagiographic by accepting and elevating the miracles attributed to him by popular imagination and devotion.

In contrast, we come across a more objective, yet sympathetic, description of Bamakshyapa's life and behaviour (during his last years sometime in the first decade of this century, before his death in 1911), by a young painter roaming the country in search of Tantrik preachers: Promode Kumar Chattopadhyay. The painter, in the course of his adventures, landed up at Tarapeeth, and had several long sessions of interviews with Bamakshyapa. The recording of these interviews, along with his graphic descriptions of Bamakshyapa's mercurial moods and behaviour, forms only one chapter of Chattopadhyay's fascinating book (*Tantrabhilashir Sadhusanga*) about his encounters with various Tantrik gurus in different parts of Bengal at the turn of this century. But this single chapter throws enough light on how Bamakshyapa in his own individualistic way was trying at one level to grapple with deep spiritual questions, as well as at another level attempting to address the existential queries and problems his rural audience confronted him with.

But despite the contrast in the environs of their experiments and the differences in the composition of their followers, the legacies left behind by both Ramakrishna and Bamakshyapa shared a common fate. Like Ramakrishna, Bamakshyapa also underwent what Toynbee once described as a 'posthumous transfiguration in the crucible of their followers' memories'.[80] Both were institutionalized by their votaries.

But the process of institutionalization in each of the two cases also shows distinct characteristics that were peculiar to the respective followers of the two preachers. It was through the efforts of Ramakrishna's most dynamic disciple, the English-educated scion of a well-known Calcutta family, Narendranath Dutta-turned-Vivekananda, that the Ramakrishna Mission emerged to institutionalize the departed anchorite's authority. Ramakrishna's approach to salvation, which laid stress on devotion to a personal deity (Kali) through prayer, meditation and acts of individual propitiation, was transmuted into the Mission's ideal of collective social activism and philanthropy combined with religious preaching. From the old temple at Dakshineshwar on the eastern side of the Hooghly, the activities of the disciples soon spread to Belur on its western bank, where a new palatial temple, constructed in memory of Ramakrishna, became the headquarters of the Mission. This was followed by a proliferation of temples and offices all over India, financed mostly by devotees in the West and manned by dedicated sannyasis of the Mission. Today, it boasts of a huge network of branches all over the world, the perennial authority of Ramakrishna having been invested in a living corporation and an organized priesthood.

Bamakshyapa had no Mahendranath Gupta among his followers who could record his sayings according to the modern norms of a written diary. More importantly, he did not have a Vivekananda among his devotees to interpret and spread his homespun preachings, both in India and abroad—that too, in English!

But, although nowhere near the massive scale of the institution-building programme undertaken by the Ramakrishna Mission, Bamakshyapa's followers—mainly from the suburban Bengali middle class, and without the benefit of international publicity and funding—have also tried in their humble way to canonize their guru. The lead was given by his trusted disciple, Nagen Chattopadhyay, who after Bamakshyapa's death deified him and created a hagiography around him, investing him with superhuman authority—and thereby also asserting his personal claim to be the sole repository of Bamakshyapa's legacy.

From a small village, consisting originally of the modestly built Tara temple enclosure and a cremation ground adjoining the mud hut where Bamakshyapa lived, Tarapeeth today has turned into a semi-urban township of sorts, dotted with numerous hermitages and memorials surrounding the main Tara temple, and shops and eating joints that draw crowds of pilgrims throughout the year— all centred around the figure of Bamakshyapa. Most of the modern buildings we see today in the Tarapeeth complex came up in the 1960s under the patronage of rich devotees, either local or Calcutta-based—indicating the rather belated attempts to institutionalize Bamakshyapa, compared to the fate enjoyed posthumously by his more illustrious contemporary Ramakrishna. In fact, the temple in the memory of Bamakshyapa in Tarapeeth was built as late as 1956. A temple to commemorate the mid-fourteenth century merchant Jaychandra who was the first to discover the spot and build the original Tara temple, came up in 1965, thanks to a club called Bamdev Sangha. A 'ratha-ghar', or room to house a chariot, was constructed in 1969. Quite a number of hermitages, dharmashalas and hotels which also sprung up during this period, continue to take care of the needs of the increasing number of pilgrims visiting Tarapeeth.

Old inhabitants of Tarapeeth remember it as a quiet village, where the Tara temple used to attract pilgrims only during an annual festival in the month of September. It is only during the last 40 years or so that it has suddenly drawn the attention of the Bengali educated middle classes and seen the proliferation of numerous religious establishments, chambers of astrologers, and temples-cum-offices of self-styled modern Tantrik preachers. Explaining the reason for this, these old timers claim that it was a Bengali film called *Sadhak Bamakshyapa,* made in 1958, that popularized the miracles and exploits of the hitherto neglected 'wise man of Tarapeeth', and encouraged the influx of visitors and pilgrims to the site of his *sadhana.* There can be some truth in the hypothesis.

The stages in the institutionalization of Bamakshyapa can be discerned from the early phase when his main disciple Nagen Chattopadhyay began to construct a hagiography around him. He spread Bamakshyapa's reputation as a thaumaturge, faith healer and Tantrik guru, which turned the non-conformist, ascetic recluse into a cynosure of public attention in and around Tarapeeth.

The worldwide popularity of Ramakrishna, brought about by Vivekananda's institutionalizion of him through the Mission, must have aroused among the descendants of Bamakshyapa's direct disciples (particularly the educated followers, like the family of Nagen Chattopadhyay) the ambition to similarly canonize him and form a network of institutions like temples, memorials, hermitages, etc. This ambition probably received a boost in the 1960s from a new generation of devotees who discovered Bamakshyapa through a form of modern media—the film—which celebrated his miracles on the screen. The educated middle-class audience of the film, searching for redemption through spiritualism, or miracles, or godmen, turned their attention to this newly discovered guru, Bamakshyapa, and began to patronize Tarapeeth and build there an elaborate complex of establishments around his memory. In the course of their own search for spiritual salvation, they salvaged Bamakshyapa from obscurity and oblivion and installed him as yet another incarnation, or avatar, of the Supreme Being in a string of tawdry memorials. The man who hated pomp and ostentation and preferred to live the life of a heretical maverick would probably have spat out stinging abuses in his usual rustic style, at the vast and glitzy enterprise built up by his modern-day followers in his old abode.

THE AMBIGUITIES OF BHARAT MATA:
A BHADRALOK GODDESS IN COLONIAL BENGAL

In the long history of interface between popular religion and the religious thoughts of the educated gentry, the emergence of a new goddess—Bharat Mata—during the period of the anti-colonial national struggle, or the Swadeshi movement, in Bengal, represents a major shift. The present essay attempts to analyse the historical background that led to the construction of the deity, its origins in the popular tradition of the mother goddess in Bengal, and its re-orientation of the ideal of human sacrifice associated with that hoary tradition to serve the interests of a latter-day militant nationalism. In the context of the latter, the essay also deals with the concept of, and attitude towards, death, as found in popular religious ideas and contemporary swadeshi politics.

While the image of the mother had always been closely associated with that of the motherland in Hindu thought and culture (e.g. *janani janmabhoomishcha swargadopi gariyashi*—the mother and the motherland are greater than even heaven), the two images came to be identified with each other much later in a concept of nationalism that evolved in British colonial India. It evolved in the context of the political relationship between the rulers and the ruled during the last decades of the nineteenth century. It was during this period that a new generation of educated middle-class Indian nationalists was trying to conceptualize a framework of nation within which they could bring together people from all parts of the country. In the precolonial era, the different communities which fought against foreign invaders, or Mughal rule (e.g. the Marathas, the Rajputs, the Sikhs, etc.) were never known to have come up with an image of a Mother India, although they might have had their mother goddesses (e.g. Shivaji worshipped Bhavani). The symbol of Bharat Mata emerged in the colonial era, when the idea of Indian nationhood was taking birth. Thus, the traditional dictum of the superiority of *janani janmabhoomishcha* (the mother and the motherland) was transformed into what we can today paraphrase as *jananeeba janmabhoomi* (the motherland is equal to the mother).

But the image of Bharat Mata that was constructed in Bengal, mainly during the last quarter of the nineteenth century and the early decades of the twentieth, from this twin concept of mother and motherland, suffered from a number of ambiguities. First, it often veered between a secular female symbol of India and the idol of a Hindu mother goddess. Secondly, even in its reincarnation as a Hindu mother goddess, it remained a divided entity—torn between the role of a benevolent mother like Annapurna and that of an aggressive, bloodthirsty mother like Kali. Thirdly, although rooted to the indigenous tradition of the mother goddess, its cultural representation at times was heavily influenced by the ideas and symbols of contemporary British patriotism. Thus, it borrowed styles of expression from the same colonial rulers to counter whom the new image of Bharat Mata was being constructed. Fourthly, it reflected a certain dichotomy in self-definition (regional/national; Bengali/Indian; Banga Janani/Bharat Janani.)

While trying to analyse these ambiguities of the concept of Bharat Mata in colonial Bengal, the essay also raises a few questions which may be relevant for understanding the re-emergence of the symbol of Bharat Mata in today's politics in India, and its reinterpretation by its modern votaries, belonging to what is commonly known as the Hindu Sangh Parivar. Looking back at the past, we might ask—why was it not possible to construct a personification of Indian nationalism in an image which could cut across religious and caste differences? By representing the Indian nation as a mother goddess with the attributes of only a Hindu idol, it left out and alienated the vast sections of the Muslim population of the country, who were no less anti-colonial than the Bengali Hindus. They were reluctant to worship the idol—not only because it hurt the sentiments of the orthodox among them opposed to idol-worshipping—but because the exclusive Hindu rituals connected with it estranged even the non-orthodox Muslims.

It should be mentioned in this connection that the latter, in common with their Hindu neighbours all over the Bengal countryside had followed a long popular tradition of worshipping certain mother deities to meet immediate needs, such as Shitala or Ola-bibi. These godlings, or little deities of popular religion, constructed by the populace on syncretistic lines, and worshipped with rituals borrowed from Hindu, Muslim and past animist traditions, continue to be worshipped by all—Hindus, Muslims, Dalits, tribals, among others. These devotees inhabit a common space and share common concerns. But the image of the new goddess—Bharat Mata—that came into being in the political scene in the late nineteenth and early twentieth century in Bengal was a far cry from these local mother goddesses. She remained exclusively a goddess of the Hindu bhadralok society, and rarely found a place in the popular religion of the rural masses. Besides, she often drove a wedge between Hindus and Muslims among the politically educated classes of Bengal.

Historical Background

Ironically, the first attempt to symbolize India as a mother goddess in nationalistic terms (according to available historical records), was made as far back as 1827, not by a Bengali Hindu, but by a young Eurasian Christian born in Bengal who identified himself with the patriotic instincts of the Bengalis. Henry Louis Vivian Derozio (1809–31), who brought up a generation of radical students during his tenure at the Calcutta Hindu College as a teacher, wrote a poem when he was eighteen, entitled 'To India, My Native Land', bewailing:

> My country! in thy days of glory past
> A beauteous halo circled round thy brow,
> And worshipped as a deity thou wast—
> Where is thy glory, where is that reverence now?[1]

It was this nostalgic pride for a 'glorious' past followed by a sense of distress at the disgraceful present, that set the tone for the future attempts to frame the image of Mother India in nationalistic terms. This picture of the contrast between an independent and idyllic motherland situated in a distant past, and a colonized and poor country in which Indians lived in the present, keeps recurring in the literature of mid-nineteenth century Bengali authors. One of the earliest Bengali poets of the nineteenth century to articulate this sentiment was Ishwar Chandra Gupta (1812–59). In a poem entitled 'Swadesh' (Motherland), he mourned how the people of this country, living in the lap of *janani-janom-bhoomi* (their motherland), have forgotten their mother.

It was, however, the establishment of the Hindu Mela in 1867 that paved the way for the construction of a more structured concept of Mother India. Nabogopal Mitra, who was one of the founders of the institution, brought together some of the leading intellectuals of the times to address annual fairs of the Hindu Mela in Calcutta to inspire a swadeshi spirit by reviving popular interest in indigenous handicraft and sports. It was on these occasions that Dwijendranath Tagore, Satyendranath Tagore and their younger brother Rabindranath (who was still in his teens) composed songs urging the children of Mother India to arise and restore the glory of their Mother. A more direct image of Mother India was projected in a play entitled *Bharat Mata*, written by Kiron Bandyopadhyay and staged by the National Theatre in 1873. Other plays written on these lines followed soon. In the songs and plays of this type, the common theme was based on a trinity of ideas: *(i)* that Mother India had fallen into bad times; *(ii)* that her children were lying deep in slumber, indifferent to her sufferings; and *(iii)* that this was a call to awaken them.

A representative example is the following song composed by Rabindranath's elder brother Dwijendranath Tagore:

Molin mukho-chandrama, Bharat tomari
Ratri diba jhorichhey lochon-bari . . .
Aaji a molin mukh kamoney nehari!
E dukkho tomar haye re sohitey na paari![2]

(Oh India, your face, beautiful as a moon, is pale today;
tears fall from your eyes through the day and night . . .
How can I look at your pale face today! I cannot bear this
pain of mine!)

Similarly, in the earlier mentioned play by Kiron Bandyo-padhyay, Bharat Mata as the heroine looks at her drowsy children and bemoans: 'they have lost their way, and are dozing with their eyes closed in the darkness of ignorance. Poor sons of mine! Deprived of food and water, they are worn out and gasping for breath like thirsty serpents. How can I still remain alive after watching all this? I must be a great Sinner'. She then tries to wake up one of her reclining sons, raises his hands and addresses him: 'Get up, my son. How can you survive by remaining like this? Remember, the days of your past glory are over. You are now subjects of a foreign ruler. Get up, rid yourself of this habit of dozing'.[3]

Or, compare Satyendranath Tagore's song:

Mile shabey Bharat Santaan
Ekotaan mano-praan
Gao Bharater-i jasho gaan.[4]

(Come together all children of India, united in mind and
soul, and sing the glory of India.)

During this period, however, the image of Bharat Mata was gradually acquiring a specifically anti-Muslim character. Thus,

Jyotirindranath Tagore, in his play *Puru-Bikram* (1874), introduced a song attacking Jabanas, the pejorative term used by Hindu intellectuals for Muslims:

> Miley shab Bharat santaan . . .
> Otho, jago beergan,
> Durdanata Jabana gan
> Grihey dekho korechhey probesh,
> Hao shabey ek-praan, matribhoomi karo traan.

(Arise, wake up, O heroes and children of India. Look, the wicked Jabanas have entered our home. Unite and rescue our motherland).

Kiron Bandyopadhyay, who, as mentioned earlier, wrote the first play on Bharat Mata in 1873, came out the next year, in 1874, with a play called *Bharatey Jabana* ('The Jabanas in India'), where Mother India calls upon her sons to rescue her from captivity by the Jabanas, and the sons declare that they will kill them all.

It has often been argued by later historians that these early nationalist authors of Bengal could not attack the British by name in their writings for fear of prosecution, and therefore chose the term Jabana as a sort of surrogate for their actual enemy. But while making allowances for such fears among the Bengali Hindu intellectuals of that period, should not historians also recognize their insensitivity to the feelings of their Muslim compatriots, who had always been quick to take offence at a term which they felt was discriminating and insulting towards them?

It was, however, left to Bankim Chandra Chattopadhyay to turn Bharat Mata into a full-fledged Hindu goddess. In 1875, he composed 'Vande Mataram'. Incidentally, the beginnings of this song can be found in an article of his on the Durga puja in his 'Kamalakanter Daptar'—a series of satirical pieces carried in his journal *Bangadarshan*—where the goddess Durga becomes Mother Bengal awaiting the awakening of her six crore children, the population of Bengal then. It may be noted that the mother goddess here is identified with Bengal only. Curiously enough, the Mother depicted in 'Vande Mataram' is primarily a benign goddess who represents fertility, knowledge, religion, the soul of mankind all bound together. It was much later that the title of this song was to turn into a battle cry and be identified with militant nationalism. In the original song, there are only four references to her military prowess and attributes: 'Bhujoir-dhrita khara-karabale' (sharp swords held in the hands), 'Bohu baladharineeng' (one who possesses immense power), 'Bahute tumi Ma shakti' (your hands, Mother, hold all power) and 'Twang hi Durga dasha praharana dharinee' (you are Durga who holds ten weapons). The main stress is on her peaceful aspects and kind virtues. But we shall come later to the transformation of this gentle goddess of 'Vande Mataram' representing the motherland in 1875, into the powerful goddess of rebellion who was worshipped by the militant nationalists at the turn of the present century.

To come back to Bankim's conception of Mother India (or Mother Bengal—for there is no specific mention of Bharat in 'Vande Mataram'), apart from her identification with Durga, there are other clear references to her as a solely Hindu goddess: 'Tomar-i pratima gori mandire mandire' (it is your image that we set up in every temple). Along with the familiar Hindu religious connotations, its composition in Sanskrit (barring a few sentences in Bengali) further reinforced its Hindu character. To non-Hindu Indians it resembled an incantation by a Brahman priest to a Hindu deity.

It is this image of a Hindu mother goddess as a symbol of an 'imagined' Indian nation that came to dominate the nationalist discourse in Bengal from the late nineteenth century onwards. The Hinduized Bharat Mata soon became the symbol of the militant nationalist movement that arose at the turn of the twentieth century. The 1905 partition of Bengal brought forth the first generation of armed revolutionaries who put the demand for independence on the agenda of the nationalist discourse. In this changed context, the image of Mother India underwent a radical transformation. The earlier generation of liberal nationalists in the 1870s fashioned her image in line with their hopes for reforms in collaboration with the British. The new generation of revolutionary nationalists discarded such hopes, and therefore constructed a different image of Mother India that symbolized their agenda.

The Roots of Ambiguities

The choice of the image of the mother as the symbol of the nation by the early generation of Bengali nationalists was inspired by the given and living tradition of the worshipping of mother goddesses (e.g. Durga, Kali, Annapurna, Bhavani, among many other manifestations of the primeval female Shakti) among the people of this country. While these goddesses could be described as a part of the 'great tradition', Bengal's countryside is littered with hundreds of local mother goddesses who belong to the 'little tradition', fulfilling special functions such as protection from disease and predatory animals. It is from these goddesses that the villagers derive the most tangible hopes—blessings that bear a relationship to the world in which they live.

Unable to eradicate these local goddesses of the 'little tradition' from the socio-religious life of the masses, the Brahman ideologues of the 'great tradition' accommodated them in their theological framework by interpreting them as the different forms of the single great mother goddess, the Adya-Shakti.

While the image of the new mother goddess Bharat Mata was constructed by the bhadralok nationalists against the backdrop of this living tradition in Bengal, the history of its development was replete with paradoxes and ambiguity. It was neither uniform nor consistent, nor was it complete. It grew out of a variety of parallel streams of patriotism, often seemingly contradictory (e.g. the liberal reformist and the militant nationalist currents).

In the Bengali educated society, the formulation of the concept was influenced not only by the Hindu religious tradition of mother goddesses, but also by the way the contemporary British rulers constructed their own image of Britannia—the ruling feminine symbol of Britain's imperial power. Similar feminine images of nationalism were to be found in other parts of Europe also (see Marianne in France). In the writings of some among the first generation of Bengali nationalists, the image of Bharat Mata was often modelled on Britannia as depicted in contemporary English literature and paintings. She was, as it were, an Indian Britannia, who once ruled over Bharat and was endowed with all the virtues and powers that were to be found in Britannia. But she had now fallen into bad times.

It seems that this generation of nationalist proponents of the concept of Bharat Mata had to contend with two mothers: one, Mother India, and the other, Queen Victoria, the living image of Britannia. They created the former to represent their concept of nation, and urged their people to worship her. But at the same time they had to display their allegiance to their colonial rulers, who were represented by a living empress. They therefore turned that empress into Mother Victoria. Both Mother India and Ma Victoria coexisted as the reigning deities in the nationalist literature of Bengal in the late nineteenth century. Mother India, or Bharat Mata, was invariably shown as a destitute woman, whose wealth had been looted by foreigners, and whose children were apathetic to her distress (e.g. the songs of Hindu Mela, plays like *Bharat Mata*, etc.). While worshipping her, the Bengali writers of this period called upon her children to arise to rescue her and restore her to her former glory. But, simultaneously these same nationalist writers appealed to the other mother—Queen Victoria—to come to the help of the destitute Mother India and save her.

A few examples may be considered. When Victoria was declared the Empress of India in 1876, and the Diamond Jubilee of her reign was held in 1897, devotees of Mother India came out with paeans of praise for her in a flow of songs and plays. Sometimes the female image Britannia replaced Victoria. Thus, in one of the exhibitions of the Hindu Mela, Nabogopal Mitra commissioned a Bengali artist to paint a huge canvas showing Indians sitting with folded hands in supplication before Britannia.[5] Or take the example of even Kiron Bandyopadhyay, who in his play *Bharat*

Mata portrayed the misery of Mother India. At the end of the play he assures Bharat Mata that the British rulers are not so bad and that they will surely rescue her. 'Our Empress (Victoria) is extremely kind . . . There is no end to her virtues. It is difficult to find another such virtuous woman among womenkind. Like your Ramchandra, she looks after all her subjects without making any distinction.'[6] Another famous theatre personality of this period, Girish Ghosh, staged *Hirak Jubilee* at Star Theatre in 1897 on the occasion of Victoria's Diamond Jubilee, in which all the Indian subjects were shown praising Mother Victoria.

A typical example of the dual loyalty to the twin mothers is a song composed by a Bengali bhadralok to welcome the nationalist leader Surendranath Banerjee on his return from England at the time of Victoria's reign:

> Orey, phirey ki bhai eli rey!
> E maa chherey, shey maar kachhey kemon adore peli rey?
> . . .
> Dekhchho ki chokh muchhechhey, smori e kangalirey?[7]
>
> (So you've come back brother! Leaving this mother, you went to the other mother. What sort of affection did you get from her? . . . Did you find her wiping away her tears while remembering this destitute?)

But there was a parallel radical nationalist stream which also developed from the end of the nineteenth century. Here the image of Mother India began to change. She came to be shaped after goddess Kali. This indicated an instinctive alliance between Hindu religion and politics, and reflected the rise of militant nationalism. Destruction, sacrifice and death—the familiar motifs associated with Kali—were transferred to the image of Mother India. Bankim Chandra Chattopadhyay who composed 'Vande Mataram' in 1875 as a hymn that celebrated the benign virtues of Mother India, transplanted it into his novel *Anandamath* (1882) written some years later. Here he turned it into a song sung by the revolutionary *santanas* (i.e. children) of Bharat Mata, who worship Mother India.

She is moulded in the image of Kali—wearing a necklace of skulls and holding a sword. Through the words of Satyananda, Bankim explains in the novel the transformation of the Mother, as she is today: 'Since the entire country has been reduced to a cremation ground, she wears a necklace of skulls. Since the country needs salvation from the foreign marauders, she is holding the sword.' Vivekananda's powerfully evocative poem 'Kali the Mother', which was written at around the same time, again emphasizes the relevance of the goddess of destruction for the contemporary times:

Come Mother, come
For Terror is thy name,
Death is in thy breath,
And every shaking step
Destroys a world for e'er.[8]

Or, take his famous saying as recorded by Nivedita: 'Deep in the heart of hearts of Her own, flashes the blood-red knife of Kali . . . I worship the Terrible . . . Let us worship the Terror for its own sake'.[9]

Vivekananda's message was to influence a whole generation of young Bengali revolutionaries, keen on destroying the colonial order, eager to embrace death. As the country woke to the twentieth century and the partition of Bengal in 1905, Bharat Mata assumed the new form of a destructive Kali, demanding sacrifice from her children. The title of Bankim's song 'Vande Mataram' was adopted by the young people as a war cry soon after a meeting in Town Hall in Calcutta on 7 August 1905, where they took the vow of Swadeshi and decided to boycott foreign goods. The British government prohibited the slogan, and cracked down on processions during which it was being shouted. Revolutionary journals like *Sandhya*, *Bande Mataram*, *Jugantar*, in the name of an aggressive Bharat Mata, urged her children to wreak vengeance on the British enemy.

Ironically, however, Bankim Chandra Chattopadhyay himself, whose song 'Vande Mataram' and concept of Mother India were borrowed by these revolutionaries of the early twentieth century, ended his *Anandamath* with the message that there was no need for violent resistance to the rulers since British rule had saved Mother India from the oppressive rule of the Jabanas! Here again we find the roots of the ambiguities that infested the Bengali nationalists and made them shape their image of Bharat Mata. Like all descendants of past traditions, they were also selective in their retention and rejection of those traditions. While retaining the message of militancy (against the British, but along with the anti-Muslim bias), they rejected Bankim's final message in *Anandamath*.

Aurobindo Ghosh, for instance, in his journal *Bande Mataram* wrote: 'What the Mother needs is hard clear steel for her sword, hard massive granite for her fortress, wood that will not break for the handle of her bow, tough substance for the axle of her chariot. For the battle is near and the trumpet ready for the signal' (23 April 1908).

The popular patriotic Bengali folk singer of this period, Mukunda Das (1878–34), in one of his songs, merged Shyama Ma (Mother Kali) with Mother India when he described her as the mother of 30 crore children (the then population of India). We should note the gradual shift from the six crore of Bengal, as found in earlier poems, to the entire population of India. It reflected the spreading of the radical nationalist trend to other parts of India, particularly Tilak's movement in Maharashtra. Referring to the adoption of 'Vande Mataram' by Bengal as the 'mantra of India's Nationalism', Tilak said that it would 'help rethrone the Mother in her own right and in her own glory.'

Bharat Mata and Changing Bengali Womanhood

Along with these two parallel political streams of nationalism and the influence of the British concept of patriotism and benevolent imperialism that went into the earlier construction of the image of Bharat Mata in colonial Bengal, there was another important social development taking place in contemporary Bengal which also in a large measure influenced this construction, and added to its ambiguities. This was the Bengali bhadralok society's attempt to redefine the role of its women in the later decades of the nineteenth century. A new generation of educated Bengali women had come of age. Although in a minority, they were coming out from their traditional 'antahpur' or inner quarters and getting exposed to the outer world, where they were increasingly participating in social and cultural affairs. News of the achievements of Kadambini Ganguly, the first woman doctor of Bengal who addressed the 1889 session of the Indian National Congress, or the poetry of Kamini Ray, who was educated at Bethune College, were reaching the Bengali women who were still confined in their antahpur. Encouraged by the alternative lifestyle followed by these sisters, these denizens of the antahpur were becoming restless. How to reconcile the traditional collective role of Bengali women as devoted housewives, with their new role as educated individuals with the potential to assert their independence? Unable to make up their minds as to how far women could be allowed to come out in the open, the Bengali bhadralok were caught up in tangles of contradictions all through these last decades of the century.

In Bengali literature of this period, we find some male writers caricaturing educated women as excessively self-assertive (e.g. in the plays of Amritalal Bose). Others speak of the virtues of female education, but remind educated women of their duty to look after their husbands and children and be ideal housewives. Even women's magazines of that period, like *Bamabodhini Patrika*, internalized this patriarchal attitude when advising their women readers. It was clearly a dilemma for the Bengali bhadralok to find ways of channellizing the new aspirations of their women.

The politics of nationalism that emerged during this period provided an avenue for some among the Bengali bhadralok politicians to resolve this social dilemma. Initially, the Hindu Mela offered a platform for involving the Bengali women of the antahpur in activities that could be harnessed to the nationalist agenda. Every year at the Mela, women's products, like embroidered textiles, carpets, etc. were exhibited, and the women artistes awarded medals. They were lauded as examples of Bengali women's artistic capacities. The organizers of Hindu Mela also commissioned artists from Krishnagar to create clay models that depicted two kinds of virtue: the grand and the heroic, and the humble and the domestic. In both, women figured prominently—the heroic represented in mythological figures, and the domestic in models of Bengali mothers and daughters engaged in their daily chores. Thus, there was a stress on women acting as benevolent mothers at home as well as playing a ministering role in society by participating in the Hindu Mela.[10]

Significantly, the image of Bharat Mata in the cultural productions of the earlier generation of Bengali nationalists has features which stress the humble and the domestic. She looks submissive, craving sympathy, as in Dwijendranath's poem, or full of motherly affection for her children, as in Kiron Bandyopadhyay's play *Bharat Mata*. This was in conformity with the contemporary Bengali middle-class male construction of Bengali womanhood. Modelled on long-suffering mythological heroines like Sita, they were required to be good mothers at home in spite of poverty or patriarchal oppression. In the male construction of Mother India, therefore, there was a simultaneous glorification of suffering, frugality, motherly affection, etc. In this new context of nationalism and its feminine symbolization as Bharat Mata, the Bengali housewife was expected to extend her nurturing capacities to inspire the menfolk to become patriots and carry out their responsibilities to the motherland. The heroic image of the Bengali woman was safely relegated to the pages of Bankim's novels, where women like Shanti or Devi Choudhurani were allowed to parade their courageous deeds outside their homes.

At the turn of this century however, as mentioned earlier, the image of Bharat Mata began to undergo a change. It was modelled on a combination of two traditions—that of the homely virtues of a mother, like affection for her children, domestic duties, religious devotion etc. and that of Kali, the goddess of destruction. It represented the newly assertive role of Mother India as a warrior leading the nation in its fight for freedom.

This image of Bharat Mata quite often merged into the role model of real life women in Bengal of that period. The life and activities of Sarala Debi Choudhurani who played an important role in the Swadeshi politics of the late nineteenth–early twentieth-century period, offer a fairly representative example of the changing concept of Indian womanhood. A niece of Rabindranath Tagore's, Sarala Devi echoed the same militant nationalistic concept of Mother India as a goddess of destruction. A poem published in *Bharati* (the family magazine of the Tagores with which she was actively involved) in 1896, entitled 'Abirbhab' ('The Advent'), portrayed Mother India as a goddess with a sword in her right hand and the bleeding, severed head of the demon Asura in her left. In her real-life situation also, Sarala Debi acted almost as a representative of this newly constructed militant image of Mother India. As early as 1904, she opened an akhara, or a gymnasium, in her house in Ballygunge, where young men took the oath of serving the country in her presence, and were trained in the use of *lathis* and daggers. In the same year, she organized the festival of Birashtami during the Durga Puja, invoking the heroic spirit of Mother Durga, where competitions in martial arts were held. She herself used to appear on the stage carrying a sword.[11] While such activities often attracted the criticism of the elder generation of Bengali males, she was immensely popular among the youth imbued with the new mood of militant nationalism.

Curiously enough, at the time when Sarala Devi was modelling herself on the militant aggressive image of Mother India, another member of her family, Abanindranath Tagore was painting a picture of Bharat Mata that celebrated the alternative image of a benign mother. Thus the two parallel streams coexisted even at the height of the anti-British national movement.

Kali, Self-Sacrifice and Death

By moulding the image of Mother India after that of Kali, the militant nationalists of early twentieth-century Bengal were falling back on a long popular historical and literary tradition.

In every traditional society in history, blood sacrifice had been a means of appeasing a deity, in order to forestall or put an end to a terrible event such as a natural calamity or an epidemic that was attributed to the deity's anger, or to gain something, like, for example, a good harvest. Both animals and human beings were sacrificed. In ancient Indian society, we find mention of men along with horses, cows, buffaloes and goats as objects of sacrifice.[12] Among the human beings, the sacrificial victims were of two kinds—enemies and one's dear ones, including one's own self. While in normal times the deity's thirst could be assuaged with the blood of enemies (e.g. ancient kings sacrificed their war prisoners at the altars of their gods), or common animals like cows, goats, or buffaloes, at times of severe crisis the deity was supposedly impressed only if the devotees could give up something of immense value. Devotees felt that their god needed some sign to satisfy him that they believed in him completely. Thus came about the idea of sacrificing the dearest of possessions. It is this that inspired the myth of Abraham's attempt to sacrifice his son to please God, a myth common to Christians, Jews and Muslims alike. Similarly, in Greek mythology, Agamemnon, to pacify the anger of Artemis, the goddess of hunting, sacrificed his daughter Iphigenia. There are parallels in ancient Indian mythology too. In the Mahabharata, we come across the story of king Somaka, who had one hundred wives, but only one son called Jantu. Desirous of having more sons, and following the advice of his priest, he sacrificed his son at a *yagna* (oblation of fire).[13] Significantly, the name of the sacrificial son was Jantu, which means animal. Is the story then a metaphor for the sacrifice of a pet animal?

But the fact remains that human sacrifice was very much a part of ancient society—and of Bengali socio-religious life even upto the nineteenth century—as indicated by numerous scriptural sources as well as historical records. The general assumption was that by being sacrificed the human being passed into the religious domain. Consecrated in death, the spirit of the sacrificed person was supposed to be released into the spiritual realm. The victim was thus seen as a privileged person. The feeling comes out clearly in the words of the Kapalik hermit in Bankim Chandra Chatto-padhyay's novel *Kapalkundala*. When about to sacrifice the hero Nabakumar, the Kapalik says to him: 'You have become worthy of your birth today. This flesh of yours will be offered for the worship of Bhairabi. What better fortune than this can a person like you expect?'[14]

How do we today look at this ancient practice? The rationale that to gain an objective, one has to offer a human life at the altar of an imagined superhuman power, should certainly be rejected as a superstitious inhuman attitude that violates modern humanitarian standards. It needs to be forcefully opposed, particularly in today's Indian society, where despite progressive laws and signs of modernization, reports of human sacrifice for petty individual gain or personal vengeance still trickle down from obscure villages.

But can we examine the tradition from another angle while reconstructing the past? The historian of popular religion has to study the way ordinary people in the past made sense of the world, and expressed it in their behaviour, however repugnant their practices might appear to us today. Let us remember that these people were trying to organize the surrounding reality in their minds into a coherent shape, provide reasons for the dangerous powers of existence, and devise strategies to cope with them. They did this with the available materials around them and the mental resources with which they were equipped at that time. At a particular stage, their rationale might have suggested the need for going beyond offering animals as sacrifice to the superhuman spirit that, according to them, caused both good and evil. Since animal sacrifice was apparently no longer able to appease the spirit, prevent natural calamities or ensure personal success, they thought of sacrificing something more important—their near ones, including their own children, or even their own selves. While this was indeed a self-destructive superstitious belief, one can also recognize in this the first stumbling effort of the mind to rise above the physical self. In the history of religion, it was this idea that later progressed and graduated to the more sophisticated concept of self-surrender to the imagined Almighty that necessitated the abandonment of all material possessions, emotional attachments and sensual desires—self-elimination in the spiritual sense (the best example of which can be found in the theology and songs of the Bhakti and Sufi movements in India).

In the Tantrik practices of Shakta religion, any sacrifice, whether of animals or human beings, had to be through bloodletting. This is in sharp contrast to the other idea of self-sacrifice that stems from Jain or other religious philosophies, which emphasizes self-denial through non-violence. Fasting as a means of reaching the objective of self-sacrifice is a typical instance. It is significant that the concept of fast-unto-death became a weapon in the hands of Gandhi (who was heavily influenced by Jain philosophy) during the later phase of the Indian national movement, while the early militant nationalists when formulating the concept of sacrifice fell back on the Shakta tradition by stressing bloodletting. Their followers were called upon either to kill the British enemy, or die as martyrs fighting them, like their ancestors who offered the lives of their enemies, or their own lives, as *balis* to the altar of the blood-thirsty mother goddess. *Balidan* or sacrifice became another synonym for martyrdom in the lexicon of militant nationalism.

The history of Bengal suggests that at moments of political upheavals and socioeconomic crisis, there had been a tendency among the people to turn towards the mother goddess. Chandi was one among them. Her name is found in the *Markandeya-purana*, as another incarnation of Adya-Shakti (in her role as the killer of the demon Chanda). But unlike in other parts of India, it is in Bengali socio-religious life that she acquired a pre-eminent position, which she still occupies. She came into prominence in poetic narratives and ballads, known as Chandimangal-kavyas, which portrayed her as an angry goddess hurling curses on those who failed to fulfil her desires, or committed any sin, and pouring happiness and good fortune (*mangal* in Bengali) upon those who propitiated her suitably. It was actually after the Turkish conquest of Bengal in the thirteenth century that the popularity of the goddess and the songs composed in her praise reached their peak. The country was passing through a period of turmoil and anarchy at the time, and a helpless population probably found solace in falling at the feet of a mother goddess to whom they attributed superhuman prowess. They could escape from a lot of mental anguish by surrendering their selves to the goddess who was expected to understand the reasons for their misfortune and save them from the chaos. Much later, looking back at the popularity of these songs during that period, Rabindranath Tagore sought to explain it in these words: 'Those who are oppressed and defeated in the world, and yet cannot find any just reason for their oppression and defeat, assume that the misplaced anger of a wanton and cruel Shakti (the divine female power) must be the cause of all their sufferings. It was the hope to appease this malicious Shakti by eulogies, by prayers, that inspired the Mangal-kavyas.'[15]

The people of Bengal faced another crisis in the eighteenth–nineteenth century with the gradual consolidation of British power. Under the colonial economic policies, the traditional rural economy collapsed, severely disrupting social life. Significantly again, this coincided with the growing popularity of Shakta religion in general and Kali in particular. Vaishnavism, which held sway over Bengal for several centuries (particularly after the rise of Chaitanya in the sixteenth century), began to beat a gradual retreat in the face of Shaktaism in social and cultural spheres during this period. This was the time when Ramprasad's songs on Kali were becoming popular both in the countryside and on the streets of the new metropolis, Calcutta. It was during these days also that the temple of Kali in Kalighat was developing from a humble altar to a prominent shrine to become the centrepiece of Bengali religious and social life. Here again, we find the familiar traces of an oppressed population seeking salvation by turning to a malevolent mother goddess. As in the past, they hoped that by propitiating her (not only through prayer, but also through human sacrifice, a practice that marked the worshipping of Kali in Bengal during the eighteenth–nineteenth century), they could put an end to the problems they were facing in a hostile socioeconomic environment. Having been ravaged by a succession of famines in the latter part of the eighteenth century, the poor people of Bengal resorted to the practice of human sacrifice in seasons of scarcity. A contemporary British official noted: 'During 1865–66 such sacrifices were had recourse to [sic] in order to avert the famine ... Among the aboriginal tribes to the south-west of Beerbhoom I heard vague reports of human sacrifices in the forests, with a view to procuring the early arrival of the rains.'[16]

The prevalence of this Shakta tradition of human sacrifice at the altar of Kali, offered the militant nationalists at the turn of the twentieth century a ready tool with which to rally their followers in their armed struggle against the British. They stressed the twin aspects of the tradition—sacrifice of the enemy, and sacrifice of one's own self, at the altar of the mother goddess.

While the Shakta concept of the mother goddess did inspire the militant nationalist movement of Bengal in the early twentieth century, it has to be acknowledged that the *Bhagavad Gita* too provided one of the main ideological bases of that movement. A few words about the relationship between the Shakta and Vaishnavite streams in the national movement may be relevant here. Chaitanya's Vaishnavism stressed the gentle and benevolent aspects of the Krishna legend—his loving kindness to his devotees in the idyllic Vrindavana—through the theological interpretation of which the Gaudiya Vaishnavite teachers propagated the message of bhakti or devotion. But the *Bhagavad Gita* revealed Krishna as a warrior saint, merciless in his exhortation to Arjuna to fight 'abhyutthanam adharmasya' (the rise of unrighteousness) and destroy the wicked. It is this facet of Krishna's character that attracted the revolutionary leaders of militant nationalism. His message could be interpreted as a call to overthrow the adharma-raj of the British, the rule of unrighteousness. Krishna thus merged easily with the warrior image of Kali, the Shakta goddesss. During the initiation ceremony of the young men who joined the armed revolution in the first decade of the twentieth century, they had to take a vow before an image of Kali, with a sword and a copy of the *Bhagavad Gita* in their hands. The British civilian J. C. Ker, who compiled facts about these revolutionaries in his book *Political Trouble in India, 1907–17*, noted that during raids on their shelters, the police found copies of both the *Gita* and the *Chandi* (hymns in praise of the mother goddess from the *Markandeya-purana*).[17]

Writing in another context, but during the same period of militant nationalism, a contemporary Bengali scholar captured the mentality of his countrymen when he observed: 'In order to properly understand the Bengalis of Bengal, it is necessary to understand this country's Vaishnav religion, as well as Tantrik religion. For, Bengalis are half-Vaishnavite and half-Tantrik.'[18]

In Tantrik concepts, blood was central to the concept of sacrifice. Even when there was no sacrifice of the human body, bloodletting remained a part of the ritual of sacrifice. Thus, we hear of a devotee cutting off his tongue as an offering to the goddess Kali at the Kalighat temple in Calcutta in 1827.[19] Self-inflicted injuries on the human body to draw blood were not only confined to Tantrik practices, but were part of certain traditional popular ceremonies that were shared in common by both Hindus and Muslims. Among the Hindus of Bengal, the custom of swinging people by iron or steel hooks suspended from a horizontal ladder during the Chadak festival continued till the late nineteenth century. Similarly, the spectacle of Shia Muslims beating and slashing their breasts with sharp weapons to commemorate the sacrifice of Hussain in Karbala in the seventh century was a common sight during Muharrum.

During the Swadeshi movement, bloodletting was revived as an ideal to be followed by the militant nationalists. A typical example is the following piece from the contemporary revolutionary journal *Jugantar*: 'The Mother is thirsty and is pointing out to her sons the only thing that can quench that thirst. Nothing less than human blood and decapitated heads will satisfy her. Let her sons, therefore, worship her with these offerings and let them not shrink even from sacrificing their lives to procure them . . .'[20]

The highest form of sacrifice was considered to be self-sacrifice, and the recruits to the armed nationalist movement were motivated to prepare themselves for death, either during encounters with the police, or at the gallows.

From Hindu Nationalism to Hindu Communalism

Thus the image of Bharat Mata constructed by the Bengali nationalists, which gained ascendancy in Bengal militant politics at the beginning of the twentieth century, was essentially based on the attributes of a Hindu mother goddess. On certain occasions, the rituals accompanying her worship were also borrowed from traditional Hindu religious customs (e.g. signing the oath of loyalty with blood). It was an exclusivist construction that left out the vast Muslim masses of Bengal.

In spite of this imperfect construction of a national symbol that stressed the features of Hindu religious customs only, it is interesting to observe that in the initial period of militant nationalism in Bengal, Muslims also participated in demonstrations that sang the praise of Bharat Mata. In the wake of the anti-1905 Bengal Partition agitation, both Hindu and Muslim students held joint processions in Calcutta. Abanindranath Tagore in his autobiography tells us how Rabindranath, during the agitation, went to Nakhoda Mosque in Chitpur in Calcutta, and tied *rakhis* on the hands of Muslims there, and the Muslims along with him sang 'Banglar Mati, Banglar Jal' which he composed during the anti-Partition movement. We learn that in Barisal, Hindus and Muslims came out together in the streets to protest against the partition, shouting 'Vande Mataram' and 'Allah-ho-Akbar' (*The Bengalee*, 23 May 1906).

But the propaganda mounted by the colonial authorities announcing benefits for Bengali Muslims after Partition weaned away large sections of the Muslims from the anti-Partition movement. Their estrangement was further reinforced by the stridently Hindu postures of the movement which increasingly took on an anti-Muslim character quite often directed against poor Muslim peasants and traders. In 1907 in Jamalpur, when Muslim tenants launched a movement against the Hindu zamindar for hiking rents, the anti-Partition Swadeshi activists who were followers of Aurobindo Ghosh were reported to have assaulted the Muslim tenants.[21] Looking back at this anti-Muslim bias of the contemporary militant nationalist movement, Rabindranath deprecated it in 1916 in his novel *Ghare Bairey*.

Explaining the gradual estrangement of the Bengali Muslims from the Swadeshi movement of the early twentieth century, one modern Bengali Muslim researcher blames it on the song 'Vande Mataram' as used by the Bengali Hindu nationalists at that time to pay obeisance to Bharat Mata. According to him:

> The adoption of the virulently anti-Muslim *Vande Mataram* as the national anthem in the anti-Partition movement made the Bengali Muslims fear that its success would lead to the ultimate disappearance of Islam as a religion as well as of Muslim culture. Because of this, the very few Bengali Muslims who joined the terrorist (i.e. the militant nationalist) movement, soon cut off all links with the Anushilan and Jugantar groups (i.e. the two main armed revolutionary groups operating in Bengal in those days).[22]

Although the song 'Vande Mataram' as such did not contain anything that was virulently anti-Muslim, it suffered by association, since it was incorporated by its author Bankim Chandra Chattopadhyay in his novel *Anandamath*, certain passages in which can certainly be construed as virulently anti-Muslim.

Muslim politicians who at the beginning expressed no objection to the singing of 'Vande Mataram' on public platforms which they shared with their Hindu compatriots, later began to express reservations. It was at the National Congress session in Calcutta in 1896, that 'Vande Mataram' was sung for the first time, by Rabindranath who set it to tune. It apparently did not evoke any opposition from Muslim delegates at that time. But in the decades that followed, Hindu–Muslim relations reached such a sensitive stage that at the 1923 Kokanad session of the National Congress, when Vishnu Digambar Palushkar rose to sing 'Vande Mataram', the President of the session, Maulana Muhammad Ali, opposed it.

Thus, the Muslim attitude towards Bharat Mata and the song 'Vande Mataram' underwent a transformation over the first two decades of the twentieth century, due to a variety of reasons: the manoeuvres of the British rulers to woo the Muslim leadership, the stridently Hindu rhetoric of the national movement with its distinctive anti-Muslim bias, and possibly in reaction to this, a tendency among the Bengali Muslim masses to assert a purist Islamic identity (which in any case they had never had, given their tradition of participation in syncretist religious practices derived from their past before they were converted to Islam) goaded by their clergy.

In such a situation, it was just a step from Hindu nationalism to Hindu communalism. Without underestimating the patriotism of the early generation of reformist nationalists, and the revolutionary zeal of the later generation of militant nationalists, we must admit that the very manner in which they fashioned the symbol of Bharat Mata during this period paved the way for its future use by the Hindu communal forces.

It is not surprising therefore to find, exactly 100 years later, a prominent member of the communal Hindu Sangh Parivar, the VHP (Vishva Hindu Parishad) appropriating Bharat Mata today for its agenda of militant Hindu communalism. It has built a Bharat Mata temple in Hardwar at an estimated cost of 10 million rupees. Incidentally, the image of Bharat Mata installed in the eight-storeyed temple recalls Abanindranath's portrait. It has, however, become more modern. Instead of four hands, the Mother now has two hands, one hand holding a milk urn, and the other sheaves of grain (symbolizing the white and green revolutions, as explained in the guidebook). While the VHP interprets this as a symbol of modern Indian nationalism calculated to appeal to all religious communities (it indeed looks like a secular symbol of the nation state), the VHP has used it primarily to rally the Hindu masses. In 1983, it organized a six-week Ekatmata Yajna (Oblation for the Unity of the Nation), accompanied with all the paraphernalia of Hindu rituals. A procession of trucks carrying the image of Bharat Mata and urns containing Ganga water, in a *ratha-yatra*, started from Hardwar and traversed various Hindu pilgrimage centres, stopping en route in villages, towns and cities, where Hindu devotees were brought to pay obeisance to the deity.[23]

Looking back at this event today, one wonders whether this *ratha-yatra* in the name of Bharat Mata in 1983 was not a dress rehearsal for the more notorious *ratha-yatra* that was organized by the same VHP a few years later, and was led by the Hindu nationalist BJP (Bharatiya Janata Party) leader L. K. Advani with the aim of constructing a Hindu temple in the so-called 'Rama-janmabhoomi'. That *ratha-yatra* of Advani's left a trail of bloody Hindu–Muslim riots and culminated in terrible communal violence in 1992 following the demolition of the Babri Masjid by the self-proclaimed Hindu votaries of Bharat Mata.

Our past mistakes come home to roost. In the Bengal of the late nineteenth–early twentieth century, when the Bengali Hindu nationalists were seeking a symbol for their incipient ideas of a fledgling nationalism, they fell back on their own Hindu tradition and invented a new mother goddess which was to be worshipped with the same old Hindu rituals. They failed to take into account the distinct religious and cultural identities of the non-Hindu communities who were no less anti-imperialist. As evident from the contemporary speeches and writings of people like Vivekananda, Aurobindo, and others, they sought to homogenize all these communities under the hegemonistic rubric of a Bharat Mata, declaring all of them subjects of the same Mother India, although she was fashioned after a Hindu goddess.

Let me hasten to add that I am not attributing any particular Hindu communal conspiratorial designs to these early proponents of nationalism. Coming from Hindu zamindari and middle-class homes, they were brought up on values which discriminated against Muslims both in economic relations (as agricultural labourers of the Hindu zamindars) and social relations (because of different religious customs). In a myopic conception of nationalism, shaped by their economic interests and cultural biases, they were naturally inclined to totally ignore the interests of both the Muslim masses, and the aboriginal people.

Conclusion

As a result of the various trends—sometimes converging, often contradictory—inherent in the vision of Bharat Mata that was envisaged by the Bengali nationalist middle classes, the Bengali quest for her was always plagued by several uncertainties. Was she Bharat Mata, or Banga Janani? Or, was she the same Mother? What could be her relationship with the Empress, Queen Victoria? Of the two female icons, who was superior? Was she the familiar benign mother of Bengali homes, or the terrible mother goddess Kali? And then, for the Bengali Muslims the moot question was: did she symbolize the common aspirations of all the Indians, including Muslims, Christians and others? Or, was she an exclusive goddess of the Hindus?

These wide-ranging political and cultural queries and doubts could perhaps explain the ambiguous relationship that sensitive Bengali intellectuals often had with the concept of a mother goddess symbolizing the country. Along with melodramatic outpourings of sympathy for Bharat Mata or Banga Janani, or revolutionary paeans in her praise, one also comes across satires lampooning the Bengali 'patriots' for their habit of making a fad of worshipping this new goddess. The same Rabindranath who at the age of 14, at the ninth session of the Hindu Mela in 1875, recited a patriotic poem in the conventional style of bewailing the fate of Mother India, in his later age mocked at Mother Bengal in the following words:

Sapto-koti santanerey, he mugdha janani,
Rekhechho bangali korey, manush karoni.[24]

(Infatuated by your seven crore children, Oh Mother,
you've left them as Bengalis, but haven't brought them up
as human beings.)

Or take Ishwar Chandra Gupta. In his poetry, love for his birth-place spontaneously identified itself with the mother. But he did not spare his compatriots who grovelled before Queen Victoria and worshipped her as Mother. The following lines addressed to the Queen Empress mock the subservience of Indians:

Tumi ma kalpatoru amra shab posha goru
Shikhini shing bankano,
Kebol khabo khol bichali ghash.
Jeno ranga amla tuley mamla
Gamla bhange na,
Amra bhushi pelei khushi habo—
Ghushi kheley banchbo na.[25]

(You are a generous mother. And we your tame cattle / We haven't even learnt to raise our horns / We'll only eat oil-cake, straw and grass / We only hope the white boss doesn't file a suit / And break our pots and pans / We'll be quite happy only with the husk / A blow will make us give up the ghost!)

These sarcastic versions remain an interesting part of Bengali cultural thinking, providing the necessary balance for an overall picture of Mother India in colonial Bengal.

CONCLUSION

These histories of popular religion offer an interesting glimpse into the continuity and changes in the system of belief and patterns of practice, as well as in the collective sensibility of their followers during a period spanning several centuries. It also stimulates further rigorous analysis and elaboration of the theories of 'popular religion'—a term which paradoxically enough is of a very recent coinage although it deals with religious creeds and customs followed by large masses of rural and urban poor in the past (in Europe and the rest of the world), and even today (mainly in the Third World countries).

A corpus of theories has developed during the last few decades around the various dimensions of these traditions. They seek to explain what is designated in the continental academic discourse as the 'history of mentalities'—the stress being on that 'which changes the least' in historical evolution.[1]

One of the major dimensions relates to the dialectical relationship between the prevailing official religion of the establishment in any given society, and the popular religion (or religions) that may be followed by the community at large, particularly the lower orders in that society. Is the relationship one of constant divide and conflict between the dominating 'elite' who patronize the official religious order on the one hand, and the dominated 'plebians' who follow certain religious customs and practices that predate theestablishment of the official religion, and which quite often contradict the precepts and norms ordained by the official religion, on the other? Or, is it one of mutual accommodation, marked by a steady acculturation over the years through assimilation of, and contamination by, the beliefs and practices of each other? Or, is popular religion simply a vulgarized version of the official religion?

Stressing the points of divide and conflict, Mikhail Bakhtin argues that popular religion and culture had always been anti-establishment and a dynamic weapon in the hands of the people to subvert the official values and norms.[2] Aron Gurevich, however, emphasizes the interlacing of the two forms of consciousness in a 'complex and contradictory synthesis' which he calls a 'dialogue conflict.'[3] Others like Etienne Delaruelle tend to dismiss popular religion as a vulgarized version of the official religion of the elite.[4]

The second major dimension over which controversies rage is about the time frame of popular religious beliefs and customs. Are they static, continuing in an unchanged form for ages, or are they dynamic enough to undergo transformation? Historians of popular culture like Emmanuel Le Roy Ladurie are inclined towards arguing for a 'history that essentially stood still' by highlighting a sense of inertia in popular psychology that resisted changes, as evident (according to their interpretations) from the persistence of certain traditional beliefs and norms of behaviour over centuries.[5] Some other continental historians and social scientists, however, have found from their examination and analysis of records (mainly from the French medieval and early modern archives) that there were 'changes in collective attitudes as a long process of evolution in the *longue durée* (long duration).'[6]

The third dimension relates to the approach which we today should adopt when discussing popular religious beliefs and practices that originated in a dimly perceived hoary past, inadequately recorded—and much of which still continues in certain parts of the world, either in its original form (if we accept the claims of the theoreticians of a static religion), or in changed form (as described by those who find popular religion following a given rhythm of change). The current debate over the modern historian's approach to popular religion should be whether to regard them as irrational (by our standards), internally rational (by the standards of the community which believed and practised them), or rational per se.

This involves the larger debate between relativists and non-relativists. Followers of the former school of thought in the field of popular culture and religion tend to argue that concepts used by the practitioners of popular religion in a certain region and at a certain time can only be understood in the context of the way of life of these peoples. What to outsiders from a distance might appear to be irrational can have an internal logic that makes sense to the practitioners.[7] While the earlier generation of anthropologists like James Frazer were inclined to treat their beliefs and practices as erroneous and irrational, there is an increasing tendency among certain historians today to discard that dismissive approach, and while accepting the argument about the relevance of internal logic in popular religious practices, to assert at the same time the need to apply certain common criteria that have developed over the ages to judge rational behaviour today. If all are equally rational, if there is no irrationality, the term 'rationality' is emptied of all meaning.[8]

In what way then, must modern historians make sense of beliefs and practices which do not prima facie conform to our standards of logic and rational behaviour? Some have suggested what has been called the 'Baptist theory' of history—a total immersion, a genuine attempt to get 'under the skin of the past'. 'We must cultivate a sociocultural history, warts and all—one in which all elements of earlier belief systems are accorded explanatory symmetry and "equal time" '.[9]

While it is certainly necessary to adopt this approach for any understanding of popular culture and religion, and to give them their due respect, we should also beware of the risks quite often involved in such 'immersion'. As Jacques Le Goff has warned: 'It would be abdication of the historian's responsibilities if he were to allow a fetishistic respect for his subject to lead to a submersion in the mentality of the era he was studying, such that he refused to apply to it other concepts than those current at the time.'[10]

From this brief summary of the current debates on popular religion and culture among academicians of the West, it becomes obvious that any theory of popular religion must grapple with the fact that its boundaries shift in response to many kinds of circumstances. It cannot be defined in terms of the purely structural characteristics of practice—which can change, or expand, beyond the original form, or even the initial objectives of its founding fathers, as we have observed, for example, in the history of the Karta-bhaja sect. For instance, some Western theoreticians argue that 'a religious phenomenon is popular when it manifests hostility to any systematic objectivization of religious belief, since it is the explosion of subjective emotions and tends to bring the divine onto the horizon of daily life'.[11] Still others have stressed the world of 'magism' of popular therapeutics, of magical actions as an essential part of popular religion.[12] Some among them seem to identify popular religion with the beliefs and practices of the peasantry only— as evident from the heavy concentration of their archival research on the rural records.[13]

Yet, if we look back at the history of the various forms of popular religion in Bengal, we find that it does not quite fit exclusively into any of the theoretical models discussed so far. While in certain respects—particularly in their earlier phase—some cults and devotees did indeed 'manifest hostility to any systematic objectivisation of religious belief' and in an 'explosion of subjective emotions brought the divine onto the horizon of daily life', their later transformation suggests major departures.The Karta-bhaja sect, for instance, ended up exactly in the same sort of objectivization—marked by the typical characteristics of a religious institution: central headquarters (in Ghoshpara); objects of ritualistic worshipping; a thriving business enterprise based on elaborate organization of fairs and rituals. Then again, what began as a religion practised by the peasants, soon began to seek its ways and modes of expression in the urban (or semi-urban) world of commercial society, and drew into its fold the elite laity. One can still, however, claim that the Karta-bhaja sect remains a popular religion, if one goes by the predominance of 'magism' and popular therapeutics at the Ghoshpara fair today, as also by the congregation of people of various religious faiths, which hark back to its syncretistic traditions.

Should one try then to look at popular religions—particularly in the Indian context—as reflections of a much more fluid and changing reality than envisaged by some of the western theoreticians? Although certainly relevant to certain historical conditions and geographical situations, and no doubt major contributions to our efforts to decode the language of popular religion and formulate a methodology to carry out the task, the theoretical framework formulated by them may not always provide adequate space for the queries which we in India may be facing while exploring our own terrain of popular culture and religion.

As stated in the introduction, popular religion is not an extinct species in Indian conditions—to be pursued as a subject for anthropological research into the curious behaviour of our ancestors, or as an object of cold academic dissection of religious practices and customs that may be still surviving among some obscure primitive communities! Popular religious beliefs and activities in India—as distinct from the strictly ordained norms of behaviour sanctioned by the established religious institutions belonging to the various orders of Hinduism, Islam, Christianity or Buddhism—have survived all these years by drawing heavily upon the rites and customs which predate the establishment of these structured religious orders, as well as by selectively accepting and rejecting the norms and practices of these established orders. Popular religion in India therefore has a long history of both continuity and transformation.

The transformation was brought about by a succession of political regimes over a period spanning thousands of years—ranging from the hoary past of the still-disputed issue of the exogenic Aryan aggression over the indigenous Dravidian population, through the historically recorded impact (on popular culture and religion) of governance by a succession of invaders from the Middle East—Turks, Pathans, Mughals—and reaching the eighteenth–ninteenth century with the consolidation of British colonial power in India. All these successive political orders left their impact on the popular religious beliefs and practices.

While the history of this transformation of various Indian popular religious cults and sects provides the historian with a fascinating chronicle of changes in collective sensibility, the continuity of popular religious customs and practices in both rural and urban Indian today poses a challenge to the Indian historian. Unlike the Western historian who can afford to look at a past without any present social obligations, any conscientious Indian historian, living in India and engaged in research in popular religious thoughts and actions, cannot escape the responsibility of moving further into exploring two more major issues of debate—(i) why do these popular religions still survive? And (ii) what are the social implications of their continuity in the everyday life of the common masses?

Poised against the backdrop of an exciting panorama of theories about popular religion, the followers of many contemporary Bengali cults and sects may appear as congenital deviants, who do not somehow fit into the conceptual framework of 'popular religion' as defined by today's historians, just as they did not fit into the religious framework as defined by the contemporary sociopolitical regime under which they were born. The relationship of these sects with the established religious orders—both Hindu and Islamic—was from the very beginning what one school of theoreticians would be tempted to claim as one of 'conflict'. But, let's hasten to add that the stress on divide and conflict was more on the part of the official Hindu and Islamic religious clergy than the sects' preceptors, who tended to avoid any open confrontation with the established religious orders.[14]

We also notice that the role of the individual—in continuation of the important position assigned to the guru or murshid in most of the popular religious cults in Bengal—appears to be less conspicuous in the history of Western popular religion, as recorded by modern historians and theoreticians.

The other distinctive feature shared by many Bengali popular religious groups is that they have been both static and dynamic. What some historians of popular religion would describe as a sense of inertia in collective psychology can be found in the persistence of certain rituals and magical beliefs even today. But, at the same time, the history of the sects, as we have observed, are of dynamic changes through acculturation and adoption of new ideas at different periods—often to the detriment of the idealism of the original belief system of the founders.

One can certainly discover an internal logic in the rituals and the popular belief in miracles found among devotees. The diseased and the disabled, as well as their relatives who bring them for treatment, have their own mode of reasoning—attributing the recovery of the patients to divine mercy, and the failure to obtain a remedy to some lapse on their part.

Modern theoretical attempts—no doubt creative and original—to define such behaviour as 'internally rational' may satisfy those historians in the West who are engaged in chronicling and analysing usually extinct popular religious beliefs and practices which do not affect them and their social environment any longer today in a major way. But in the modern Indian context, merely recognizing internal logic in popular beliefs and behaviour patterns and stopping at that point, entails the risk of an *a priori* rejection of the other part of popular religion—the fears and prejudices born of the 'sleep of reason' which can create the 'monsters' ruthlessly derided by the late eighteenth–early nineteenth-century Spanish painter Goya in his famous series of engravings entitled 'Los Caprichos' (literally meaning 'caprices').[15] The scenes engraved by Goya—showing devout women with rolling eyes worshipping a scarecrow, priests pouring oil into a lamp (held by a standing woman in the shape of a goat), starry-eyed old pilgrims dragging their way to the 'Miraculous Fountain of San Isidore'—are not fantasies in modern India. Their Indian counterparts are to be found in certain communities which brand women as witches and kill them, or in some far-flung village where a peasant sacrifices a child to propitiate a local goddess, or among the pilgrims who drag disabled people to Ghoshpara and duck them in the Himsagar tank hoping for recovery. No Indian historian therefore can escape the responsibility of explaining the persistence of such popular religious practices, and analysing their implication—social or otherwise—for collective psychology and behaviour.

NOTES

1 See for instance the works of Emmanuel Le Roy Ladurie, *Mind and Method of the Historian* (Cambridge: Cambridge University Press, 1978); Jacques Le Goff, *Time, Work and Culture in the Middle Ages* (Chicago: University of Chicago Press, 1980); Aron Gurevich, *Medieval Popular Culture: Problems of Belief and Perception* (Cambridge: Cambridge University Press, 1988); and Michel Vovelle, *Ideologies and Mentalities* (Cambridge: Polity Press, 1990) among others. In India, one of the pioneering efforts in recent years to evaluate the different streams of popular religion in the country was made in the course of the project, 'Socio-Religious Movements and Cultural Networks in Indian Civilization', which was undertaken by the Indian Institute of Advanced Study (IIAS), Shimla, in 1991–92, and brought together scholars from different parts of India and abroad.

2 See Stewart Elliott Guthrie, *Faces in the Clouds* (New York: Oxford University Press, 1993); and Donald Wiebe, *The Irony of Theology and the Nature of Religion* (Montreal: McGill-Queens University Press, 1991).

3 Karl Marx, Introduction to 'Contribution to the Critique of Hegel's Philosophy of Law' in Marx and Engels, *On Religion* (Moscow, 1976), p. 38.

4 See 'Early Bengali Literature and Newspapers', *Calcutta Review*, 13(25) (1850):141.

5 Jack Goody, *The Logic of Writing and the Organization of Society* (Cambridge: Cambridge University Press, 1986), pp. 9–16.

6 Etienne Delaruelle, *La Piete populaire du moyen age* (Turin, 1975), p. *xv.*

7 Le Goff, *Time, Work and Culture*, p. 185.

8 Mikhail M. Bakhtin, *Rabelais and His World* (Cambridge, MA: MIT Press, 1968).

9 Gurevich, *Medieval Popular Culture*, pp. 179–80.

10 Abanindranath Tagore, *Banglar Brata* (Calcutta: Visva-Bharati, 1995[1943]), pp. 8 and 18. See also, among others, Dineshchandra Sen, *Bangabhasha O Sahitya* (Calcutta, Pashchimbanga Rajya Pustak Parshad, 1986[1896]), and D. D. Kosambi, *Myth and Reality: Studies in the Formation of Indian Culture* (Bombay: Popular Prakashan, 1962).

11 For an interesting analysis of this trend in Gaudiya Vaishnavism, see Ramakanta Chakravarty, *Vaishnavism in Bengal* (Calcutta: Sanskrit Pustak Bhandar, 1985), and his essay 'Chaitanyer Dharmandolan', *Baromash* (April 1986).

12 Ladurie, *Mind and Method of the Historian*, p. 24.

13 Vovelle, *Ideologies and Mentalities.*

14 John C. Marshman, *The Life and Times of Carey, Marshman and Ward: Embracing the History of the Serampore Mission* (1859), quoted in Raja Binaya Krishna Deb, *The Early History and Growth of Calcutta* (Calcutta: Riddhi, 1977).

15 *Bengal Past and Present, Journal of the Calcutta Historical Society* I (July–December, 1907): 214.

16 See Robert D. Storch (ed.), *Popular Culture and Custom in Nineteenth Century England* (London: Croom Helm, 1982). Also Eileen and Stephen Yeo (eds), *Popular Culture and Class Conflict 1590–1914: Explorations in the History of Labour and Leisure* (Sussex: The Harvester Press, 1981).

17 Akshoy Kumar Dutta, *Bharatbarshiya Upasak Samproday*, VOL. I (Calcutta: Karuna Prakashani, 1987[1870]), p. 230.

18 Dutta, *Bharatbarshiya Upasak Samproday*, VOL. I, p. 230. Also see Sudhir Chakravarty, *Bala-Harhi Samproday O Tader Gan* (Calcutta: Pustak Bipani, 1986), p. 10.

19 Sudhir Chakravarty, *Panchagramer Karcha* (Calcutta: Pratikshan Publications, 1995), pp. 54–5.

20 For an exhaustive analysis of their concepts, see Sudhir Chakravarty, *Bratya Lokayata Lalan* (Calcutta: Pustak Bipani, 1992).

21 Aime Cesaire, *Poetry and Cognition* (1944), quoted by Robin D. G. Kelley in 'A Poetics of Anticolonialism', *Monthly Review* 51(6) (November 1999): 1–21.

22 Quoted by Chakravarty, *Bala-Harhi Samproday*, p. 117.

23 Carlo Ginzburg, *Myths, Emblems, Clues* (London: Hutchinson Radius, 1990[1986]), p. 125.

24 See Shashibhushan Das Gupta, *Obscure Religious Cults* (Calcutta: Firma K. L. M, 1962), pp. 413–24.

25 See Dinendra Kumar Ray, 'Nadiya Jelar Siddhajogi', *Aryavarta* 1(6) (1910).

26 See Sudhir Chakravarty, 'Gabhir Nirjan Pathey', *Ekshan* (Autumn 1985).

27 Wakil Ahmed, *Unish Shatokey Bangali Musalmaner Chinta Chetonar Dhara* (Dhaka: Bangla Academy, 1983), pp. 83–4.

28 Max Weber, 'The Sociology of Religion' (1963); reprinted in *Economy and Society*, VOL. 2 (New York: Bedminster Press, 1968), pp. 30 and 80.

29 Sir James George Frazer, *Apollodorus* (London, 1921), pp. *xxvii–xxxi*.

30 Paul Saye White, Preface in Ernesto De Martino, *Primitive Magic: The Psychic Powers of Shamans and Sorcerers* (Dorset: Prism Press, 1988), p. 1.

31 Robert Oppenheimer, *The Flying Trapeze: Three Crises for Physicists* (London: Oxford University Press, 1964), pp. 2–3.

32 Marc Bloch, *The Historian's Craft* (Manchester University Press, 1967[1954]), p. 38.

33 Roy Porter, Perface in Piero Camporesi, *Bread of Dreams: Food and Fantasy in Early Modern Europe* (Cambridge: Polity Press, 1989), pp. 1–16; here, pp. 3–4.

34 I have in mind the well-meaning efforts made by the Delhi-based cultural organization SAHMAT, and other secular-minded individuals and groups, to foster amity among Hindus and Muslims in

the wake of the communal disturbances following the demolition of the Babri Masjid.

35 Susan Sontag, *Against Interpretation* (London: Vintage, 1994), p. 250.

36 I am referring here particularly to some of the observations made by Ashis Nandy in his various essays, especially in his 'An Anti-Secularist Manifesto' (*Seminar* 314[1985]). Also: 'those showing respect to the satisthal (the place of sati) are not applauding murder; they are applauding the idea of self-sacrifice and the rare human ability to transcend self-interest and fear of death' (Ashis Nandy, *The Sunday Times of India* [New Delhi, 21 November 1999]). In the next sentence, Nandy demonizes rationality by equating it with self-interest when he explains the behaviour of the large crowds of devotees who throng the place of sati to show respect to the dead widow: 'They want to reconfirm their belief that, even today, it is not all a matter of rationality or self-interest.'

37 See Upendra Kumar Das, *Shastramoolak Bharatiya Shakti Sadhana*, VOL. 2 (Santiniketan: Visva-Bharati, 1988), pp. 673–75 and Promode Kumar Chattopadhyay, *Tantrabhilashir Sadhusanga* (Calcutta: Bishwabani Prakashani, 1983), pp. 184–90, for descriptions and analyses of such sexual rites. For a critique of Kabir from today's gender point of view, see Amita Sharma, 'Kabir, Caste and Women' (unpublished paper, available at the Indian Institute of Advanced Study, Shimla).

38 Ginzburg, *Myths, Emblems, Clues*, p. *viii*.

39 Camporesi, *Bread of Dreams*, p. 17.

Changing Role of Kali

1   Sister Nivedita, *Kali The Mother* (Pithorgarh: Advaita Ashrama, 1950[1897]).

2   Gurevich, *Medieval Popular Culture*.

3   Reports of animal, and even human, sacrifice at the altars of these goddesses of death in the villages of nineteenth-century Bengal appeared in contemporary newspapers. See Brajendranath Bandyopadhyay (ed.), *Sambadpatrey Sekaler Katha*, 2 VOLS (Calcutta: Bangiya Sahitya Parishat, 1949). For an interesting analysis of the development of the goddess Rankini, see Nrisinghaprasad

Bhaduri, *Shyamamayer Charitkatha, Shyamamayer Gan* (Calcutta: Antaranga Prakashana, 1993), p. 9.

4 Niharranjan Ray, *Bangalir Itihas: Aadi Parba* (Calcutta: Dey's Publishing, 1993), p. 481.

5 Heinrich Zimmer, *The Art of Indian Asia,* VOL. I (New York: Pantheon Books, 1960), p. 94.

6 Quoted in Ray, *Bangalir Itihas,* p. 490.

7 Bhaduri, *Shyamamayer Charitkatha,* p. 9.

8 *Samachar Darpan* (4 February 1837). Quoted in Bandyopadhyay, *Sambadpatrey Sekaler Katha,* VOL. 2, p. 533.

9 W. W. Hunter, *The Annals of Rural Bengal* (Calcutta: R. D. Press, 1965[1868]), p. 73.

10 Bakhtin, *Rabelais and His World,* p. 319.

11 Quoted in Upendrakumar Das, *Shastramoolak Bharatiya Shakti Sadhana,* VOL. I (Calcutta: Visva-Bharati, 1984), pp. 72–3.

12 Kumudnath Mullick, *Nadia Kahini* (Calcutta, 1986), pp. 116–17.

13 See Shashibhushan Das Gupta, *Bharater Shakti Sadhana O Shakta Sahitya* (Calcutta: Sahitya Samsad, 1965).

14 Quoted in Das, *Shastramoolak Bharatiya Shakti Sadhana,* p. 500.

15 Georges Bataille, *L'erotisme* (1957). Quoted in Jerry Aline Flieger, *The Purloined Punch Line* (Baltimore: Johns Hopkins University Press, 1991).

16 Bhaduri, *Shyamamayer Charitkatha,* pp. 22–4.

17 Das, *Shastramoolak Bharatiya Shakti Sadhana,* p. 476.

18 Das, *Shastramoolak Bharatiya Shakti Sadhana,* p. 135.

19 Dineshchandra Sen, *Brihat Banga,* VOL. I (Calcutta: Dey's Publishing, 1993), p. 8.

20 A. K. Ray, *A Short History of Calcutta* (Calcutta: Riddhi, 1982[1902]), p. 12.

21 As narrated by Aghori during an interview, in Pramode Kumar Chattopadhyay, *Tantrabhilasheer Sadhusanga* (Calcutta: Bishwabani Prakashani, 1983), pp. 199–200.

22 Panchkari Bandyopadhyay, *Banglar Tantra* (Calcutta: Bengal Publishers Ltd., 1982), pp. 124–5.

23 See P. Thankappan Nair (ed.), *Calcutta in the 17th Century* (Calcutta: Firma KLM, 1986), pp. 29–32.

24 Ray, *A Short History of Calcutta*, p. 14.

25 Ray, *A Short History of Calcutta*, p. 27.

26 Quoted in Deb, *The Early History and Growth of Calcutta*, pp. 64–5.

27 Deb, *The Early History and Growth of Calcutta*, pp. 65–6.

28 See Prankrishna Dutta, *Kolikatar Itibritta* (Calcutta: Pustak Bipani, 1981), pp. 133–4.

29 Ray, *A Short History of Calcutta*, p. 22. Also Nair (ed.), *Calcutta in the 17th Century*, p. 31.

30 Suprakash Ray, *Bharater Krishak Bidroha O Ganatantrik Sangram* (Calcutta: DNBA Brothers, 1972), pp. 363–5.

31 See Eric Hobsbawm's books and articles on social banditry and primitive rebellions, for instance, E. J. Hobsbawm and George Rudé, *Captain Swing* (New York: W. W. Norton and Company, 1975[1969]); E. J. Hobsbawm, *Bandits* (Harmondsworth: Penguin, 1985[1969]); *Revolutionaries* (London: Orion Books, 1994[1973]); *Uncommon People* (London: Little Brown, 1999[1998]); and the first six *Subaltern Studies* volumes edited by Ranajit Guha (New Delhi: Oxford University Press).

32 Gyanendramohan Das (ed.), *Bangala Bhashar Abhidhan* (Calcutta: Sahitya Samsad, 1986[1916]), p. 1443.

33 See the entry on *Thugee* in *Vishwakosh* (Nagendranath Basu comp, and ed.) (Calcutta, 1988[1886]).

34 For a discussion on the difference between the 'naked' and the 'nude', see Kenneth Clark, *The Nude* (London: Pelican Books, 1960), pp. 1–25, and John Berger, *Ways of Seeing* (London: BBC, 1979), p. 54.

35 Durgadas Lahiri (ed.), *Bangalir Gan* (Calcutta, 1905), p. 28.

36 Lahiri, *Bangalir Gan*, p. 27.

37 Lahiri, *Bangalir Gan*, p. 29.

38 Lahiri, *Bangalir Gan*, p.6.

39 Sister Nivedita, *Kali the Mother*, p. 54.

40 W. J. Wilkins, *Modern Hinduism* (Calcutta: Rupa, 1975[1887]), p. 340.

41 Ritwik Ghatak, 'Chalachhitra Chinta', *Chitrabikshan* (special issue on Ghatak) (January–April 1976): 53

42 Ghatak, 'Chalachhitra Chinta', p. 41.

'Pir' and 'Narayana'

1 '[E]thnology modifies history's chronological perspectives . . . it proposes a history made up of repeated or expected events, such as festivals on the religious calendar . . . Through this shift in interest towards the life of ordinary men, historical ethnology leads naturally to the study of mentalities, considered as "that which changes least" in historical evolution' (Le Goff, *Time, Work and Culture in the Middle Ages*, pp. 228–35).

2 Among the various publications in which they are quoted, the following are important sources: Basu, *Bangla Vishwakosh*, VOL. 18, pp. 154–61; Sen, *Bangabhasha O Sahitya*, VOL. 2, pp. 467–597; Girindranath Das, *Bangla Pir Sahityer Katha* (Barasat, 1976), pp. 447–98; Sukumar Sen, *Bangla Sahityer Itihas*, VOL. 1, SECTION 2 (Calcutta: Modern Book Agency, 1948); Muhammad Enamul Huq, *A History of Sufi-ism in Bengal* (Dhaka: Asiatic Society of Bangladesh, 1975), pp. 290–2. About 150 manuscripts narrating the folktale have been traced so far from different parts of Bengal.

3 See Huq, *A History of Sufi-ism in Bengal*, p. 2.

4 Sen, *Bangabhasha O Sahitya*, VOL. 1, p. 129.

5 Sen, *Bangabhasha O Sahitya*, VOL. 2, pp. 312–17.

6 For a description of these literary compositions, see Sen, *Bangabhasha O Sahitya*; Wakil Ahmed, *Bangla Sahityer Purabritta* (Dhaka: Khan Brothers and Co., 1974); Jagadish Narayan Sarkar, *Banglay Hindu-Musalman Samparka, Madhyajug* (Calcutta: Bangiya Sahitya Parishat, 1981).

7 Le Goff, *Time, Work and Culture in the Middle Ages*, p. 26.

8 The Satyapir folklore and the ritual are inseparable, since most of the texts direct the devotees to listen to the tales of the deity following the ritual of the votive offering of shirni. See *Satyanarayaner Panchali* by Shankaracharya: 'Pujante Bratakatha shunibey jatoney.' (At the end of the worship, listen carefully to the recitation of the auspicious tale). See Vladimir Propp on folktales in the West, in *Theory and History of Folklore*: 'The tale is part of the

ritual; it is attached to the rite' (Manchester: Manchester University Press, 1984), p. 119.

9   Propp, *Theory and History of Folklore*, p. 75.

10   Shankaracharya, *Sri Sri Satyanarayaner Panchali* (Calcutta: Rajendra Library, n.d.).

11   *Satyapirer Punthi* attributed variously to Wajed Ali and Garibullah, quoted in Das, *Bangla Pir Sahityer Katha*, p. 450.

12   Faizullah, *Satyapirer Panchali* quoted in Huq, *A History of Sufi-ism in Bengal*, p. 291.

13   A term used by the French social historian Emmanuel Le Roy Ladurie, quoted in Robert Darnton's *The Great Cat Massacre* (Harmondsworth: Penguin, 1985), p. 32.

14   Quoted in Sen, *Bangabhasha O Sahitya*, pp. 55–7. Modern research suggests that the treatise could have been composed in the fifteenth–sixteenth centuries.

15   Reprinted in Akshoy Kumar Maitreya (ed.), *Aitihashik Chitra*, 1(1) (January, 1899), quoted in Anima Mukhopadhyay, *Atharo Shataker Bangla Punthitey Itihas Prasanga* (Calcutta: Sahityalok, 1987), p. 127.

16   Huq, *A History of Sufi-ism in Bengal*, p. 90. Hallaj was killed by orthodox Muslims in 922 AD for his claim to divine manifestation.

17   See Munshi Abdul Karim's introduction to Ballav's *Satyanarayaner Punthi* (seventeenth century) in *Bangiya Sahitya Parishat Patrika* (1915), quoted in Das, *Bangla Pir Sahityer Katha*, p. 447.

18   Huq, *A History of Sufi-ism in Bengal*, p. 124.

19   Shankaracharya, *Sri Sri Satyanarayaner Punthi*.

20   Quoted in Das, *Bangla Pir Sahityer Katha*, p. 483.

21   Quoted in Das, *Bangla Pir Sahityer Katha*, 457.

22   The ritual, with slight modifications, followed by the narration of the tale of Satyanarayana, is still observed in Bengali villages. There is no fixed date for the worshipping of the deity. Any auspicious evening (e.g. a full-moon night, or the last day of a Bengali month) is usually chosen.

23   See Faizullah, *Satyapirer Panchali*, quoted in Das, *Bangla Pir Sahityer Katha*, p. 453.

24   Das, *Bangla Pir Sahityer Katha*, p. 470.

25 Shankaracharya, *Sri Sri Satyanarayaner Punthi*.

26 Huq, *A History of Sufi-ism in Bengal*, p. 292.

27 Kalia Ranjan Kanungo in 'Islam and its Impact on India', quoted by Musa Kalim in *Madhyajuger Bangla Sahitye Hindu-Muslim Samparka* (Calcutta, 1988), p. 129.

28 Huq, *A History of Sufi-ism in Bengal*, pp. 289–90.

29 Sen, *Bangabhasha O Sahitya*, pp. 583–5.

30 Huq, *A History of Sufi-ism in Bengal*, p. 289.

31 Das, *Bangla Pir Sahityer Katha*, p. 452.

32 Quoted in Gurevich, *Medieval Popular Culture*, p. *xxii*.

33 Le Goff, *Time, Work and Culture*, p. 235.

34 Keith Thomas, *Religion and the Decline of Magic* (London: Weidenfeld and Nicholson, 1973).

Radha and Krishna

1   The other terms often used to describe these two currents apart from 'elite' and 'popular', are 'urban' and 'rural', or 'written' and 'oral'. No doubt, these binary terms define categories which sometimes overlap at certain levels, thus making them appear as inadequate tools of precise definition. But then, the very nature of the historical development of the two traditions makes it difficult to imprison them into two watertight compartments.

2   We can mention in this connection the numerous types of folk songs about Radha and Krishna that were prevalent in Bengal prior to the advent of Chaitanya (e.g. *Krishna-dhamali, jager gan,* jhumur, etc.), as well as the padabalis of Chandidas and Vidyapati.

3   Writing towards the end of the nineteenth century, Bengali scholar Akshoy Kumar Dutta listed at least 56 Vaishnavite or semi-Vaishnavite sects flourishing in Bengal between 1870–80, some of them tracing their ancestry to the seventeenth–eighteenth centuries. See *Bharatbarshiya Upasak Sampraday*, VOL. I.

4   Radha's name does not appear in the *Srimad Bhagavata*, the ancient Sanskrit Purana composed in the ninth or tenth century, the tenth chapter of which forms the basis of the Vaishnavite theological system. Here she looms vaguely in the background as one among the *gopinis* described as *anaya radh itah* (one who

propitiated him, i.e. Krishna). The word *radh* from it was extrapolated by later Vaishnavite scholars to claim that this gopini was Radha. As a consort of Krishna's, she figures under the name of Lakshmi in the later Puranas like *Brahmavaivarta* and *Padma*.

5 For critical commentaries on these various stages in Radha's development in religion and literature, see Shashibhushan Das Gupta, *Sree Radhar Kramabikash* (Calcutta: A Mukherjee, 1963); Satyavati Giri, *Bangla Sahitye Krishnakathar Kramabikash* (Calcutta: Pustak Bipani, 1988); Gouri Bhattacharya, *Bangla Loksahitye Radha Krishna Prasanga* (Calcutta: Rabindra Bharati University, 1989); and Sumanta Banerjee, *Appropriation of a Folk-Heroine: Radha in Medieval Bengali Vaishnavite Culture* (Shimla: Indian Institute of Advanced Study, 1993).

6 See *Chaitanya Charitamrita* by Krishnadas Kabiraj (1496–1583); *Chaitanya Bhagavat* by Vrindavan Das (1507–1609?); and *Chaitanyamangal* by Jayananda (1512–?).

7 See Satyavati Giri, *Bangla Sahitye Krishnakathar Kramabikash*, pp. 217–20.

8 Hirendranarayan Mukhopadhyay (ed.), *Ujjalaneelamani* (Calcutta, 1965).

9 See Sushil Kumar Dey, *Early History of the Vaishnava Faith and Movement in Bengal* (Calcutta, 1961), pp. 448–520.

10 See Ramakanta Chakravarty, *Vaishnavism in Bengal* (Calcutta, 1985), pp. 181–2.

11 See Banerjee, *Appropriation of a Folk-Heroine*, pp. 40–2.

12 Chakravarty, *Bala-harhi Sampraday*.

13 See Dineshchandra Sen, *Bangabhasha O Sahitya*, VOL. II, p. 554. Narrating his experiences while searching for manuscripts, Dineshchandra Sen observed: 'I have moved from one district to another looking for ancient manuscripts. There are not many Bengali manuscripts in the homes of the educated gentry; but they can be found in heaps in the houses of the lower orders. The extreme care with which they have preserved the ancient manuscripts should make the Bengali litterateurs grateful to them.'

14 See Shantikumar Dasgupta and Haribandhu Mukhoti (eds), *Ishwar Gupta Rachanabali*, VOL. I (Calcutta: Sanskrita Pustak Bhandar, 1977), p. 110.

15 The Bengali nouveau riche played an important role in the gradual
    secularization of the Radha-Krishna legend in these newly evolved
    urban cultural representations and performances, which were
    increasingly moving away from the original religious motivations.
    A typical contemporary example was the annual *Rash-jatra*, held
    in the month of November, in Calcutta and its suburbs. It was
    derived from the description of Krishna's dance with the gopinis—
    the *Rash* dance in the *Srimad Bhagavata* and the hallisha dance in
    Harivamsa (which were meant to celebrate Krishna's performance
    as the god of all rasas, or the various devotional and aesthetic
    instincts). But the *Rash-jatras* of nineteenth-century Calcutta and
    its neighbourhood, mainly organized by the city's rich gentry,
    became occasions for popular participation in a carnival of sorts,
    with songs and dances, carousals and gambling (reports in
    Samachar Darpan [11 and 18 November 1837], quoted in Bandy-
    opadhyay, *Sangbadpatrey Sekaler Katha*, VOL. 2, pp. 277–8).

16 See Sumanta Banerjee, *Appropriation of a Folk-Heroine*.

17 A lucid explanation of the allegorical implications of the Radha-
    Krishna fable can be found in Shashibhushan Das Gupta, *Obscure
    Religious Cults* (Calcutta: Firma K. L. Mukhopadhyay, 1962), p. 124.

18 Sen's *Bangabhasha O Sahitya*, VOL. 2, Chapter Eight, analyses the
    domestication of these divinities in the medieval Mangal-kavyas.
    Also compare the following description by a late nineteenth-
    century observer of a village scene in Bengal on the last day of the
    popular religious festival Durga puja (On this day, the image of the
    goddess Durga—another name for Parvati—is immersed in the
    river Ganges, a gesture symbolic of sending her back to her hus-
    band Shiva's home in the Himalayas): 'when the village housewife
    with tears in her eyes, and in a choked voice, bade goodbye to the
    Mother (i.e. Durga), no one seemed to remember the great,
    omnipotent goddess. It was as if the sad scene of seeing off a vil-
    lage bride on her way to her father-in-law's house had just been
    re-enacted' (Debaprasad Sarbadhikari, *Smritirekha* [Calcutta:
    Nikhilchandra Sarbadhikari, 1933], p. 83.

19 For a critical analysis of the theological controversy over *para-
    kiyabad*, see Hitesh Ranjan Sanyal, *Bangla Kirtoner Itihas* (Calcutta:
    K. P. Bagchi for the Centre for Studies in Social Sciences, 1989),
    p. 228.

20 Shashibhushan Das Gupta in his *Obscure Religious Cults* (pp. 113–14) analyses the relationship between Bengali Vaishnavism and the Sahajiyas.

21 If however one believes that these gods of the Hindu pantheon were recast from original rural community deities (like Shiva, who was especially associated with agriculturist devotees, or Krishna who was the god of the Yadava or cowherd community), one can argue that the attributes of Shiva and Krishna that we find in folklore were built into the popular conception of these deities from the beginning. From this argument, one can conclude that the folklorists did not demystify or distort their deities, but retained them as their community or domestic gods and goddesses with limited powers over their respective followers, as they had always been in their tradition. That it was the later Brahman theologians who changed the character of these folk deities when they incorporated them into their pantheon and endowed them with universal omnipotent powers and deeper spiritual essence. For a discussion on this transaction between folk religion and Brahmanical theology, see Sumanta Banerjee, *The Parlour and the Streets:* Elite and Popular Culture in Nineteenth-Century Calcutta (Calcutta: Seagull Books, 2018[1989]) p. 104–105.

22 Theoretical explanations for the tendency to desecrate the omnipotent divinities in folk cultures of medieval Europe can be found, among others, in Bakhtin's *Rabelais and His World* and Gurevich's *Medieval Popular Culture*. See also Sumanta Banerjee, 'Bogey of the Bawdy: Changing Concept of "Obscenity" in 19th century Bengali Culture', *Economic and Political Weekly* 22(29) (18 July 1987): 1197–1206 for an analysis of similar desecration in Bengali folk literature.

23 For an exhaustive history and critical analysis of kobi-gan, see Prafulla Pal, *Pracheen Kobiwalar Gan* (Calcutta: University of Calcutta, 1958).

24 The other five states of minds are *abhisarika* (when Radha goes out to seek her lover); *basaka-sajjika* (when Radha adorns herself at home awaiting her lover); *utkanthita* (when Radha gets worried at the delay in her lover's arrival); *kalahantarita* (when Radha feels remorse after having spurned her repentant lover); and *swadhinbhartrika* (when Radha totally controls the lover who serves her).

25 The manuscript of *Srikrishnakirtan* carries the date 1682, but Sukumar Sen in *Bangla Sahityer Itihas* (Delhi, 1987) speculates that it
   could have been written in the fifteenth century.

26 Bodu Chandidas, *Srikrishnakirtan* (Calcutta, 1954), p. 63.

27 Dasgupta and Mukhoti (eds), *Ishwar Gupta Rachanabali*, pp. 148–
   9. It should be noted that the nineteenth-century Bengali urban
   poet chose to discard the literary style of his predecessor, the
   medieval poet Bodu Chandidas, who introduced elaborate excuses,
   couched in flattering erotic terms, to help Krishna seduce Radha.
   Ram Bosu, instead, has Krishna get down to business straight-
   away—a reflection of the no-nonsense, fast-paced urban lifestyle.

28 The khemta-walis were women dancers from the lower orders,
   whose dances to light musical airs were marked by swinging steps,
   swaying hips and flashing limbs, in sharp contrast to the slow
   movements of the richer class of baijis who were usually north
   Indian, and whose nautch, or dance, performances graced aristo-
   cratic Bengali homes in the nineteenth century.

29 *Hutom Penchar Naksha O Anyanya Samajchitra* (Brajendranath
   Bandyopadhyay and Sajanikanta Das eds) (Calcutta: Bangiya
   Sahitya Parishad, 1977[1862]). p. 38.

30 Mitra, *Sadhabar Ekadoshi*, Act II, Scene I (first EDN Calcutta, 1866).

31 Dasgupta and Mukhoti (eds), *Ishwar Gupta Rachanabali*, p. 200.

32 Dasgupta and Mukhoti (eds), *Ishwar Gupta Rachanabali*, pp. 153–
   4.

33 Baishnabcharan Basak, *Bharatiya Sahasra Sangeet* (Calcutta: Basak,
   n.d.[early twentieth century]), p. 257.

34 Peter Burke, *Popular Culture in Early Modern Europe* (London: Temple Smith, 1978), p. 60.

35 Basak, *Bharatiya Sahasra Sangeet*, p. 272. The word *daphaye* can
   have two meanings: one, which means 'in phases' (implying that
   Krishna will receive the court order in instalments), and the other,
   meaning 'undoing' (of Krishna) as used in the popular Bengali
   term *dapha-rapha*.

36 For a brief account of the life and poetry of this flamboyant character of early nineteenth-century Calcutta, see Ramakanta
   Chakravarty, *Bismrita Darpan* (Calcutta, 1971]), pp. 32–7.

37 Durgadas Lahiry, *Bangalir Gan* (Calcutta, 1905), p. 403.

38 Lahiry, *Bangalir Gan*, pp. 403–4. The allusion is to the mythological story of Krishna as a child stealing butter from his mother's cupboard.

39 Bakhtin describes how on such occasions of carnival in medieval Europe, the common people 'mimicked serious rituals' and 'laughed and scoffed at the deity', and then explains the role of the comic in folk culture: 'laughter liberates not only from external censorship but first of all from the great interior censor; it liberates from the fear that developed in man during thousands of years, fear of the sacred, of prohibitions, of the past, of power' (*Rabelais and His World*, pp. 93–4).

40 Jhumur songs were usually accompanied by female dancers, known as jhumurwalis. The jhumur form developed from tribal song and dance performances in the border areas of West Bengal-Bihar, and became a part of the Radha-Krishna kirtan narrative; see Ashutosh Bhattacharya, *Banglar Lokanritya* (Calcutta: A. Mukherjee and Co., 1982), p. 90. The musical style of jhumur however should not be confused with the term jhumar, which is usually used to describe the epilogue of a conventional Vaishnavite pala-kirtan. See Haridas Das, *Sree Sree Gaudiya Vaishnav Abhidhan*, VOL. 2 (Nabadwip, 1957), p. 1096.

41 Lahiry, *Bangalir Gan*, p. 1041.

42 *Chandidas Padabali* (Calcutta, n.d.), p. 74.

43 Meghnad Gupta, *Rater Kolkata*, p. 10.

44 Dutta, *Kolikatar Puratan Kahini O Pratha*, pp. 24–5.

45 *Bangadarshan* (Kartick, 1280 B.S. [1873]). For those not acquainted with the names of some of the mythological characters quoted here (apart from the better known Krishna, Radha, Ravana and Sita), Kaikeyi was Rama's stepmother, at whose behest Rama was sent into exile for fourteen years, and Dasaratha was his father.

46 For discussions on the theoretical concept of the 'world upside down' in folk culture, see Barbara A. Babcock (ed.), *The Reversible World* (Ithaca: Cornell University Press, 1978).

47 'A Hindoo on the Drama', *Morning Chronicle* (January 1855).

48 *Bangadarshan* (Kartick, 1280 B.S. [1873]).

49 Hur Chunder Dutt, *Bengali Life and Society: A Discourse* (Calcutta, 1853), pp. 10–11.

50 Mahendranath Dutta, *Kolikatar Puratan Kahini O Pratha*, pp. 29–30.

51 For an analysis of the impact of English education on the new generation of Bengali intellectuals in nineteenth-century Calcutta, see Banerjee, *The Parlour and the Streets*, pp. 176–8. The trend among young educated Bengali Hindus to convert to Christianity (e.g. famous poet Michael Madhusudan Dutt), or gravitate towards the new reformist religion of Brahmo Samaj, posed a threat to the orthodox Hindu society. Bankim Chandra Chattopadhyay represented the other trend among educated Hindus of re-interpreting Hinduism and attempting to establish its superiority by trying to adopt the methodology of Western rational enquiry.

52 Bankim Chandra Chattopadhyay, 'Krishna-charitra' in *Bankim Rachanabali* (Calcutta: Sahitya Samsad, 1954), p. 476.

53 Rabindranath Tagore, 'Panchabhoot' in *Rabindra Rachanabali*, VOL. 2 (Calcutta: Visva-Bharati, 1984), p. 631.

54 Tapan Raychaudhuri, *Europe Reconsidered: Perceptions of the West in Nineteenth Century Bengal* (New Delhi: Oxford University Press, 1988), p. 149.

55 Rabindranath Tagore, *Lokasahitya*, VOL. 2 (Calcutta: Visva-Bharati, 1984), p. 82.

56 For a detailed account of working conditions of the labouring poor, and their entertainments in nineteenth-century Calcutta, see Banerjee, *The Parlour and the Streets*.

57 Gurevich, *Medieval Popular Culture*, pp. 179–80.

58 Required to be vegetarians under the strict Vaishnavite norms, many among these priests could not resist the temptation of eating fish on the sly! Their hypocrisy was lampooned in a famous Kalighat *pat* (painting done on cheap paper by folk painters who settled near the Kali temple in south Calcutta) which showed a cat with the familiar *rasokali* (the Vaishnavite longish 'U' sign) painted on the bridge of his nose, holding a prawn between his teeth. See W. G. Archer, *Bazaar Paintings of Calcutta* (London: Victorian & Albert Museum, 1953), p. 49.

Aulchand

1 See Ramakanta Chakravarty, 'Chaitanyer Dharmandolan', *Baromash* (April 1986).

2. See Chakravarty, 'Chaitanyer Dharmandolan' and Ramakanta Chakravarty, *Vaishnavism in Bengal* (Calcutta: Sanskrit Pustak Bhandar, 1985).

3 Akshoy Kumar Dutta, *Bharatbarshiya Upasak Sampraday*, VOL. I (Calcutta: Karuna Prakasani, 1987[1870]).

4 I am grateful to my friend Sudhir Chakravarty (former Professor, Krishnanagar College, Nadia, West Bengal) for bringing to my notice (through his articles and books) the activities of many of these sects which still survive in the villages of Bengal. See *Bala-Harhi Sampraday O Tader Gan* and *Bratya Lokayata Lalan*.

5 Arnold Toynbee, *An Historian's Approach to Religion* (London: Oxford University Press, 1979), pp. 265–6

6 The available sources are Akshoy Kumar Dutta, *Bharatbarshiya Upasak Sampraday*; Debendranath Dey, *Karta Bhaja Dharmer Itibritta* (Calcutta: Jijnasa, 1968); and Manulal Mishra, *Bhaber Geet* (Calcutta, 1877).

7 The Auls are one of the many Vaishnavite sects with much in common with the Bauls, Darbeshi, Khushibishwashi, Shahebdhani and similar Sufist sects. According to one scholar, the term *aul* could have been associated with the Arabic word *awliya* (plural of *wali*, a word originally meaning 'near', which is used for 'friend' or 'devotee') that refers to a class of perfect men. See Shashibhushan Das Gupta, *Obscure Religious Cults*, p. 161.

8 See Dutta, *Bharatbarshiya Upasak Sampraday*, pp. 220–1. The list of original disciples, according to another source, also included a Muslim, Etawari Biswas (see Debendranath Dey, *Karta-bhaja Dharmer Itibritta*, p. 28).

9 Dutta, *Bharatbarshiya Upasak Sampraday*, pp. 221–2.

10 Dey, *Karta-bhaja Dharmer Itibritta*, p. 22.

11 Chakravarty, *Vaishnavism in Bengal*, p. 354.

12 For exhaustive historical accounts and analyses of the composite cultural output in Bengali literature which resulted from the interaction between the Islamic influence (following the Muslim conquest) and the traditional belief systems (ranging from animist to

Brahmanical), the following texts can be consulted: Sen, *Banga-bhasha O Sahitya*; Sukumar Sen, *Bangla Sahityer Itihas*, VOL. 2 (Calcutta: Ananda Publishers, 1975); Das Gupta, *Obscure Religious Cults*; Wakil Ahmed, *Bangla Sahityer Poorabritta* (Dhaka: Khan Brothers and Co., 1974); Jagadish Narayan Sarkar, *Banglaye Hindu-Musalman Samparka* (Calcutta: Bangiya Sahitya Parishat, 1981)

13 Haq, *A History of Sufi-ism in Bengal*, p. 308.

14 Das Gupta, *Obscure Religious Cults*, p. 170.

15 Jasimuddin, *Mursheeda Gan* (Dhaka: Bangla Academy, 1979), p. 250.

16 Dey, *Karta-bhaja Dharmer Itibritta* p. 22.

17 Chakravarty, *Vaishnavism in Bengal*, pp. 358–59.

18 Dey, *Karta-bhaja Dharmer Itibritta*, p. 36. One of the disciples, Kanai Ghosh, set up his own *gadi* near that of Ramsharan.

19 W. W. Ward in *Asiatick Researches*, VOL. 2, quoted in Dey, *Karta-bhaja Dharmer Itibritta*.

20 Jayanarayan Ghoshal, in his famous book of verses *Karaunanidhan Bilas* (1813), placed Ramsharan on the same pedestal as Guru Nanak and Jesus Christ. He later wrote to Ramdulal asking to be made a disciple, in reply to which Ramdulal sent him a note in the form of a poem inviting him to Ghoshpara (see Dey, *Karta-bhaja Dharmer Itibritta*, pp. 31–4). Among other important nineteenth-century Bengali personalities who became admirers of the Karta-bhaja sect was the Brahmo social reformer Sashipada Bandyo-padhyay, engaged in educational activities among the factory workers, and founder of a working-men's club in 1870 in Barana-gar, an industrial suburb near Calcutta. In 1894, during a visit to the Ghoshpara fair, the poet Nabinchandra Sen came across a number of bhadraloks who were 'mostly graduates, well-educated, and occupying high positions in their professions . . . They included Brahmins, Vaids, Kaisthas, gold-merchants and all other castes' (*Nabinchandra Granthabali: Amar Jeeban*, VOL. 4 [Calcutta: Bangiya Sahitya Parishat, 1959], p. 186).

21 See Dey, *Karta-bhaja Dharmer Itibritta*, p. 34. An old poem claims that Rammohan Roy and Alexander Duff (the Scottish Christian missionary) visited Ramdulal and benefited from his advice (quoted in Dey, *Karta-bhaja Dharmer Itibritta*, p. 86).

22 Quoted in Ramakanta Chakravarty, *Vaishnavism in Bengal*, p. 359.

23 See Ratan Kumar Nandy, *Karta-bhaja Dharma O Sahitya* (Calcutta, 1984); referred to in Dey, *Karta-bhaja Dharmer Itibritta*, p. 86. See also Tushar Chattopadhyay, 'Karta-bhaja O Chicago's Amantran', *Anandabazar Patrika* (29 April 1979).

24 Satyabrata Dey in his addendum in Dey, *Karta-bhaja Dharmer Itibritta*, p. 87. Another modern scholar speculates: 'He (Ramdulal) composed most of the songs for circulation among the urban new rich, and carefully used a jargon and imagery which they might easily understand. In fact Dulalchand (another name of Ramdulal) talked both shop and mysticism' (Chakravarty, *Vaishnavism in Bengal*, p. 361).

25 Quoted in Dey, *Karta-bhaja Dharmer Itibritta*, p. 29.

26 *Calcutta Review*, 6: 407.

27 *Somprakash* (4 April 1864). Quoted in Dey, *Karta-bhaja Dharmer Itibritta*, p. 29.

28 Kumudnath Mullick, *Nadia Kahini* (Calcutta, 1986[1910]), p. 185.

29 Sen, *Nabinchandra Granthabali*, VOL. 4, p. 187.

30 Benoy Krishna Deb, *The Early History and Growth of Calcutta* (Calcutta: Riddhi, 1977[1905]), p. 48. Also, Pramathanath Mullick, *Sachitra Kolikatar Itihas* (Calcutta, 1935), p. 125.

31 Kumudnath Mullick, *Nadia Kahini*, p. 186

32 Dey, *Karta-bhaja Dharmer Itibritta*, p. 67.

33 Christina Larner, *Witchcraft and Religion: The Politics of Popular Belief* (London: Basil Blackwell, 1984).

34 Keith Thomas, *Religion and the Decline of Magic*.

35 While Aulchand died in 1799 (according to some sources), Ramsharan (Sati-Ma's husband) died in 1783, and Ramdulal (her son) in 1833. She lived till 1839.

36 *Samvad Prabhakar* (18 Chaitra 1254 B.S. [1847]). Quoted in Benoy Ghosh (ed.), *Samayik Patrey Banglar Samajchitra*, VOL. I (Calcutta: Papyrus, 1978), pp. 137–8.

37 *Somprakash* (20 Chaitra 1270 B.S. [1863]). Also: 'Although many educated gentlemen are engaged in this (the practices of the Karta-bhaja sect) . . . but the majority are the vulgar masses and women' (Dutta, *Bharatbarshiya Upasak Sampraday*, p. 226).

38 Joseph Campbell, *The Masks of God: Creative Mythology* (Arkana, 1968), p. 149.

39 According to her last wishes, Sati-Ma's body was buried in a part of the ancestral house of the Pals. The spot has become a pilgrimage centre.

40 Dey, *Karta-bhaja Dharmer Itibritta*, p. 37.

41 Dey, *Karta-bhaja Dharmer Itibritta*, p. 105.

42 Dutta, *Bharatbarshiya Upasak Sampraday*, pp. 223–24.

43 According to some latter-day observers, the choice of Friday as an auspicious day could have also been influenced by the Muslim practice of respecting the 'Juma-bar'. Among other similar Muslim influences on 'Karta-bhaja' religious practices, is the obligation to repeat the name of the deity five times a day—like the 'namaz' prayers. See Dey, *Karta-bhaja Dharmer Itibritta*, p. 4 and p. 54.

44 Rev. J. J. Weitbrecht, *Protestant Missions in Bengal*, quoted in P. Thankappan Nair (ed.), *Calcutta in the 19th Century: Company's Days* (Calcutta: Firma KLM, 1989), pp. 864–5.

45 Nair (ed.), *Calcutta in the 19th Century*, pp. 863–4.

46 Choice of partners as well as change of partners following mutual agreement, are quite common among the heterodox Vaishnavite sects. The companionship—whether temporary or lasting—is inaugurated by what is known as *kanthi-badal*, or a mutual exchange of a necklace of beads.

47 Dey, *Karta-bhaja Dharmer Itibritta*, p. 51.

48 Dey, *Karta-bhaja Dharmer Itibritta*, p. 51

49 Tripti Brahma, *Lokajeebaney Banglar Loukik Dharmasangeet O Dharmiya Mela* (Calcutta, 1982), p. 166.

50 Brahma, *Lokajeebaney Banglar Loukik Dharmasangeet*, p. 166.

51 Brahma, *Lokajeebaney Banglar Loukik Dharmasangeet*, pp. 165–6.

52 Brahma, *Lokajeebaney Banglar Loukik Dharmasangeet*, pp. 165–6.

53 Brahma, *Lokajeebaney Banglar Loukik Dharmasangeet*, p. 160.

54 *Samvad Prabhakar* (18 Chaitra 1254 B.S. [1947]), quoted in Ghosh, *Samayik Patrey Banglar Samajchitra*, VOL. I, p. 137.

55 Report of Ghoshpara fair in *Utsamanush* (April 1982). Quoted in Tapan Chakravarty and Bhabaniprasad Sahi (eds), *Dui Banglar*

Kushanshkar—Birodhi Bigyan Chinta (Calcutta: Deep Prakashan, 1993), pp. 129–30. Similar accounts of physical coercion of disabled pilgrims are available from early twentieth-century reports (e.g. Kumudnath Mullick, *Nadia Kahini* and Nagendranath Basu (ed.), *Vishvakosh* 3 (1886–1911), under the entry 'Karta-bhaja'), as well as from recent literature, the most graphic account of a Ghoshpara fair being the travelogue *Kothaye Shejone Achhe* by the late Samaresh Basu, the well-known Bengali novelist, published in 1389 B.S. [1982].

Bamakshyapa

1 For the different versions of Bamakshyapa's birth date, see Aditya Mukhopadhyay, *Tarapeether Katha* (Birbhum: Malancha, 1994), p. 13; and Shambhukinkar Chattopadhyay, *Tarapeeth* (Birbhum, 1994), p. 36.

2 As narrated to Nagendranath Chattopadhyay, grandfather of Shambhukinkar Chattopadhyay, who recorded the reminiscences in his *Tarasharan Bamacharan* (Calcutta: Sarat Book House, 1972), p. 6.

3 Chattopadhyay, *Tarasharan Bamacharan*, p. 7.

4 Chattopadhyay, *Tarasharan Bamacharan*, p. 7.

5 Chattopadhyay, *Tarasharan Bamacharan*, p. 5.

6 These experiences of Bama are described in detail in the popular legends about him, as well as in his own reminiscences, as narrated and recorded by his disciples in the books mentioned above.

7 Although the term 'kaula' has different connotations in Tantrik scriptures, here it is meant to describe a Tantrik preceptor who has acquired spiritual powers through the arduous practice of Kaulachaar (Upendra Kumar Das, *Shastramoolak Bharatiya Shakti Sadhana*, VOL. I [Calcutta, 1984], pp. 580–90).

8 Chattopadhyay, *Tarasharan Bamacharan*, pp. 35–6.

9 Mukhopadhyay, *Tarapeether Katha*, p. 23.

10 Rani Rashmoni was the daughter-in-law of Piritram Marh, founder of the Janbazar Raj family in central Calcutta.

11 For a critical assessment of Ramakrishna's role in the socioreligious life of the Bengali urban middle class, see Sumit Sarkar, *An*

Exploration of the Ramakrishna Vivekananda Tradition (Shimla: Indian Institute of Advanced Study, 1993).

12 Ray, *Bangalir Itihas*, pp. 533–7; 595–6.

13 Ray, *Bangalir Itihas*, p. 537.

14 Within Bengal, in the Birbhum district alone, apart from the popularly acclaimed *peetha* of Tarapeeth, there are four officially recognized *peethas*—Nalhati (where Sati's forehead was supposed to have fallen); Attahash (the site of Sati's lips); Nandipur (the site of her bones); and Bakreshwar (where the portion between her two brows supposedly fell).

15 Chattopadhyay, *Tarasharan Bamacharan*.

16 Mukhopadhyay, *Tarapeether Katha*, pp. 8–9. The origins of the goddess Tara are usually traced to Buddhist scriptures.

17 Das, *Shastramoolak Bharatiya Shakti Sadhana*, VOL. I, p. 168.

18 Chattopadhyay, *Tarapeeth*, p. 17.

19 Chattopadhyay, *Tarapeeth*, pp. 9–20.

20 Chattopadhyay, *Tarapeeth*, pp. 22–4.

21 Chattopadhyay, *Tarapeeth*, pp. 30–4. The tradition continues even today at Tarapeeth, where one finds every day hordes of pilgrims sitting in rows in the afternoon and evenings, being served prasad—usually khichri (gruel made of rice and pulses) with a vegetable dish.

22 Mukhopadhyay, *Tarapeether Katha*, p. 23.

23 Chattopadhyay, *Tarasharan Bamacharan*, p. 138.

24 Pramode Kumar Chattopadhyay, *Tantrabhilashir Sadhusanga* (Calcutta: Bishwabani Prakashani, 1983), p. 289.

25 Upendra Kumar Das, *Shastramoolak Bharatiya Shakti Sadhana*, VOL. I, pp. 464 and 567; VOL. 2, p. 635.

26 Chattopadhyay, *Tarapeeth*, pp. 25–26.

27 By the early nineteenth century, Tarapeeth seemed to have acquired a structured network of services, with a number of sevayats, or managers-cum-head-priests of the various mini temples that had grown around the main temple of Tara; a host of pandas or guide-cum-priests who charged the pilgrims for taking them on a tour around the complex and instructed them on how to offer prayers;

and of course, the ubiquitous community of Doms, who dominated the cremation ground, thanks to their occupational expertise
in burning the corpses.

28 Chattopadhyay, *Tantrabhilashir Sadhusanga*, p. 296.

29 Das, *Shastramoolak Bharatiya Shakti Sadhana*, VOL. 2, pp. 662, 664
and 670.

30 Das, *Shastramoolak Bharatiya Shakti Sadhana*, VOL. 2, p. 1061.

31 Panchkori Bandyopadhyay, *Banglar Tantra* (Calcutta: Bengal Publishers Ltd., 1982), pp. 12–13.

32 Chattopadhyay, *Tantrabhilashir Sadhusanga*, p. 319.

33 Chattopadhyay, *Tantrabhilashir Sadhusanga*, p. 319.

34 Das, *Shastramoolak Bharatiya Shakti Sadhana*, VOL. 2, pp. 934 and
948.

35 Chattopadhyay, *Tantrabhilashir Sadhusanga*, p. 314.

36 Chattopadhyay, *Tantrabhilashir Sadhusanga*, pp. 314–15.

37 Chattopadhyay, *Tantrabhilashir Sadhusanga*, p. 316. In this context,
a story about Bamakshyapa's encounter with a prostitute may be
of interest to the readers.

The collector of revenue of Tarapeeth, Neelmadhab, was reported
to have sent a prostitute to Bamakshyapa to seduce him when he
was deep in meditation. Her embrace woke him up, and sensing
the purpose of her visit, Bamakshyapa greeted the prostitute with
the words: 'Mother (meaning Tara), so you have arrived at last!'
and began to suck at her breasts like a child. At this, the prostitute
fell at his feet and wept saying that she was a sinner. Bamakshyapa
then lifted her up and assured her that Mother Tara would take pity
on her. See Haricharan Gangopadhyay, *Sree Bam-leela* (Calcutta:
Sri Guru Press, 1934), p. 178.

38 Chattopadhyay, *Tantrabhilashir Sadhusanga*, p. 324. The term
'chakra' in Tantrik scriptures has various meanings. But in the
context in which Bamakshyapa used it in the above quote, it refers
to six wheels, which are assumed by Tantrik theologians to be
located in a hierarchical order inside the Sushumna artery
(through which the Kundalini is supposed to creep up to the brain)
of the human body. The *shat-chakra*, or six wheels, start from the
lowest Muladhar based at the root of the spinal cord (which, as
explained earlier nests and nurtures the sexual instincts and

procreative powers). From this basic chakra, the Kundalini moves up through the next four wheels (described in the following order: *Swadhishthan-chakra, Manipur-chakra, Anahata-chakra* and *Bishuddha-chakra*—corresponding respectively in a general sense—to what are termed by modern physiologists as 'sacral plexus', 'solar plexus', 'cardiac plexus' and 'laryngeal plexus' in the network of vessels in the living body). The Kundalini finally reaches the last and sixth chakra at the top of this ladder—*Agya-chakra*, located inside between the two eye-brows of the human body. Agya, which means command, is thus quite appropriately situated at the apex of the human body (Das, *Shastramoolak Bharatiya Shakti Sadhana*, VOL. 2, pp. 948–58.)

39 Chattopadhyay, *Tantrabhilashir Sadhusanga*, p. 324.

40 Chattopadhyay, *Tantrabhilashir Sadhusanga*, p. 339.

41 Chattopadhyay, *Tantrabhilashir Sadhusanga*, p. 193.

42 Chattopadhyay, *Tantrabhilashir Sadhusanga*, pp. 326–27.

43 Chattopadhyay, *Tantrabhilashir Sadhusanga*, pp. 192–93.

44 Incidentally, two interesting features need to be noted while examining these two Bengali godlings. First, both are female and fashioned in images of the traditional mother-goddess. Secondly, their worship in rural Bengal cuts across religious barriers. While Muslims along with their Hindu neighbours propitiate Shitala during the outbreak of small-pox, Hindus do the same at the time of cholera with respect to Ola-bibi (of Muslim origin, as evident from the suffix 'bibi').

45 Some of the diseases were indeed foreign to the Bengali physiology. Malaria, for instance, became an epidemic in rural Bengal following the stagnation of river waters caused by the laying down of railway lines by the British administration in the mid-nineteenth century. Cholera broke out for the first time in 1817 (*Calcutta Review* 13(25) [January–June 1850]: 141). Even Western modes of medication to fight diseases, like inoculation against cholera, vaccination against small-pox, etc., were perceived by the people as alien, as yet another form of invasion of the body by external forces. Opposition to, and suspicion of, vaccination and inoculation persisted in Bengali rural society for quite a long time. Forcible penetration of the body by needles and injection of foreign fluids into it, as introduced by Western physicians, were different from herbal

medication like poultices of leaves on wounds, or the sick person's willingness to submit him/herself to a regimen, or faith cure, to which Bengali rural society had been used for generations.

46 Das, *Shastramoolak Bharatiya Shakti Sadhana*, pp. 1034–5.

47 Chattopadhyay, *Tarasharan Bamacharan*, p. 17.

48 Chattopadhyay, *Tarasharan Bamacharan*, pp. 50–7.

49 Chattopadhyay, *Tantrabhilashir Sadhusanga*, p. 293.

50 Chattopadhyay, *Tarasharan Bamacharan*, pp. 71–2.

51 Chattopadhyay, *Tantrabhilashir Sadhusang*, pp. 543–5.

52 Chattopadhyay, *Tantrabhilashir Sadhusang*, pp. 291–5.

53 Upendra Kumar Das, *Shastramoolak Bharatiya Shakti Sadhana*, VOL. I, p. 485.

54 Das, *Shastramoolak Bharatiya Shakti Sadhana*, VOL. I, pp. 490–3.

55 A. K. Ray, *A Short History of Calcutta*, p. 14.

56 'The devotee should pray and practice to attain his goal, in secret; his sadhana is not meant for the public . . . Only worshipping can be done in public gaze. But the devotee's sadhana has to be done in absolute secrecy so that no one comes to know about it; once it is known, it is foiled' (Bamakshyapa, quoted in Das, *Shastramoolak Bharatiya Shakti Sadhana*, VOL. I, p. 600).

57 *Shastramoolak Bharatiya Shakti Sadhana*, VOL. 2, p. 688.

58 *Nirukta-tantra*, quoted in Das, *Shastramoolak Bharatiya Shakti Sadhana*, VOL. I, p. 495.

59 Das, *Shastramoolak Bharatiya Shakti Sadhana*, VOL. I, p. 495.

60 Chattopadhyay, *Tarapeeth*, p. 64.

61 Waterborne diseases like dysentry and gastro-enteritis, common during the monsoons, were often fatal in those days.

62 Gangopadhyay, *Sree Bam-leela*, pp. 46–7.

63 Vovelle, *Ideologies and Mentalities*, p. 79.

64. Chattopadhyay, *Tarapeeth*, pp. 68–9.

65 Das, *Shastramoolak Bharatiya Shakti Sadhana*, VOL. I, p. 495.

66. Chattopadhyay, *Tarapeeth*, p. 66.

67 Camporesi, *Bread of Dreams*, p. 128.

68 Das, *Shastramoolak Bharatiya Shakti Sadhana*, VOL. 2, p. 642.

69 Das, *Shastramoolak Bharatiya Shakti Sadhana*, VOL. 2, p. 608.

70 Chattopadhyay, *Tarapeeth*, p. 66.

71 Das, *Shastramoolak Bharatiya Shakti Sadhana*, VOL. 2, pp. 646–8; 660–1.

72 Chattopadhyay, *Tarasharan Bamacharan*, p. 92.

73 Das, *Shastramoolak Bharatiya Shakti Sadhana*, VOL. 2, p. 643.

74 Chattopadhyay, *Tarapeeth*, pp. 57–8.

75 Chattopadhyay, *Tarasharan Bamacharan*, pp. 127–31.

76 Gangopadhyay, *Sree Bam-leela*, p. 185.

77 Lahiri, *Bangalir Gan*, p. 45.

78 Das, *Shastramoolak Bharatiya Shakti Sadhana*, VOL. 2, p. 1044.

79 Gangopadhyay, *Sree Bam-leela*, p. 185.

80 Toynbee, *An Historian's Approach to Religion*, pp. 265–6.

Bharat Mata

1 Quoted in Arabinda Poddar, 'Renaissance in Bengal: Quests and Confrontations 1800–1860' (Shimla: Indian Institute of Advanced Study, 1970), p. 116 [published later as *Renaissance in Bengal: Search for Identity* (Shimla: IIAS, 1977)].

2 Lahiri, *Bangalir Gan*, p. 608.

3 Quoted in Prabhat Kumar Bhattacharya, *Bangla Natakey Swadeshikatar Prabhab* (Calcutta: Sahitya Sree, 1979), p. 277.

4 Lahiri, *Bangalir Gan*, p. 612.

5 Dwijendranath Tagore's memoirs in Bipin Behari Gupta, *Puratan Prasanga* (Calcutta: Vidyabharati Publications, 1966) p. 298.

6 Bhattacharya, *Bangla Natakey Swadeshikatar Prabhab*.

7 Baishnavcharan Basak, *Bharatiya Sahasra Sangeet* (Calcutta, n.d.; probably early twentieth century), p. 485.

8 Quoted in Sister Nivedita, *Kali The Mother*, p. 111.

9 Sister Nivedita, *The Master As I Saw Him* (Calcutta: Udbodhan Karyalay, 1987), p. 135.

10 Jogesh Chandra Bagal, *Hindu Melar Itibritta* (Calcutta, 1945).

11 Ghosh, *Jagaran O Bishphoron*, p.116.

12 Shatapatha-Brahmana, quoted in Das, *Shastramoolak Bharatiya Shakti Sadhana*, VOL. 2, p. 917.

13 Mahabharata: Vana-parba, Sections 127 and 128, Bengali version by Kaliprasanna Sinha (Calcutta: Basumati Sahitya Mandir, 1965), pp. 553–4.

14 Bankim Chandra Chattopadhyay, *Kapalkundala* (1866). For scriptural evidences of human sacrifice, see Das, *Shastramoolak Bharatiya Shakti Sadhana*, VOL. 2, pp. 916–18, and Dutta, *Bharatbarshiya Upasak Sampraday*, VOL. 2, p. III, for a discussion on the practice of human sacrifice among some of the popular religious cults in nineteenth-century Bengal. For incidents of human sacrifice at the altars of local mother-goddesses during that period in villages near Calcutta, see Brojendranath Bandyopadhyay (ed.), *Sangbadpatrey Sekaler Katha*, VOL. I (Calcutta: Bangiya Sahitya Parishat, 1970).

15 Quoted in Arun Kumar Basu, *Shaktigeet Padabali* (Calcutta, 1964), p. 5.

16 Hunter, *The Annals of Rural Bengal*, p. 73.

17 Quoted in Dilip Bose, *Bhagavad-Gita and Our National Movement* (New Delhi: People's Publishing House, 1981), p. 23.

18 Panchkari Bandyopadhyay, *Banglar Tantra* (Calcutta: Bengal Publishers Ltd., 1982, p.130.

19 *Samachar Chandrika* (21 April 1827).

20 Quoted in Sedition Committee Report, 1918. Interestingly enough, the stress on bloodletting as a symbol of self-sacrifice had continued to mark the rhetoric of Bengali revolutionaries even in the post-Swadeshi period, at times almost to the point of an obsession. In the 1940s, Subhash Bose inspired his followers with the message: 'Give me blood, and I shall give you freedom.' Three decades later, a Communist revolutionary of Bengal, Charu Mazumdar, the leader of the Naxalite movement, came up with the slogan: 'He who has not dipped his hand in the blood of class enemies can hardly be called a communist.'

21 Suprakash Ray, *Bharater Baiplabik Sangramer Itihas*, quoted in Tajul Islam Hashmi, *Ouponibeshik Bangla* (Calcutta: Papyrus, 1985), p. 36.

22 Hashmi, *Ouponibeshik Bangla*, pp. 35–6.

23 Lise McKean, 'Bharat Mata' in John Hawley and Donna Wulff (eds), *Devi: Goddesses of India* (Delhi, 1998).

24 It is interesting to note the change in Rabindranath's attitude towards the concept of Bharat Mata. In 1905, following the partition of Bengal and the movement against it, Rabindranath composed at least seven Swadeshi songs, where he visualized Bengal as a Mother, on the lines of Bankim's 'Vande Mataram'. One of these songs, 'Amar Sonar Bangla', was to become the national anthem of Bangladesh. Still later, in his novel *Gora* (1910), the hero addresses his mother (who had adopted him) in these words: 'It is you who is my India.' But at his increasing frustration with the exclusivist Hindu orientation of the votaries of Bharat Mata, Rabindranath not only distanced himself from their movement, but also criticized their concept of worshipping the country as a mother, as evident in his novel *Ghare Bairey* (1916).

25 Dasgupta and Mukhoti (eds), *Ishwar Gupta Rachanabali*, VOL. I, Introduction, p. 11.

Conclusion

1 Le Goff, *Time, Work and Culture in the Middle Ages*, p. 235.

2 Bakhtin, *Rabelais and His World*.

3 Gurevich, *Medieval Popular Culture*.

4 Etienne Delaruelle, *La Piete Populaire du moyen age* (Turin: Bottega d'Erasmo, 1975).

5 Le Roy Ladurie, *Mind and Method of the Historian*.

6 Vovelle, *Ideologies and Mentalities*, p. 111.

7 Peter Winch, 'Understanding Primitive Society' in Bryan R. Wilson (ed.), *Rationality* (Oxford: Blackwell, 1979), pp. 1–17; E. E. Evans Pritchard, *Witchcraft, Oracles and Magic among the Azande* (Oxford, 1937).

8 Alasadair MacIntyre, 'Is Understanding Religion Compatible with Believing?' in Wilson, *Rationality*, pp. 62–77.

9 Porter, in Camporesi, *Bread of Dreams*, pp. 3–4.

10 Le Goff, *Time, Work and Culture in the Middle Ages*, p. 82.

11 Quoted in Vovelle, *Ideologies and Mentalities*, p. 82.

12 Thomas, *Religion and the Decline of Magic.*

13 Vovelle, *Ideologies and Mentalities* and Le Goff, *Time, Work and Culture in the Middle Ages.*

14 The hostile attitude of the Brahman religious leaders can be found in 'The Disreputable Guru-worshipping sects of Bengal' in *Hindu Castes and Sects* written and published by Jogendranath Bhattacharya, president of the Nabadwip 'pundits' association in 1896. A few years later, orthodox Muslim leaders launched an offensive against the Karta-bhaja sect in the pages of *Islam-Pracharak* (January 1903), a journal edited by Mohammad Reazuddin Ahmed. See Dey, *Karta-bhaja Dharmer Itibritta,* p. 77 and pp. 88–9.

15 For these engravings, Goya used the famous adage 'El sueno de la razon produce monstrous' (The sleep of reason produces monsters).

SELECT BIBLIOGRAPHY

'A Hindoo on the Drama'. *Morning Chronicle* (January 1855).

AHMED, Wakil. *Bangla Sahityer Poorabritta*. Dhaka: Khan Brothers and Co., 1974.

———. *Unish Shatakey Bangali Musalmaner Chinta-Chetonar Dhara*. Dhaka: Bangla Academy, 1983.

APOLLODORUS. *The Library*, 2 VOLS (Sir James George Frazer trans.). London: William Heinemann, 1921. Now available as Volume 121 of the Loeb Classical Library.

ARCHER, W. G. *Bazaar Paintings of Calcutta*. London: Victoria & Albert Museum, 1953.

BABCOCK, Barbara A. (ed.). *The Reversible World*. Ithaca: Cornell University Press, 1978.

BAGAL, Jogesh Chandra. *Hindu Melar Itibritta*. Calcutta, 1945.

BAKHTIN, Mikhail M. *Rabelais and His World*. Cambridge, MA: MIT Press, 1968.

BANDYOPADHYAY, Brajendranath (ed.). *Sambadpatrey Sekaler Katha*, 2 VOLS. Calcutta: Bangiya Sahitya Parishat, 1949.

BANDYOPADHYAY, Panchkari. *Banglar Tantra*. Calcutta: Bengal Publishers Ltd., 1982.

BANERJEE, Sumanta. 'Bogey of the Bawdy: Changing Concept of "Obscenity" in 19th century Bengali Culture'. *Economic and Political Weekly* 22(29) (18 July 1987): 1197–1206.

———. *Appropriation of a Folk-Heroine: Radha in Medieval Bengali Vaishnavite Culture*. Shimla: Indian Institute of Advanced Study, 1993.

———. *The Parlour and the Streets: Elite and Popular Culture in Nineteenth Century Calcutta* (Calcutta: Seagull Books, 2018[1989])

BASAK, Baishnabcharan. *Bharatiya Sahasra Sangeet*. Calcutta, n.d.

BASU, Arun Kumar. *Shaktigeet Padabali*. Calcutta: n. p., 1964.

BERGER, John. *Ways of Seeing*. London: BBC, 1979

BHADURI, Nrisinghaprasad. *Shyamamayer Charitkatha, Shyamamayer Gan*. Calcutta: Antaranga Prakashana, 1993.

BHATTACHARYA, Gouri. *Bangla Loksahitye Radha Krishna Prasanga*. Calcutta: Rabindra Bharati University, 1989.

BHATTACHARYA, Prabhat Kumar. *Bangla Natakey Swadeshikatar Prabhab*. Calcutta: Sahitya Sree, 1979.

BLOCH, Marc. *The Historian's Craft*. Manchester University Press, 1967.

BOSE, Dilip. *Bhagavad-Gita and Our National Movement*. New Delhi: People's Publishing House, 1981.

BRAHMA, Tripti. *Lokajeebaney Banglar Loukik Dharmasangeet O Dharmiya Mela*. Calcutta: n. p., 1982.

BURKE, Peter. *Popular Culture in Early Modern Europe*. London: Temple Smith, 1978.

CAMPBELL, Joseph. *The Masks of God, Volume 4: Creative Mythology*. New York: Penguin, 1991[1968].

Chaitanya Bhagavat by Vrindavan Das (1507–1609?)

Chaitanya Charitamrita by Krishnadas Kabiraj (1496–1583)

Chaitanyamangal by Jayananda (1512– ?)

CHAKRAVARTY, Ramakanta. *Vaishnavism in Bengal*. Calcutta: Sanskrit Pustak Bhandar, 1985.

——— (ed.) *Bismrita Darpan*. Calcutta: Sanskrit Pustak Bhandar, 1971.

CHAKRAVARTY, Sudhir. 'Gabhir Nirjan Pathey'. *Ekshan* (Autumn 1985).

———. *Bala-Harhi Samproday O Tader Gan*. Calcutta: Pustak Bipani, 1986.

———. *Bratya Lokayata Lalan*. Calcutta: Pustak Bipani, 1992.

——. *Panchagramer Karcha*. Calcutta: Pratikshan Publications, 1995.

CHAKRAVARTY, Tapan and Bhabaniprasad Sahi (eds.). *Dui Banglar Kushanshkar: Birodhi Bigyan Chinta*. Calcutta: Deep Prakashan, 1993.

CHANDIDAS, Bodu. *Srikrishnakirtan*. Calcutta, 1954.

CHATTOPADHYAY, Bankim Chandra. *Kapalkundala*. 1866.

——. 'Krishna-charitra' in *Bankim Rachanabali*. Calcutta: Sahitya Samsad, 1954.

CHATTOPADHYAY, Pramode Kumar. *Tantrabhilasheer Sadhusanga*. Calcutta: Bishwabani Prakashani, 1983.

CHATTOPADHYAY, Nagendranath. *Tarasharan Bamacharan*. Calcutta: Sarat Book House, 1972.

CHATTOPADHYAY, Shambhukinkar. *Tarapeeth*. Birbhum, 1994.

CHATTOPADHYAY, Tushar. 'Karta-bhaja O Chicago's Amantran'. *Anandabazar Patrika* (29 April 1979).

CLARK, Kenneth. *The Nude*. London: Pelican Books, 1960.

DARNTON, Robert. *The Great Cat Massacre*. Harmondsworth: Penguin, 1985.

DASGUPTA, Shantikumar and Haribandhu Mukhoti (eds.). *Ishwar Gupta Rachanabali*, VOL. I. Calcutta: Sanskrit Pustak Bhandar, 1954.

DAS GUPTA, Shashibhushan. *Obscure Religious Cults*. Calcutta: Firma K. L. M, 1962.

——. *Sree Radhar Kramabikash*. Calcutta: A Mukherjee, 1963.

——. *Bharater Shakti Sadhana O Shakta Sahitya*. Calcutta: Sahitya Samsad, 1965.

DAS, Girindranath. *Bangla Pir Sahityer Katha*. Barasat, 1976.

DAS, Gyanendramohan (ed.). *Bangala Bhashar Abhidhan*. Calcutta: Sahitya Samsad, 1986[1916].

DAS, Haridas. *Sree Sree Gaudiya Vaishnav Abhidhan*, VOL. 2. Nabadwip, 1957.

DAS, Upendra Kumar. *Shastramoolak Bharatiya Shakti Sadhana*, 2 VOLS. Santiniketan: Visva-Bharati, 1984, 1988.

DE, Sushil Kumar. *Early History of the Vaishnava Faith and Movement in Bengal*. Calcutta: Firma K. L. M., 1961.

DEB, Raja Binaya Krishna. *The Early History and Growth of Calcutta.* Calcutta: Riddhi, 1977.

DELARUELLE, E. *La Piete populaire du moyen age.* Turin: Bottega d'Erasmo, 1975.

DEY, Debendranath. *Karta Bhaja Dharmer Itibritta.* Calcutta: Jijnasa Agencies Ltd., 1968.

DUTT, Hur Chunder. *Bengali Life and Society: A Discourse.* Calcutta, 1853.

DUTTA, Akshoy Kumar. *Bharatbarshiya Upasak Sampraday*, VOL. I. Calcutta: Karuna Prakasani, 1987[1870].

DUTTA, Mahendranath. *Kolikatar Puratan Kahini O Pratha.* Calcutta: Mahendra Publishing Committee, 1973.

DUTTA, Prankrishna. *Kolikatar Itibritta.* Calcutta: Pustak Bipani, 1981.

EVANS-PRITCHARD, E. E. *Witchcraft, Oracles and Magic among the Azande.* New York: Oxford University Press, 1976.

FLIEGER, Jerry Aline. *The Purloined Punch Line: Freud's Comic Theory and the Postmodern Text.* Baltimore: Johns Hopkins University Press, 1991.

GANGOPADHYAY, Haricharan. *Sree Bam-leela.* Calcutta: Sri Guru Press, 1934.

GHATAK, Ritwik. 'Chalachhitra Chinta'. *Chitrabikshan* (special issue on Ghatak) (January–April 1976).

GHOSH, Benoy (ed.). *Samayik Patrey Banglar Samajchitra*, VOL. I. Calcutta: Papyrus, 1978.

GHOSH, Kalicharan. *Jagoran O Bishphoran.* Calcutta: n. p., 1973.

GINZBURG, Carlo. *Myths, Emblems, Clues* (London: Hutchinson Radius, 1990[1986]).

GIRI, Satyavati. *Bangla Sahitye Krishnakathar Kramabikash.* Calcutta: Dey's Publishing, 1988.

GOODY, Jack. *The Logic of Writing and the Organization of Society.* Cambridge: Cambridge University Press, 1986.

GUHA, Ranajit (ed.). *Subaltern Studies I–V.* New Delhi: Oxford University Press, 1982–89.

—— (ed.). *A Subaltern Studies Reader: 1986–1995.* Minneapolis: University of Minnesota Press, 1997.

—— and Gayatri Chakravorty Spivak (eds). *Selected Subaltern Studies*. New York: Oxford University Press, 1988.

GUPTA, Bipin Behari. *Puratan Prasanga*. Calcutta: Vidya Bharati Publications, 1966.

GUPTA, Meghnad. *Rater Kolkata*. Calcutta: Hemanta K. Roy, 1923.

GUREVICH, Aron. *Medieval Popular Culture: Problems of Belief and Perception*. Cambridge: Cambridge University Press, 1988.

GUTHRIE, Stewart Elliott. *Faces in the Clouds*. New York: Oxford University Press, 1993.

HASHMI, Tajul Islam. *Ouponibeshik Bangla*. Calcutta: Papyrus, 1985.

HOBSBAWM, E. J. *Bandits*. Harmondsworth: Penguin, 1985.

——. *Revolutionaries*. London: Orion Books, 1994.

——. *Uncommon People*. London: Little Brown, 1999.

—— and George Rudé. *Captain Swing*. New York: W. W. Norton and Company, 1975.

HUNTER, W. W. *Annals of Rural Bengal* (Calcutta: R. D. Press, 1965[1868])

HUQ, Muhammad Enamul. *A History of Sufi-ism in Bengal*. Dhaka: Asiatic Society of Bangladesh, 1975.

JASIMUDDIN. *Mursheeda Gan*. Dhaka: Bangla Academy, 1979.

KALIM, Musa. *Madhyajuger Bangla Sahitye Hindu-Muslim Samparka*. Calcutta, 1988.

KELLEY, Robin D. G. 'A Poetics of Anticolonialism'. *Monthly Review* 51(6) (November 1999): 1–21.

KOSAMBI, D. D. *Myth and Reality: Studies in the Formation of Indian Culture*. Bombay: Popular Prakashan, 1962.

LAHIRI, Durgadas. *Bangalir Gan* (Asitkumar Bandyopadhyay ed.). Calcutta: Paschim Banga Bangla Academy, 2001[1905].

LARNER, Christina. *Witchcraft and Religion: The Politics of Popular Belief*. London: Basil Blackwell, 1984.

LE GOFF, Jacques. *Time, Work and Culture in the Middle Ages*. Chicago: University of Chicago Press, 1980.

LADURIE, Emmanuel Le Roy. *Mind and Method of the Historian* (Sian Reynolds and Ben Reynolds trans). Chicago: University of Chicago Press, 1981.

LONG, James. 'Early Bengali Literature and Newspapers'. *Calcutta Review*, 13(25) (1850): 124–61.

MacINTYRE, Alasadair. 'Is Understanding Religion Compatible with Believing?' in Bryan R. Wilson (ed.), *Rationality* (Oxford: Blackwell, 1979), pp. 62–77.

Mahabharata (Kaliprasanna Sinha trans.). Calcutta: Basumati Sahitya Mandir, 1965.

MARSHMAN, John C. *The Life and Times of Carey, Marshman and Ward: Embracing the History of the Serampore Mission*, 2 VOLS. London: Longman, Brown, Green, Longmans, and Roberts, 1859.

MARX, Karl. Introduction to 'Contribution to the Critique of Hegel's Philosophy of Law' in Karl Marx and Friedrich Engels, *On Religion* (Moscow, 1976), **p. 38**.

McKEAN, Lise. 'Bharat Mata: Mother India and her Militant Matriots' in John S. Hawley and Donna M. Wulff (eds), *Devi: Goddesses of India*. New Delhi: Aleph Book Company, 2017[1998], pp. 250–80.

MISHRA, Manulal. *Bhaber Geet*. Calcutta, 1877.

MUKHOPADHYAY, Aditya. *Tarapeether Katha*. Birbhum: Malancha, 1994.

MUKHOPADHYAY, Anima. *Atharo Shataker Bangla Punthitey Itihas Prasanga*. Calcutta: Sahityalok, 1987.

MUKHOPADHYAY, Hirendranarayan (ed.). *Ujjalaneelamani*. Calcutta, 1965.

MULLICK, Kumudnath. *Nadia Kahini*. Calcutta: n. p., 1910.

MULLICK, Pramathanath. *Sachitra Kolikatar Itihas*. Calcutta: Sri Prabodh Krishna Bandyopadhyay, 1935.

NAIR, P. Thankappan (ed.). *Calcutta in the 17th Century*. Calcutta: Firma K. L. M., 1986.

—— (ed.). *Calcutta in the 19th Century: Company's Days*. Calcutta: Firma K. L. M., 1989.

NANDY, Ashis. 'An Anti-Secularist Manifesto'. *Seminar* 314 (1985): 14–24.

NANDY, Ratan Kumar. *Karta-bhaja Dharma O Sahitya*. Calcutta: Bangiya Sahita Samsad, 1984.

OPPENHEIMER, Robert. *The Flying Trapeze: Three Crises for Physicists*. London: Oxford University Press, 1964.

PAL, Prafulla. *Pracheen Kobi-walar Gan.* Calcutta: University of Calcutta, 1958.

PODDAR, Arabinda. *Renaissance in Bengal: Search for Identity.* Shimla: Indian Institute of Advanced Study, 1977.

PORTER, Roy. Perface in Piero Camporesi, *Bread of Dreams: Food and Fantasy in Early Modern Europe.* Cambridge: Polity Press, 1989, pp. 1–16.

PROPP, Vladimir. *Theory and History of Folklore.* Manchester: Manchester University Press, 1984.

RAY, A. K. *A Short History of Calcutta.* Calcutta: Riddhi, 1982[1902].

RAY, Dinendra Kumar. 'Nadiya Jelar Siddhajogi'. *Aryavarta* 1(6) (1910).

RAY, Niharranjan. *Bangalir Itihas: Aadi Parba.* Calcutta: Dey's Publishing, 1993.

RAY, Suprakash. *Bharater Krishak Bidroha O Ganatantrik Sangram.* Calcutta: DNBA Brothers, 1972.

RAYCHAUDHURI, Tapan. *Europe Reconsidered: Perceptions of the West in Nineteenth Century Bengal.* New Delhi: Oxford University Press, 1988.

SANYAL, Hiteshranjan. *Bangla Kirtoner Itihas.* Calcutta: K. P. Bagchi, for the Centre for Studies in Social Sciences, 1989.

SARBADHIKARI, Debaprasad. *Smritirekha.* Calcutta: Nikhilchandra Sarbadhikari, 1933.

SARKAR, Jagadish Narayan. *Banglay Hindu-Musalman Samparka, Madhyajug.* Calcutta: Bangiya Sahitya Parishat, 1981.

SARKAR, Sumit. *An Exploration of the Ramakrishna Vivekananda Tradition.* Shimla: Indian Institute of Advanced Study, 1993.

SEN, Dineshchandra. *Bangabhasha O Sahitya.* Calcutta: Pashchimbanga Rajya Pustak Parshad, 1986[1896]).

——. *Brihat Banga*, VOL. I. Calcutta: Dey's Publishing, 1993.

SEN, Nabinchandra. *Nabinchandra Granthabali: Amar Jeeban*, VOL. 4. Calcutta: Bangiya Sahitya Parishat, 1959.

SEN, Sukumar. *Bangla Sahityer Itihas*, VOL. I. Calcutta: Modern Book Agency, 1948.

——. *Bangla Sahityer Itihas*, VOL. 2. Calcutta: Ananda Publishers, 1975

SEN, Sukumar. *Bangla Sahityer Itihas.* Delhi, 1987.

SHANKARACHARYA, *Sri Sri Satyanarayaner Panchali*. Calcutta: Rajendra Library, n.d.

SHARMA, Amita. 'Kabir, Caste and Women' (unpublished paper, available at the Indian Institute of Advanced Study, Shimla).

SINHA, Kaliprasanna. *Hutom Penchar Naksha O Anyanya Samajchitra* (Brajendranath Bandyopadhyay and Sajanikanta Das eds). Calcutta: Bangiya Sahitya Parishad, 1977.

SISTER NIVEDITA, *Kali The Mother*. Pithorgarh: Advaita Ashrama, 1950[1897].

———. *The Master As I Saw Him*. Calcutta: Udbodhan Karyalay, 1987.

SONTAG, Susan. *Against Interpretation*. London: Vintage, 1994.

STORCH, Robert D. (ed.). *Popular Culture and Custom in Nineteenth Century England*. London: Croom Helm, 1982.

TAGORE, Abanindranath. *Banglar Brata*. Calcutta: Visva-Bharati, 1995[1943].

TAGORE, Rabindranath. 'Panchabhoot' in *Rabindra Rachanabali*, VOL. 2. Calcutta: Visva-Bharati, 1984.

———. *Lokasahitya*, VOL. 2. Calcutta: Visva-Bharati, 1984.

THOMAS, Keith. *Religion and the Decline of Magic*. London: Weidenfeld and Nicholson, 1973.

TOYNBEE, Arnold. *An Historian's Approach to Religion*. London: Oxford University Press, 1979.

Vishwakosh (Nagendranath Basu comp, and ed.). Calcutta, 1988[1886].

VOVELLE, Michel. *Ideologies and Mentalities*. Cambridge: Polity Press, 1990.

WEBER, Max. 'Religious Groups (The Sociology of Religion)' (1963) in *Economy and Society: An Outline of Interpretive Sociology* (Guenther Roth and Claus Wittich eds). Berkeley: University of California Press, 1978, pp. 399–634.

WHITE, Paul Sayce. Preface in Ernesto De Martino, *Primitive Magic: The Psychic Powers of Shamans and Sorcerers*. Dorset: Prism Press, 1988.

WIEBE, Donald. *The Irony of Theology and the Nature of Religion*. Montreal: McGill-Queens University Press, 1991.

WILKINS, W. J. *Modern Hinduism*. Calcutta: Rupa, 1975[1887].

WINCH, Peter. 'Understanding Primitive Society' in Bryan R. Wilson (ed.), *Rationality* (Oxford: Blackwell, 1979), pp. 1–17

YEO, Eileen and Stephen (eds). *Popular Culture and Class Conflict 1590–1914: Explorations in the History of Labour and Leisure.* Sussex: The Harvester Press, 1981.

ZIMMER, Heinrich. *The Art of Indian Asia,* VOL. I. New York: Pantheon Books, 1960.

Chakravarty, Ramakant A. 'Chaitanyer Dharmandolan'. *Baromash* (April 1986): 18.

MAITREYA, Akshoy Kumar (ed.). *Aitihashik Chitra* 1(1) (January, 1899).

Periodicals

Bangadarshan (Kartick, 1280 B.S. [1873])

Bengal Past and Present, Journal of the Calcutta Historical Society I (July–December, 1907)

Calcutta Review, 6

Calcutta Review 13(25) (January–June 1850)

Indian Studies: Past and Present (Calcutta 1965)

Samachar Chandrika (21 April 1827)

Samachar Darpan (4 February 1837)

Samvad Prabhakar (18 Chaitra 1254 B.S. [1847])

Somprakash (20 Chaitra 1270 B.S. [1863])

Somprakash (4 April 1864)

INDEX

Adhikari, Gobinda 119

Adya-Shakti 36, 60, 142, 171, 177, 215, 225

Agambagish, Krishnananda 40–1, 50, 51 *Brihattantrasar* 51; *Tantrachuramoni* 51

Akbar Shah Ali 69

akhara 138, 144, 146, 222

Alauddin Hussain Shah, Sultan 68

alcohol, consumption of 53, 193–4, 195–6, 197; in Shakta tradition 53–4, 183, 194, 194, 195–6

Anandamath (Bankim Chandra Chattopadhyay) 61, 217, 219, 230

Anandananth 167

animism 3–4, 13, 69, 71, 74–5, 129, 133, 198, 210

Annada 35, 196

Annapurna 35, 36, 64, 209, 215

Anushilan. *See also* nationalism: militant

Asiatic Society of Bengal, The 9

Aul 9, 134, 258n7

Aulchand 13, 127, 128, 130–4, 135–40, 142–4, 149, 153, 154, 260n35

Babri Masjid 25, 232, 245–6n34

babu 99, 105, 109, 112, 119

baiji 108, 225

Bakhtin, Mikhail 5, 39, 236, 254n22, 256nn39

Bala-Harhi 11

Balaram Harhi 13, 16–17, 127, 135

Balarami 13, 16, 97, 127

Bamabodhini Patrika 220

Bamakshyapa 18, 30, 155–64, 167, 168–85, 174, 189, 190, 191–6, 197, 198–207, 262n1, 262n6, 264n37–8, 266n56

Bana-bibi 4, 19, 47. *See also* mother goddesses: in agrarian/tribal society

Bandyopadhyay, Kiron 211, 212, 213, 216–217, 221; *Bharat Mata* 211, 212, 213, 216–217, 221; *Bharatey Jabana* 213

Banerjee, Surendranath 217

Bangadarshan 122, 213

Baul 11, 14, 15, 16, 17–18, 23, 32, 79, 97, 127, 133, 134–5, 139, 145, 147, 258n7

bawdy 115–6, 118–121, 256n37

Benaras 55, 196

Bentinck, Lord William 57